Power Politics, Banking Union and EMU

This book examines the politics of Banking Union and EMU reform in the EU, and draws lessons for what it means for international politics, both in Europe, and for international relations more broadly. It demonstrates that most of the reforms in Europe to break free of the Eurozone and banking crises in which Europe continues to find itself focus on building up the capacities of national authorities rather than European ones. The result is that national authorities remain largely in control of the decisions and funds that are to be deployed to prevent economic disaster if a single EU bank fails. The likely outcome is an accelerated balkanization of the European market for the foreseeable future.

The book also contends that power politics, and realism in particular, is a defining feature of European politics with coercion and enforced national responsibility at the demand of Germany; the dominant form of institution-building that established the responsible sovereignty model, and shut down the possibility of alternatives. In making this case, the book demonstrates that the dominant view in international relations, that power politics best explains the behaviour of states, also apply to the EU.

This text will be of key interest to scholars and students of the Eurozone crisis, EU politics, economic policy, and more broadly to political economy, public policy and international relations.

Shawn Donnelly is Assistant Professor of International relations and European Studies at the University of Twente, the Netherlands.

Routledge/UACES Contemporary European Studies
Edited by Chad Damro, University of Edinburgh, UK, Elaine Fahey, City University London, UK, and David Howarth, University of Luxembourg, Luxembourg, on behalf of the University Association for Contemporary European Studies

The primary objective of the new Contemporary European Studies series is to provide a research outlet for scholars of European Studies from all disciplines. The series publishes important scholarly works and aims to forge for itself an international reputation.

The Dynamics of EU External Energy Relations
Fighting for Energy
Francesca Batzella

Claiming Citizenship Rights in Europe
Emerging Challenges and Political Agents
Edited by Daniele Archibugi and Ali Emre Benli

The Contested Diplomacy of the European External Action Service
Inception, Establishment and Consolidation
Jost-Henrik Morgenstern-Pomorski

Power Politics, Banking Union and EMU
Adjusting Europe to Germany
Shawn Donnelly

For more information about this series, please visit: www.routledge.com/Routledge-UACES-Contemporary-European-Studies/book-series/UACES

Power Politics, Banking Union and EMU

Adjusting Europe to Germany

Shawn Donnelly

Routledge
Taylor & Francis Group
LONDON AND NEW YORK

UACES

First published 2018
by Routledge

2 Park Square, Milton Park, Abingdon, Oxfordshire OX14 4RN
52 Vanderbilt Avenue, New York, NY 10017

Routledge is an imprint of the Taylor & Francis Group, an informa business

First issued in paperback 2020

British Library Cataloguing-in-Publication Data
A catalogue record for this book is available from the British Library

Library of Congress Cataloging-in-Publication Data
Names: Donnelly, Shawn, author.
Title: Power politics, Banking Union and EMU : adjusting Europe to Germany / Shawn Donnelly.
Description: Abingdon, Oxon ; New York, NY : Routledge, 2018. | Series: Routledge/UACES contemporary European studies ; 41 | Includes bibliographical references and index.
Identifiers: LCCN 2017053098 | ISBN 9781138572300 (hardback) | ISBN 9780203702130 (ebook)
Subjects: LCSH: Economic and Monetary Union. | Monetary policy—European Union countries. | Financial institutions—Government policy—European Unions countries. | Banks and banking, Central—European Union countries. | Germany—Foreign relations—European Union countries. | European Union countries—Economic policy. | European Union countries—Politics and government.
Classification: LCC HG930.5 .D66 2018 | DDC 332.1094—dc23
LC record available at https://lccn.loc.gov/2017053098

ISBN: 978-1-138-57230-0 (hbk)
ISBN: 978-0-367-59171-7 (pbk)

DOI: 10.4324/9780203702130

The authors gratefully acknowledge the provision of funding of Open Access by the Faculty of Behavioural, Management and Social Sciences at the University of Twente.

Contents

Acknowledgements

This book has come out later than expected as EMU reform and Banking Union have unfolded, and benefited from the valued help of colleagues who have read and commented on parts of it in one form or another.

Particular thanks go out to Rachel Epstein, David Howarth and Richard Deeg, who have had the most profound impact through reflection, feedback and encouragement. There are a number of others who have helped significantly along the way as well – Lucia Quaglia, Aneta Spendzharova, Martin Rhodes, Randall Germain, Huw Macartney, Zdenek Kudrna, Jakob Gren, Michele Chang, David Mayes, Scott James, Sebastian Heidebrecht, Ad van Riet, Manuela Moschella, Stijn Verhelst, Ismael Emre Bayram, Marina Huebner, Pawel Tokarski, Joachim Schild, Patrick Leblond, Dora Piroska, Ioannis Asikmoakopoulos, Matthias Wohlfahrt, Florian Brandt, Iain Hardie, Geoffrey Underhill, Waltraud Schelkle, Ismail Erturk, Juliet Johnson, Michel Goyer, Jana Grittersova, John Zysman, Mark Cassell, and Joseph Grieco. Some of these inputs were intense, others brief, but all were valuable and appreciated. The mistakes, as usual, are mine.

1 Introduction

Do international institutions shape the behaviour of powerful states or do those institutions adjust to their wishes? Can great powers step outside established institutions to alter the existing status quo? The European Union (EU) was shaped to tie Germany's hands after reunification, but changed after 2008 to reflect Germany's priorities. New EU institutions of macroeconomic governance were introduced to change state behaviour of states, but German-led institutions were also established outside the EU that bypass its legal and institutional order and force the EU to adjust. This strategy magnified German capacity to secure its goals over the objections of other countries within and without the EU. The result is a German Europe (Beck 2013) more than a European Germany. This took place in a contentious environment in which EU and international institutions, France and Southern Europe pushed for the EU to develop supranational institutions and a federal government to combat the Eurozone Crisis (EZC), and in which Germany and Northern Europe sought to impose national responsibility for financial stability and public finances.

The Great Financial Crisis (GFC) and the EZC that followed shifted power resources and vulnerabilities in Europe in ways that enhanced Germany's power, allowing this strategy to succeed. Germany remained economically strong and resilient, a fact that financial markets amplified by treating German securities as a safe haven in turbulent times. Southern European countries, in contrast, were dragged down by declining demand and scarcer credit, which financial markets amplified by withdrawing and withholding investment to the point where neither banks nor sovereigns could borrow – imposing a full stop on economic prospects. France, meanwhile, with the strongest EU investments in Southern Europe of any country, came out weakened and nearly as vulnerable to a Southern European collapse as those countries themselves.

As a result of these changes in relative power, German capacity to determine outcomes in Europe's adjustment process rose dramatically. The relative power of Southern Europe should have been minimal. That of France, which traditionally lobbies to soften German demands for austerity on the rest of the Eurozone, should have been weakened as well, resulting in a modified Eurozone architecture reflecting German interests. Although this happened to some degree, EU institutional rules blocked German proposals or watered them down sufficiently that Germany

DOI: 10.4324/9780203702130-1

remained dissatisfied. In response, Germany pushed the establishment of a new institutional architecture outside the EU to overcome resistance to its demands over the terms of financial stability within the European Economic and Monetary Union (EMU). Germany still found itself confronted with resistance from national governments and parliaments, but could better impose its preferences.

In this context, the range of tools that Germany used to achieve its goals grew after 2008 from hard bargaining, a staple of intergovernmental politics in the EU, to include coercion and imposition of its own terms on other states through non-EU institutions, practices that are decidedly not and that strain European legitimacy (Piattoni 2015; Fabbrini 2017). Germany's dominance is limited to the realm of financial policy, where its interest in its neighbours and how they govern themselves (lest they hurt Germany's own financial interests) is direct and intense, and its capacity to bring pressure to bear on others is greatest.

This capacity to direct outcomes can nevertheless be seen in Banking Union (BU) and the reform of European economic governance as well, particularly the rules surrounding EMU membership. The present book focusses on the last two issues.

Germany's power resources are important in explaining outcomes, as are the distributional interests, but its ideas about what is right and wrong in public policy matter as well for the nature of Europe and of European states (Hall 2012; Dullien & Guerot 2012). In Banking Union and EMU, German conviction is high that others must emulate their ideas of financial prudence and self-sufficiency in macroeconomic policy and institutions, but also bank and financial market regulation – the institutional sinews of modern economies.

What is remarkable about German initiatives inside and outside the EU is that they move Europe further away from the organized chaos and compromises that are the traditional hallmark of European public policy making and impose direction, and above all *order* more compatible with its conceptions of its own interests. Also remarkable is that the voluntarism and national prerogatives that persisted well into the 21st-century EU were significantly displaced by new ordering principles for the EU stressing obligation and punishment. Those principles start out with the notion of responsible sovereignty (Piattoni 2017) – national responsibility for carrying out policy within pre-defined parameters (rather than in a fully discretionary manner), and then increasingly escalate to country-specific recommendations, then demands made under coercion and finally direct imposition on governments that resist.

The core mechanisms of German policy that break with the past are coercion – intrusion into the domestic internal policy of EU member states – and the willingness to abandon EU institutions and use other mechanisms that increase German leverage over other states. The principal mechanisms are not only international treaties like the Treaty on Stability, Coordination and Governance (TSCG), which requires the signatory states to balance their budgets, but also the establishment of institutionalized instruments of power outside the EU like the European Stability Mechanism (ESM) and the Single Resolution Fund (SRF), which provide emergency funds for states and banks in financial distress. The

ESM, with a German veto, imposes conditions for loans over the opposition of states requiring assistance, without violating the EU's principles that member states are still ultimately in control of their own policy and commitments. The threshold to demand important constitutional (Wiener 2008) and policy changes from others is lower, as in the TSCG, but in the case of the ESM, conditionality, coercion and imposition become the primary means of interacting with target states. These powers exceed anything the EU has ever used against member states, even though the legal framework to do so was introduced after the EZC (on Germany's insistence).

What happened instead since the onset of the GFC has been the construction of a different Europe. It has been built on principles and using methods that European area study specialists failed to foresee and continue to have difficulty squaring with their understanding of how Europe 'should' work, based on their observations of past behaviour. But things have changed. Although Germany seeks voluntary agreement from its fellow states, and engages in traditional intergovernmental bargaining and decision-making to achieve its ends within coalitions within the EU, it is no longer willing to accept deadlock if its concerns are not met. It resorts to more coercive and intrusive methods to get what it wants.

The fate of Europe is instructive for our understanding of international relations more broadly. Without going so far to conclude that Europe's transformation proves realist assumptions about great powers, institutions and international order, we can contend that it worked out that way. This is neither classical nor structural realism, however. Classical and structural realists expected the EU to fall apart at the end of the Cold War without the external security pressure to stick together – but institutionalized Europe is very much alive. European area study specialists explained this as evidence of sticky institutions exerting influence over states. Liberal institutionalists see a Europe dominated by national governments who maintain it for commercial interest, while neofunctionalists, akin to complex interdependence theorists, see a highly supranationalized and transnationally interdependent Europe from which no country can extract itself or exert any meaningful control. This did not happen. Instead of EU institutions, it got German ones. How do we account for this?

This outcome naturally has consequences for the practical nature of Europe in the international system, but even more importantly, gives us food for thought regarding the role of states, power and international institutions like the EU. The EU is the exception in international relations in the establishment of supranational institutions, but primarily a body of rules and regimes that commit the member states to particular policies, limiting their sovereignty in ways that international organizations generally do not. Until recently EU law and institutions were still widely based on voluntary agreement. That which failed to attract consensus support or a strong supermajority did not proceed. Recent developments have changed that and again covered new territory found nowhere else in the world. Where other regional institutions exist – NAFTA, ASEAN etc. – they have assiduously protected the principle of national sovereignty, with the result that the regional international organizations are associations of sovereign member states.

I generally expect institutions to be built that incorporate formal respect for national sovereignty while focussing on rules of the game, as in ASEAN or NAFTA. The post-2008 European focus on intrusive institutionalism stems from the need to reshape existing institutions in the interest of a great power (possibly with a supporting coalition) over the objections of other actors while maintaining a high degree of interdependence. This outcome is the consequence of Germany having made compromises on the rule structure and membership of EMU that allowed more national budgetary leeway than it preferred (Dyson & Featherstone 1999; Donnelly 2005), and later helped to roll back (Heipertz & Verdun 2010). Dissatisfaction grew to the point where Germany pushed back to impose its own priorities and principles. Ironically, in the attempt to avoid taking financial responsibility for the entire Eurozone, a step that it equates with hegemonic status in the EU, Germany felt compelled to install that status by institutional means – by establishing principles of national economic self-sufficiency and institutionalized steps of command and control to achieve it within Europe. Given the uniqueness of this historical institutional legacy, the force required in other situations should also be less. It is therefore unlikely that what has happened in Europe could happen elsewhere. Although great powers seek to institutionalize relations with other states, the institutional demands on states need not be particularly thick.

I contend below that the contemporary trajectory of Europe can best be expressed as realist institutionalism (RI). RI rests on well-established realist assertions of how great powers seek to organize the international system, with particular attention to their neighbours. The European experience is characterized by the German desire to take an existing set of institutional commitments that impose semi-sovereignty on the member states, but in a chaotic and compromise-based way that does not reflect German preferences, and to move it forward to restrict sovereignty even further for other states as a means of correcting the chaos. In which 'correcting' means forcing other states in the EU to adjust to German preferences rather than accepting the status quo (lack of further agreement) or moving in another direction (more voluntary integration – which would result in a fiscal union with a different distributional outcome (Krasner 1991). This behaviour reflects the high degree of interdependence brought about by the single currency, the high potential cost of stabilizing it, and the highly ineffectual budget constraints on national governments. This makes it practically impossible for Germany to escape from a bad situation by emulating NAFTA or ASEAN or even UK preferences for the EU, which strip down interdependence into cooperation between fully sovereign states. The way forward is to coerce the others, particularly Eurozone members, if necessary to row the boat in the direction Germany lays out.

It is also important to outline the limits of what is being tested in the European case. The German transformation of Europe reflects the emergence of a financial and political great power, but not a military one. Germany lives in an environment in which military security is still provided by the United States and NATO, in which geopolitical order is structured primarily by the conflict between NATO and Russia, followed by a destabilized Middle East and North Africa. This means that Germany is not a regional hegemon. But it is nevertheless a resurgent financial great power that has translated its economic resources into political power over its neighbours at a turning point in the order of Europe (Dyson 2016).

The study of that transformation is nevertheless important because it demonstrates the drive of great powers to shape their environments to the extent of their capabilities. The capacity of great powers to shape international order and its institutions is therefore not dependent on the full spectrum of power resources and capabilities. It is layered. Realist institutionalism is reflected equally in the economic and financial realm: the restructuring of those other institutions and interdependencies that make Europe work.

This book is organized as follows. Chapter 2 outlines the case for realist institutionalism, outlines alternatives and sets out the research design. Chapters 3 through 6 test the hypotheses on the reform of economic governance in the EU, primarily rules regarding national government budgets and macroeconomic imbalances on the one hand, and the various components of Banking Union (BU) on the other. Chapter 7 concludes, outlines the implications for the EU and the world and makes suggestions for further research. The rest of this chapter outlines the case investigated in this book and the impact the outcome has on Europe and the rest of the world. It makes the introduction longer, but provides insight into the challenge facing Europe for those without a background in financial stability.

Financial stability

Financial stability refers to the capacity of banks (and other financial institutions) to meet the demands of their creditors and depositors on a daily basis.[1] This capacity applies not only for retail customers with simple bank and investment accounts, but for commercial enterprises as well, including banks. Three meltdowns of the international financial system in Europe, in 2008, 2011 and 2012, took place when the interbank market in loans collapsed. One of the key functions of financial stability mechanisms is to ensure that threats to the integrity of the entire financial system, whether well-founded or imagined, emanating from within banks or from the broader economic environment, are not permitted to spread from one bank to another. Ideally they also minimize the likelihood of a single bank getting into trouble in the first place. They also help suppress contagion between banks and between national banking systems (Balogh 2012).

Stability requires not only sound economic fundamentals on bank balance sheets, but also confidence in the soundness of the bank's procedural and institutional structures for managing that business, and on other outside factors that ensure it a sure source of income at any moment that access to capital becomes necessary to meet demand. It also depends, in a diffuse sense, on the general economic conditions that undermine the financial capacity of the bank or banks in question. The lower the confidence, the greater the need for guarantees that outside capital will assume the risk of shortfalls in income and asset value. Those outside factors may include the degree of reliable personal and corporate connections that can provide liquidity in times of crisis, but the most important are general public confidence in the banking institution, general public confidence in the banking sector as a whole, and in the willingness of public authorities, whether governments or central banks, to provide access to credit in time of banking crisis. In sum, financial stability relies on both the quality of individual bank management, and on its access to outside sources of capital. The greater the strain on the overall banking system, that is to say to the extent that economic problems or crises of confidence extend beyond individual institutions, the more generalized and massive the line of credit to the banking sector has to be to fulfil this function sufficiently. This is why public actors in a capacity as lenders or creditors of last resort are often seen as indispensable parts of a governance framework that provides for financial stability.

The symptoms of financial instability are illiquidity, insolvency, the collapse of interbank loans, zombie banks, which lead to a stagnant or declining economy, and very prevalent in the Eurozone crisis that started in 2010, a symbiosis of state- and private-sector debt, which leads to successive rounds of financial overextension between banks and sovereigns and possible collapse. Illiquidity refers to a bank being short of cash, but sufficiently rich in assets that ensure long-term ability to pay. Insolvency, a much more serious condition, refers to a bank's long-term inability to fulfil its obligations. Zombie banks, which in the European case have gone hand in hand with the symbiosis of state and private-sector debt, are liquid and solvent in part by virtue of state intervention, and continued uncertainty about liabilities and the quality of assets. Whilst uncertainty about those figures would lead to the collapse of the bank without state aid, its provision allows the banks to continue functioning in the absence of general confidence regarding economic fundamentals or corporate governance and risk management measures.

Microeconomic measures taken to restore financial stability are recapitalization, reorganization, including the establishment of a bad bank to absorb the toxic assets of a bank, resolution, in which a bank is closed, and nationalization. In all of these cases in the early days of the Eurozone crisis, the only authorities capable of providing the monetary and regulatory resources to banks to continue doing business were national governments. The reasons for this are found in the institutional and political requirements for ensuring financial stability, coupled with the weakness of the EU in these areas. Beyond these microeconomic measures, macroeconomic intervention is important for providing improved access to capital in the form of general fiscal stimulus and monetary accommodation, both for the economy as a whole and for the banking sector in particular.

Macroeconomic institutional requirements for ensuring financial stability are of a financial and of a regulatory nature. The financial category, covering monetary and fiscal policy, is essential to crisis management, when emergency liquidity must be provided into the system by a central bank or central government. There are two kinds of institutions that are crucial to ensuring financial support for financial stability: a central bank that can make liquidity generally available to the economy, and specifically to the banking system (i.e. act as a lender or creditor of last resort); and a central public authority that can provide targeted financial injections (a public backstop for the banking system). In the EU, where the capacity of national governments to provide a public backstop varies widely, an additional requirement consists of fiscal transfers that allow capital to flow to the countries that most need it to prop up their banking systems.

The above requirements mean that the same institutional requirements for operating a successful monetary union also are necessary for financial stability. Where they are absent at the European Union level where banks operate across national borders, either the system breaks at the point of its weakest link (normally where public sector capacity to raise funding to cover bank debts is at its weakest), or functional necessity drives those powers to the member states at the continued expense of the Union, with some countries performing better than others, based on resources as much as willingness to adapt. This is the case for budgetary policy and fiscal transfers across member states within EMU and for most measures involving public funds in Banking Union.

Because the Treaties and the interpretation by the Commission restrict the degree to which both the European Central Bank and national central banks can provide a lender of last resort function, and because the EU's own budget is tiny and subject to intergovernmental negotiation that is hostile to expansion, the EU lacks the institutional capacity for an extended period to serve as a lender or creditor of last resort. This in turn intensifies the primacy of national governments as guarantors of financial stability through their fiscal capacity, whilst entrenching inequalities in their capacity to do so. Financial centres in the old member states remain stable and supported by financial markets that see them, in relative terms, as safe havens under conditions of market uncertainty. The potential vulnerability of the EU's single market to bankruptcies is strongest in Europe's established member states, whose governments are the main providers of state aid, and the recipients of Commission permission to do so.

Europe's institutional underdevelopment and its reliance on member state resources are also visible in bank regulation, which deals with crisis prevention rather than management. Part of the EU's initial answer to the financial crisis was the establishment of the European Banking Authority (EBA), which was given formal powers to supervise and investigate banks and conduct stress tests to determine their hardness or resilience – the likelihood that a credit event (normally a sharp drop in economic activity, the failure of a financial institution or the default of a member state on its national debt) could lead to the bank becoming insolvent – and to issue orders for improvement, primarily directed at national authorities. It was also tasked with developing a Single Rulebook on supervision standards for its members. However, the EBA's purported independence from political influence gave way to complaints that national governments, captured by their own banks, interfered strongly in the EBA's affairs to preserve their own banks at the expense of cleaning up financially insolvent institutions. This led analysts to diagnose a symbiosis of private and public interests that plays a much stronger role than EU rules, with the result that proper supervision was not taking place. The EBA, for example, refused to incorporate a possible default of the Greek government on its debt obligations into its stress test modelling, despite the fact that heads of government were discussing precisely that in European Council meetings within the same time frame in 2011. Although the UK made it clear that it did not want banking supervision to be robust, its fellow member states proved to be not much more ambitious in the realm of regulatory oversight of banking institutions.

The institutional requirements of ensuring financial stability in turn rely on political prerequisites. A certain degree of solidarity across member states, whether seen as wholehearted or as a necessary evil, is required to underpin the development of a fiscal union that transfers money to where debts need to be paid. The TSCG is not a fiscal union in that it focusses on budgetary discipline of the recipient states, while the European Financial Stability Facility and its successor, the European Stability Mechanism are built on the presumption that financial flows to countries in trouble are loans under Troika control. National governments are placed under EU/IMF/ESM administration and the money flows directly back to the banks headquartered in countries that are arranging the loans. None of these actions evidence a political context of solidarity. Indeed, by demanding that all Eurozone member states extend credits to Greece and Portugal, which in turn flow to the banks of established financial centres in the EU, a further concentration of financial activity is protected and promoted, rather than diminished. The questions remain: what does the outcome tell us about the nature of international relations in the EU and the capacity of EU institutions to survive? What is the enduring role of the state within the institutional framework that Europe adopted during the crisis, and what was the role of Germany in making those institutions happen?

The case: institutionalizing financial stability in Europe

This book examines the German-led reforms to provide financial stability in Europe in the wake of the GFC. This encompasses changes to EMU, the introduction of BU, and the politics responsible for them taking the shape that they have. It assesses how far the Europeans have come, and what the implications are for financial stability in Europe and worldwide. Not only do these reforms impact growth, employment and financial stability in Europe, they impact the value of American and other global investments in Europe and channels of financial contagion worldwide.

The acid test of BU and the reforms of EMU it is intended to buttress is to what extent they increase the resiliency of the European financial system – its ability to steer clear of future crises, and to weather them when they do come. This means improving the state of banking itself, not just of bank regulation and oversight, and improving the resiliency of public finances in Europe. This book examines each of the individual components of banking and monetary union under discussion, and reaches beyond the headlines to examine the details of what has been agreed, and whether it contributes sufficiently to resilience.

BU mimics the trajectory of EMU as a hybrid of supranational and national elements within the EU, and elements outside the EU and is likely to suffer from the same weaknesses. Monetary union, meanwhile, remains fragile. As then, distributional conflict prevents cross-national stabilizing transfers. Financial stability, meanwhile, ultimately depends on an institution making loans and imposing conditions from outside the EU, as well as an interventionist ECB. What remains is incapable of fully tackling bank-centred financial stability.

EMU was established with a strong, independent ECB with significant powers to set and carry out a stability-oriented monetary policy. But it also entrenched the primacy of national control over fiscal and broader economic policy, regardless of the commitments made on paper to abide by common rules. The reason, then as now, was to prevent the establishment of a European federal budget with fiscal transfers from rich states to poor ones, making individual governments responsible for their own financial solvency within the single currency. BU follows the same pattern. The ECB becomes the lead supervisor of European systemically important banks (SIBs) and helps set the Single Rulebook that national authorities use to supervise other banks. Resolution is coordinated on European lines. However, important aspects remain in largely national hands – resolution planning and implementation (Véron 2017), deposit insurance, public backstops and components of stress testing that form part of supervision (Quaglia & Spendzharova 2017a). The costs associated with providing for bank solvency remain with national authorities as strongly as in monetary union.

What determines the strength and weakness of the components of EMU and BU components *within the EU*, where intergovernmental bargaining still takes place, is the degree of German political backing on the one hand and the degree of permissive consensus within the European Council on the other. German support for a strong ECB to contain the growth of credit in other countries for which Germany might otherwise be liable with Monetary Union, and then Banking Union were core components of an acceptable outcome under conditions of increased financial interdependence. For EMU, this meant credit creation in the macroeconomy – preventing an undesirable growth in the money supply through the establishment of an independent central bank with a mission of stability. For BU, this meant credit creation in the banking sector – by exposing the extent of toxic assets in European banks and preventing their future proliferation. If this credit growth could not be controlled, then Germany and countries like it could find themselves transferring funds in the future to stabilize the weakest links of the European economy. Doing this meant rejecting calls from nearly every corner for further European financial powers (an EU fiscal transfer union) and imposing national responsibility as an ordering principle of EU affairs, alongside enforcement by the ECB. In other areas, however, EU reforms did not go nearly far enough in their control of national government fiscal policy to satisfy the German government (or any of the main opposition parties). Voting rules and the lack of consensus made this possible, with the result that Germany moved further outside the EU to make up for perceived weaknesses.

This means that intergovernmentalism is alive and well as a normal process of EU politics alongside new developments. To the extent that Germany could push its own version of state responsibility and EU powers within the EU, it relied on coalition partners, in typical intergovernmental style. Together with Finland and the Netherlands, and joined later by Slovakia, Estonia and the other Baltic countries, Germany successfully defended against distributional losses and demanded national responsibility for the financial consequences of bank failure and protected key national aspects of bank resolution and deposit insurance that strengthen instability in the Eurozone, particularly the negative feedback loop between states and sovereigns.

One purpose of this book is to show exactly of what the structure of BU and EMU reform consists. Another is to show how that result differs from alternatives pushed by supranational institutions and transnational coalitions. It provides an analysis of what experts at the IMF, Financial Stability Board (FSB), OECD (Olivares-Caminal 2011; Blundell-Wignall 2012), the European Central Bank, the European Systemic Risk Board and others agree on as the essential requirements of a Banking Union that can contribute meaningfully to financial stability, shows how the established Banking Union differs from that benchmark, and provides insight into why that is. In the process, it provides an introduction into the world of financial stability in plain English that is accessible for readers without a background in that area. This is not just about eliminating jargon, but in making the analysis clearer of what Banking Union does well, and where it is likely to do poorly, just as in EMU.

This book outlines as well that key aspects of Banking Union, and the fiscal treaties and bank resolution funds that were established alongside it, were created outside the EU at the behest of the German government (and only the German government), establishing a shadow European Union (that might not eclipse the EU but seriously alter it) with grave consequences for member states. The Shadow EU is a set of international treaties and institutions that run parallel to EU treaties, that restrict national fiscal policy, that make broader demands on economic policy to introduce structural reforms and other measures that minimize so-called macroeconomic imbalances that Germans deem just as much to blame for Europe's banking and sovereign debt crisis as the excessive borrowing of the EU's southern periphery. It also controls all common emergency funds to stabilize EMU in a crisis. This shadow structure was set up so that Germany and its allies, fed up with the behaviour of Southern European EMU member states and blaming them for the banking crisis, could coerce them into accepting restraints on national economic policy in return for cooperation in resolving the crisis in an orderly fashion. In other words, it meant managing the effects of interdependence during a crisis on German terms, with a focus on distributional issues, using tools unavailable within the EU to reach those ends. A paradigm of living within one's means, of borrowing modestly and earning money first before spending it (export-led development) was what Germany sought to institutionalize. Rather than accept a necessary compromise with Southern Europe within the possibilities of EU voting rules, Germany forced Europe to adjust to it, not only in specific votes but in the entire macroeconomic architecture.

An EU solution would have required compromises to reach agreement amongst the heads of state and government of all 28 member states on the text of a treaty change. By orchestrating an international treaty to balance budgets, and a European version of the IMF, Germany could set and achieve its agenda in ways not possible within the EU. In this context, the vulnerability of Southern

European countries to negative press in financial markets could be exploited as the German-led coalition proposed one measure after the other for resolving the crisis in an orderly fashion (Lapavitsas 2012; Matthijs & McNamara 2015). In this way, coercion could be effectively deployed to get all Eurozone member states, above all reluctant Southern European countries, to say yes to German demands. The alternative would not only be dire for the finances and the financial stability of the German-led coalition, but doubly so for the countries suffering capital flight at the first sign of political unwillingness to adhere to the demands being made.

EMU reform and Banking Union are also the institutional foundations for promoting the principle of national responsibility, or responsible sovereignty as an ordering principle of international politics in Europe, and an alternative to the increasing federalization expected as part of 'ever closer union'. The institutionalization of responsible sovereignty steers a middle course between two alternatives that Germany finds undesirable: a fully-fledged fiscal union which opens the door to automatic transfers from surplus countries to deficit countries,[2] and an uncontrolled collapse of the Eurozone, starting with uncontrolled defaults of national governments in Europe's southern periphery.

The distributional consequences of these ordering principles are clear. National responsibility for financial stability reduces costs for Germany in preventing the collapse of the Eurozone, but the unevenness of available financial resources across countries means a decline in stable banking activity in the Eurozone. To reduce instability even further, Banking Union also forces private (for the most part institutional) investors to accept heavy reductions in the value of their investments in Southern Europe during bank insolvencies. This minimizes the need for public money from northern Europe to step in for southern losses, but ensures that investments retain some of their value. Banking Union and EMU reforms further introduce measures to prevent risk-acceptant behaviour which led to the crisis from recurring, both in the banking sector and in public finances. This package of measures serves the interests of Germany and its allies who feared that if Europe chose a fiscal union to avoid the catastrophe of a collapse of the Eurozone that it would face permanent transfers to others and what it saw as the irresponsible accumulation of debt by governments and banks in the south in the 2000s.

EMU reform and BU, as real political enterprises, lay in concrete, exogenous, geoeconomic events. The financial and economic crisis that gripped the world from 2008 onward was not sufficient to nudge European governments to consider Banking Union, nor was the insolvency of Ireland, Greece and Portugal (2010), though it did lead to first steps in 2011 to improve macroeconomic policy reviews. It was the impending collapse of the much larger Spanish financial system, and the incapacity of the Spanish government to borrow money on financial markets to prevent the collapse alone, that prompted the establishment of the ESM, which would provide loans to countries that needed them to buttress their banking systems – subject to strict conditionality of the creditor countries, and Banking Union. Bargaining over what features should be included, under what conditions, and above all, how much of the package would be European or national ensued. By European, I mean EU-level institutions for supervising banks, and EU funds for deployment in the event of a banking crisis, much like the United States has such institutions and funds to manage its own banking system. By national, I mean not only each member state on its own, but EU-level agreements that are designed to ensure that national authorities remain in control of their own banking systems, even as they agree in principle to cooperate and coordinate.

Negotiations on Banking Union generated institutions that followed a political logic of establishment, selected by Germany and its allies to minimize costs, rather than promote broader political consensus or adopt expert advice on what was required to sort out Europe's chronic financial problems. The IMF, FSB, G20, OECD, the ECB, European Systemic Risk Board, the Basel Committee, the United States government and important think tanks like Bruegel, the Centre for European Policy Studies and the Peterson Institute showed remarkable unity in favour of establishing strong European institutions and financial resources, while Germany preferred to keep funds outside the EU in international bodies where it had veto rights, and while most member states preferred that their national institutions did much of the work of regulating banks, and sorting out the affairs of insolvent ones (Donnelly 2016). Rather than truly federal institutions and funds, EU institutions coordinate and oversee national efforts for the most part, while non-EU institutions provide financial resources on an ad hoc basis on the recommendation of the Eurogroup, where German governments could control payouts. The ECB became a direct supervisor for the Eurozone's 128 largest SIBs, but relied on national authorities and the intergovernmentally focussed EBA to handle the other 6000. The SRB oversees efforts made at the national level. And the ESM and SRF remain outside EU competence.

The rest of this chapter starts by briefly outlining the overall vision of a new approach to international relations and European integration I call realist institutionalism. It considers what the institutional and political developments in Europe since 2010 mean more broadly for our understanding of how international relations are expected to work under stress, even in highly institutionalized environments. Why is there a need for such a new viewpoint? These points are brought into contrast with the expectations of other theories of international relations and European integration, with an eye to the puzzles contained in Europe's reform of EMU and its construction of Banking Union.

Realist institutionalism and the new European order

This book tests the assumption that international politics in Europe entered a new phase after 2010, during the process of establishing Banking Union and EMU reform – in which unilateral moves by a single great power were able to significantly reshape the region's institutional and political order. This observation does not seek to refute the insights of liberal intergovernmentalism or of the new intergovernmentalism that followed it, but to note that Europe's institutional transformation since 2010 appears to reflect a further evolution of international politics in Europe, in which existing institutions matter less and the power of single states (rather than coalitions of states working within the EU) matter more than previously. It is that development that sets this new era apart from previous ones in which governments negotiated over the establishment of supranational institutions to make credible commitments in commercial and macroeconomic policy (Moravcsik 1993; Pollack 2003; Howarth & Quaglia 2016), or after 1992, when they turned increasingly toward a new intergovernmentalism based on collective management, policy debate and decentralized responsibility for policy implementation by national executives and their agents (Bickerton, Hodson & Puetter 2015).

The basis of this assertion lies in the observation that Germany took its own initiatives to move outside the EU after 2010 to accomplish its goals with regard to the behaviour of other EU states. It indeed tried first to achieve its goals within the EU, but moved outside them when traditional intergovernmentalism failed to bear fruit. It insisted on the establishment of new institutions beyond the reach of EU bodies and procedures once its demands on others to reshape EMU in its interests and construct Banking Union in ways that would have been possible within the EU itself failed. In other words, Germany forced the EU to adjust to it rather than the other way around. Had this not been the case, the outcome of negotiations over these two projects would have incorporated compromises similar to previous bouts of institutional creation and establishment that would have formed the foundation of very different outcomes. Instead of compromises, Germany has successfully established institutions outside the EU that were used to establish ongoing leverage over other EU states, and force a reshaping of EMU itself to suit its own preferences.

Grappling with these developments is difficult from within the confines of European integration theory, but relatively easy within the context of international relations theory, where the relative weight of state power and international institutions are commonplace considerations.

I refer to this new era of international relations as realist institutionalism. It is close to, but different than the two dominant schools of intergovernmentalism by virtue of its assumption that great powers can and do change the rules of the game, and the game itself, when confronted with outcomes that are unacceptable to them. Of these two, it is closest to liberal intergovernmentalism (LI) by virtue of the (latter's) status as a general theory of international relations in which hard bargaining and the use of power resources to determine outcomes is emphasized. LI is fully compatible with the possibility of conflict between states, even with coercion and the possibility of powerful states walking away from existing regimes and institutions or attempting to establish alternatives that this book takes as starting points. But LI literature doesn't normally expect or stress the development of institutional orders that challenge and coerce the existing ones. What this book does is stress what the new developments mean for those new developments in the international politics of Europe, and how the lessons might apply more broadly to international relations elsewhere.

It merits underlining that the curiosity of this book lies in the nature of the institutions that have been built in Europe, and who controls them. Neofunctionalism, a Europe-specific variation of international relations theory, views all European institutions as proof of path dependent cooperation between European states and supranationalism above them. The nature of the institutionalized order is of secondary importance if any at all. And even more so than liberal intergovernmentalism, it underestimates the duress that a single great power was willing to exert over a great number of other countries to gain agreement on an institutionalized order that was established against the latter's will. It is the combination of coercion and the establishment of a new order that this book seeks to understand and to seek explanatory tools for in international theory.

Realist institutionalism is a strand of realism that brings back state power and the willingness to use it to secure national goals through international institutions of their own choosing, even over the objections of other states, and supranational actors. States organize international relations into institutionalized systems, and new powers rework them or sideline them to suit their own preferences. Institutions rise and fall with the capacity of great powers to protect and promote them. It refutes the idea that international relations are always consensual and path dependent. It also refutes the tendency of liberals and of some realists to portray realism as exclusively anarchic and unorganized. Instead, it focusses on the realist expectation, dating back to Thucydides, adopted by hegemonic stability theory and incorporated into realist analyses of power in the institutions of global economic governance (Drezner 2007; Koppel 2010; Germain 2016; Helleiner 2004; Kirton 1989; Quaglia & Spendzharova 2017b), that great powers typically seek to organize, to institutionalize and to provide order to their environments in ways that serve their interests. Institutions can change to reflect changes in the club of great powers, their interests and demands on other states or they can be rendered irrelevant or secondary by great powers creating alternatives to take their place (Strange 1998) or reinforce the aspects they want at the expense of other priorities (Streeck & Thelen 2005). Institutional changes on their own are compatible with liberal institutionalism and liberal intergovernmentalism, both of which accept the centrality of states and power in determining international agreement on establishing, maintaining and adjusting international institutions. However, expectations that states may resort to coercion and insist simultaneously on radical change in the institutionalized principles of international order are not. Realist institutionalism seeks to capture institutional upheavals, especially related to principles of international order that the others do not.

Since 2000, a growing body of realist literature underlines the importance of material resources in determining which national governments can take control of international bodies at the centre of global governance. Since the financial crisis of 2008, some attention has been focussed on the new role those bodies have played in building up state capacity at the national level, modelled on the practices of the world's most powerful economies. But the additional components of direct coercion, made possible in part by the willingness of a powerful state to impose its preferences on others, and to bypass existing institutions to increase its leverage over others as it creates a new regional international order and institutions based on new ordering principles to suit its own needs, and to remake other states in its own image is new. This book reflects on these important developments, empirically and with regard for the implications they have for the way we think about international relations.

The realist institutionalism outlined in Chapter 2 as follows takes recent theoretical moves further in at least two key ways: by reintroducing the element of intent alongside power as a key determinant in understanding what kind of order a powerful state is willing to accept and demand; and by placing more emphasis on the malleable nature of international order and institutions as a result. This puts it in stark contrast to alternative explanations built on sticky institutions. The first move reflects on the failure of the French strategy of institutional anchoring and restraint of German power through the establishment of the euro. German politicians, voters and epistemic communities harboured deep reservations about the policy preferences of most EMU member states, to the point where they demanded change by those states to their constitutions, institutions, laws and economies (Dyson 2016). The German intent to constrain and shape the national sovereignty of others through international treaties, and to forge ahead outside the EU when existing institutions and the countries that stood behind them would not yield are not only noteworthy, but revolutionary in the evolution of European politics. It is doubtful whether one could accurately contend that European politics was realist before 2012, and for how long the realist moment will continue – but it certainly took hold in 2012 and has strengthened to the present day. This book takes account of those developments and seeks reference points for how durable that new order is likely to be. While Moravcsik's seminal work in particular made great strides in outlining, developing and testing a general theory of international relations applicable to the EU and other regions and the empirical evidence supported those claims at the time he formulated the theory, the politics of providing order to Europe have changed with a resurgent Germany and the way that it goes about securing its goals. That requires an adjustment in how far theory expects great powers to go in achieving their aims, and how strongly weaker states must succumb to those demands. If anything, the self-restraint implicit in LI's work is something that realist institutionalism discounts.

If the German attempt at creating order is successful, it will generate powerful structural incentives for national governments to change the way they do business, domestically and internationally. Europe's new Germanified institutions create large incentives for national governments to take matters into their own hands in ensuring financial stability rather than relying on the institutions and fellow member states of the EU to help them out. This expectation to adapt is based on the principle of responsible sovereignty – that national governments are to take responsibility for national financial stability by fulfilling newly strengthened, monitored and if necessary enforced commitments in budget and banking policy. European financial stability depends not on federal institutions, as found in the United States, but on a collection of strong national policies and institutions agreed to in intergovernmental agreements (Buras 2013; Bickerton, Hodson &

Puetter 2015; Schimmelfennig 2016; Verdun 2015; Manoli & Maris 2015). The reasons for this outcome is distributional conflict between countries that weakens common institutions within the EU and makes revolutionary changes extremely unlikely, even in the face of strong incentives to act otherwise. The result is that the key components of bank regulation and state intervention to avert disaster will continue to be supplied at the national level, where they cannot act effectively to stabilize cross-border institutions and financial flows. This in turn strengthens global trends toward the balkanization of finance, in which national regulators shut down opportunities for foreign banks to act under the responsibility and regulation of another state. The ultimate consequence is a renewed symbiosis between state and banking systems in the one place where internationally minded politicians and technicians hoped to establish and entrench cross-border activity and interdependence. The next chapter develops an analytical structure for investigating these phenomena and embeds it in existing relevant literature.

Notes

1 It is therefore not the same as ensuring a certain level of credit/money/potential for growth within the economy. High or low levels of credit provision and attendant economic activity are compatible with financial stability per se.
2 This itself is not technically the bazooka of monetary and fiscal stimulus that US Secretary of the Treasury Geithner promoted, but would be the ultimate result, as Germany and other surplus countries would pay down Eurobond debt that financed deficit countries.

References

Balogh, P. (2012) *Macroprudential banking supervision: - objectives, means and specific techniques*. Cluj: Unpublished doctoral thesis, Babes-Bolyai University.

Beck, U. (2013). *German Europe*. Cambridge: Polity Press.

Bickerton, C. J., Hodson, D., & Puetter, U. (2015) The new intergovernmentalism: European integration in the post-Maastricht era. *JCMS: Journal of Common Market Studies* 53, 4: 703–22.

Blundell-Wignall, A. (2012) Solving the financial and sovereign debt crisis in Europe. *OECD Journal: Financial Market Trends* 2011, 2.

Buras, P. (2013) *The EU's silent revolution*. ECFR/87. London: European Council on Foreign Relations, September.

Donnelly, S. (2005) Explaining EMU reform. *JCMS: Journal of Common Market Studies* 43, 5: 947–68.

Donnelly, S. (2016) Expert advice and political choice in constructing European banking union. *Journal of banking regulation, 17*, 1–2: 104–18.

Drezner, D. (2007) *All Politics is Global: explaining international regulatory regimes*. Princeton: Princeton University Press.

Dullien, S., & Guérot, U. (2012) *The long shadow of ordoliberalism: Germany's approach to the euro crisis*. European Council on Foreign Relations (ECFR).

Dyson, K. (2016). Germany, the Euro crisis, and risk management: Europe's reluctant and vulnerable hegemonic power. In D'Ottavio, G. & Saalfeld, T. eds., *Germany after the 2013 elections: Breaking the mould of post-unification politics?* Abingdon: Routledge: 49–66.

Dyson, K., & Featherstone, K. (1999) *The road to Maastricht: Negotiating economic and monetary union.* Oxford: Oxford University Press.

Fabbrini, S. (2017) The euro crisis through two paradigms: Interpreting the transformation of the European economic governance. *European Politics and Society* 18, 3: 318–32.

Germain, R. (2016). Locating authority: Resolution regimes, SIFIs and the enduring significance of financial great powers. *Journal of Banking Regulation, 17*, 1–2: 34–45.

Hall, P. A. (2012) The economics and politics of the euro crisis. *German Politics* 21, 4: 355–71.

Heipertz, M., & Verdun, A. (2010) *Ruling Europe: The politics of the stability and growth pact.* Cambridge: Cambridge University Press.

Helleiner, E., & Pickel, A. (eds.) (2005). *Economic nationalism in a globalizing world.* Ithaca: Cornell University Press.

Howarth, D., & Quaglia, L. (2016) Internationalised banking, alternative banks and the Single Supervisory Mechanism. *West European Politics* 39, 3: 438–61.

Kirton, J. (1989) Contemporary concert diplomacy: the seven-power summit and the management of international order. Paper prepared for the annual meeting of the British International Studies Association, London, 29 March-1 April.

Koppel, J. (2010) *World Rule: accountability, legitimacy and the design of world governance*. Chicago: University of Chicago Press.

Krasner, S. D. (1991) Global communications and national power: Life on the Pareto frontier. *World Politics* 43, 3: 336–66.

Lapavitsas, C. (2012) *Crisis in the Eurozone*. Verso Books.

Manoli, P., & Maris, G. (2015) The role of the European Parliament in managing the international economic crisis. In Stavridis, S. & Irrera, D. eds., *The European parliament and its international relations*. Abingdon, Routledge: 70–91.

Matthijs, M., & McNamara, K. (2015) The Euro crisis' theory effect: Northern Saints, Southern Sinners, and the demise of the eurobond. *Journal of European Integration* 37, 2: 229–45.

Moravcsik, A. (1993) Preferences and power in the European community: A liberal intergovernmentalist approach. *Journal of Common Market Studies* 31: 473–.

Olivares-Caminal, Rodrigo. (2011) The EU architecture to avert a sovereign debt crisis. *OECD Journal: Financial Market Trends* 2.

Piattoni, S. (2015) The European Union: Legitimating values, democratic principles, and institutional architectures. In Piattoni, S. ed., *The European Union: Democratic principles and institutional architectures in times of crisis*. Oxford: Oxford University Press: 3–28.

Piattoni, S. (2017) The European Union between intergovernmentalism and 'shared and responsible sovereignty': The haptic potential of EMU's institutional architecture. *Government and Opposition* 52, 3: 385–411.

Pollack, M. A. (2003) *The Engines of European integration: Delegation, agency and agenda-setting in the EU.* Oxford: Oxford University Press.

Quaglia, L., & Spendzharova, A. (2017a) The conundrum of solving 'too big to fail' in the European Union: Supranationalization at different speeds. *JCMS: Journal of Common Market Studies* 55, 5: 1110–26.

Quaglia, L., & Spendzharova, A. (2017b) Post-crisis reforms in banking: Regulators at the interface between domestic and international governance. *Regulation & Governance, 11*, 4: 422–437.

Schimmelfennig, F. (2016) A differentiated leap forward: Spillover, path-dependency, and graded membership in European banking regulation. *West European Politics* 39, 3: 483–502.

Strange, S. (1998) *States and markets* (2nd ed.). London: Bloomsbury Academic.
Streeck, W., & Thelen, K. (2005) *Beyond continuity institutional change in advanced political economies*. Oxford: Oxford University Press.
Verdun, A. (2015) A historical institutionalist explanation of the EU's responses to the euro area financial crisis. *Journal of European Public Policy* 22, 2: 219–37.
Véron, N. (2017) *Europe's fourfold union: Updating the 2012 vision*. Bruegel Policy Contribution Issue n° 23| September 2017.
Wiener, A. (2008) *The Invisible Constitution of Politics*. Cambridge: Cambridge University Press.

2 Realist institutionalism

Power, institutions and international order

Do international institutions shape the behaviour of states, or is it the other way around? International relations theorists, taking into account developments in global governance, have moved closer together in the core and specific assumptions about what to expect in this regard. Realists and liberal institutionalists accept that institutions exist to manage interdependence, and that relative power determines how conflicts are resolved and authoritative decisions taken. However, realists are more likely than liberals to view the continued existence of institutions as contingent on great power preferences. Abandoning institutional rules of the game to pursue alternatives are real choices available to great powers, particularly if those rules cannot be redirected to support what they deem to be the national interest.

For liberal institutionalists, the changes are more modest. Great powers may threaten to walk away from existing rules and institutions as part of hard bargaining, but face real disincentives to take these threats too far. Transaction costs and opportunity costs of managing interdependence in alternative ways have to be subtracted from the benefits of establishing a radical new status quo, with the result that compromises within the existing rule structure are more likely.

Much like liberal institutionalists, European integration theorists, as a subset of international relations, have come up with their own answers to the institution-great power debate. Neofunctionalists assert that supranational institutions and transnational coalitions guide national governments to accept more supranational governance in the face of common problems that individual countries cannot handle alone. Liberal intergovernmentalists, like their liberal institutionalist counterparts, see national governments pursuing mutually beneficial *economic* gains through collective action, particularly delegation of new powers in selected areas to supranational institutions. New Intergovernmental theorists, meanwhile, treat liberal intergovernmentalism as a phase of intergovernmental politics that was replaced after the 1992 Maastricht Treaty by a new intergovernmentalism: one in which national governments remain in control, but manage new collective policy areas by themselves rather than delegating to supranational institutions. Deliberative policy discourse across national executives on politicized issues and de novo institutions within the EU that governments create to help with coordination are the hallmarks of a new stage of integration (Bickerton et al. 2015).

DOI: 10.4324/9780203702130-2

International relations and European integration theories can be thought of as inhabiting a spectrum regarding their expectations of whether institutions constrain great powers or not. Starting at the institutional end of the spectrum, in which institutions have the strongest influence on state behaviour and that of other actors, we have neofunctionalism, followed by liberal institutionalism. Then follow the theories that place more emphasis on state power behind institutional development: liberal intergovernmentalism, then realist institutionalism, hegemonic stability theory, new intergovernmentalism (with its focus on weak institutions and soft coordination) and finally both classical and structural realism, which expect few institutions in an anarchic environment.

Placing realist institutionalism alongside these other standard theories within this spectrum helps clarify its contribution to understanding how international order is institutionalized. There are improvements in fit between empirics and theory that can be obtained by drawing on realist theory to explain current developments within the EU, however. How can we explain the simultaneous establishment of strong institutions and treaties outside the EU, with its legal and bargaining environment, when hard bargaining inside the EU has failed? How do we explain the simultaneous establishment of strong institutions within the EU (in contradiction to new intergovernmentalist expectations) in a context of new non-EU treaties and institutions that provide direction to them? Why strong institutions in one corner of a policy designed to deal with a common problem and weak ones in another? Who decides and why? This chapter is designed to construct a testable set of assumptions and hypotheses that inform the rest of the analysis in this book. That construct, outlined as follows, is placed within the realist paradigm, using institutionalist assumptions and hypotheses that fit the empirical events, both in Europe and elsewhere – and that can be tested at other times and in other places.

Realist institutionalism has a long and robust history in international relations theory, and was extensively developed in the early years of the 21st century, although it never has been so named. This chapter outlines, discusses and builds on that realist body of literature to establish it as a means for understanding and explaining the construction of international order and institutions, to situate it within the contemporary debate on international relations theory and on national responsibility to act in accordance with new commitments contained in the new institutions to take that debate further. The rest of the book will test its capacity to shed light on the reordering of international institutions in Europe, and to apply those lessons elsewhere. As the name implies, it acknowledges that realism, liberal institutionalism and complex interdependence theorists have drawn closer together as the product of competitive theory building and testing, research, analysis and reflection on new developments in global governance. However, more can be done to make the claims broadly applicable across time and space, testable and in a rigorous way. This chapter sets out what realist institutionalism entails, what it means and how it can be tested against key competing theories. It then makes the case that it is applicable in Europe by outlining what it leads to it in the European context. It then outlines the research design to be used in the rest of the book.

Realist institutionalism maintains that great powers seek to establish order in the international system that suits their preferences and compels lesser powers to follow. Great powers – countries with a preponderance of power resources relative to other states in the international system – seek to organize relations with their geopolitical neighbours and if they are powerful enough, further abroad, until they encounter other great powers that are doing the same and prevent them from continuing. The institutions of international relations range from conventions of recognition, war and diplomacy (the institutions of international society: Buzan 1993) to rules of international finance and commerce, to formal international law and organizations, to international standard-setting bodies in the public and private sector. They also extend in practical international relations to standing expectations of whether lesser states are bound to support one great power over another in matters of war and peace (Gray 2013). In doing so, great powers attempt to restrict the range of behaviour that others engage in, thereby managing the impact of interdependence on relations between countries, and forcing others to adjust to their own wishes rather than the other way around. Their ability to do so, to compel others to comply, is greatest and the degree of institutionalization thickest when dealing with lesser powers within their sphere of influence.[1] Correspondingly, it is weakest between great powers, in which institutions may only arise and be maintained by mutual agreement.

If there is no effective opposition, the establishment of international order can extend geographically and across issue areas to the point of hegemony, in which one great power determines the processes, institutions, policy demands and general character of world affairs for the others (Kindleberger 1986; Agnew 2005). Within this context, global interdependence can increase exponentially as states and private actors within them interact within the established international order. This provides further opportunities for great powers, hegemons especially, to exploit country-specific expertise and knowledge as power resources in managing interdependence.[2]

However, all hegemonic positions eventually decline, and rising powers seek institutions that better reflect their own interests. New great powers are those powerful enough to attack or leave the existing institutional order of the international system or demand that it be changed to accommodate their wishes. They must also be strong enough to set up their own arrangements. Regardless of how institutional change happens and whether it is comprehensive or incremental (Streeck & Thelen 2005), and whether the outcome is coherent or not, they are expected to seek an international order that reflects their preferences.

As the distribution of power in the international system changes decisively, so too will the demands of emerging great powers on incumbent powers and the institutions of international order they protect. Should they collide, incumbent international institutions backed by an incumbent hegemon will suffer at the hands of new great power initiatives – whether those are directed at establishing a new institutional order or simply allowing the established institutional order to fall apart through defection, erosion or disuse as countries act unilaterally in contravention of established rules. Given that establishing a new institutional order requires far more power resources to be brought to bear, we should expect radical change to be a rare thing, preluded by the crumbling of the order and institutions that preceded it.

The institutional focus of realist institutionalism therefore takes the spectrum of possible institutional arrangements to be quite broad. It covers all conceivable manifestations of how great powers organize international affairs, from respect for hierarchical control (empire or sphere of influence) to regimes based on formal equality but a set of expectations that less powerful states have to abide by (within a sphere of influence) to horizontal relations between real equals (other great powers) that are dominated by minimal obligations but often rules of the game that make survival possible, as posited by English School theorists of international relations.

The premises of realist institutionalism can be summed up in three propositions, or core assumptions. They are general in nature, and expanded on afterward with regard to how they are manifested in the existing international system, and then within Europe (where they embody the same principles). These propositions are presented below and contrasted with contending international relations theories to contrast the distinctive points.

Proposition 1

> *Great powers seek to manage interdependence by institutionalizing and providing order to their environments in ways that serve their interests.*

Interdependence is present in all situations, affecting survival and welfare of the state to some degree (even in a state of anarchy characterized by security dilemmas) and therefore leads great powers to seek to institutionalize their relationships with others. Doing so allows them to increase predictability, to secure their goals of survival and position in the international system, and to do so on their own terms. It is the inherent interdependence of states that drives them to institutionalize their environments.

Interdependence ranges from security dilemmas (requiring basic institutions and rules in the sense propagated by English School theorists) to economic, social and political systems forms of interaction that states deliberately permit or support through regimes and organizations (managing public affairs involving governments and private affairs involving others such as trade, investment and migration flows)(Gowa 1989).

Institutions refer to the rules and norms and organizations by which state and private behaviour is steered, interdependence thereby managed (Krasner 1983a; Hasenclever, Mayer & Rittberger 1997; Buzan & Lawson 2015) and unrestrained power struggles between states suppressed. The economic, political and security advantages of organizing other states inspires great powers to do so where they can. These institutions may have regional or global reach depending on the resources of the great power involved. They may have benign (Kindleberger 1986) or exploitative effects (Cox 1987; Stopford, Strange & Henley 1991; Agnew & Corbridge 2002), and they may be thicker or thinner in their demands on state behaviour (depending on the asymmetry of power between states) but great powers reliably want and do establish institutions that are aligned with their own preferences where they are able.[3]

Great powers thus seek to shape international order through institutions. Institutions range from formal and hard law (used rarely) to regimes, soft law and informal international governance. Harder institutions are costlier in all sorts of ways (achieving consent, monitoring and enforcing compliance), but soft institutions guide behaviour sufficiently. Hard institutions are more likely to be found in rare cases where great powers see interdependence very badly affected. The pursuit of lower transaction costs (agreement on ideas, details that vary with the strength of commitment desired) allows for deals in a liberal context without realism, but some decisive questions can and are solved through more forceful realist ways.

Realist institutionalism therefore focusses on the primacy of order, power and distributional issues in the international system, including the international economy (Grieco 1988, 1995; Krasner 1976, 1991; Ruggie 2002; Barnett & Duvall 2004). It shares the assumption of liberal institutionalist theory that states seek to manage interdependence institutionally, but is decidedly focussed on how power politics (not institutional engineering or expertise) determines the supply of order and the shape of that order given functional incentives to do so. Asymmetric power plays a key role in overcoming national impediments to cooperation, whether between great powers and lesser ones, or between hegemons and others, including lesser great powers (Snidal 1985; Eichengreen 1987). Economically suboptimal situations are inherently possible as are highly skewed outcomes (Krasner 1991) that liberal institutionalists have since come to accept (Milner & Keohane 1996; Jervis 1999: 46), and that within European integration theory, liberal intergovernmentalism has always espoused (Moravcsik 1993; Pollack 2003; Quaglia 2007).

Proposition 1 also engages contemporary analysis and research on the institutionalized nature of international relations today. While transnational networks, agencies and international institutions lead complex interdependence theorists (Zürn 1998; Mattli & Büthe 2003; Büthe & Mattli 2011; Mattli & Woods 2009; Rosenau & Czempiel 1992; Hall & Biersteker 2002; Cerny 2010) to conclude that ultimate power and control over world affairs lies beyond the nation state once established, realist research provides evidence that great powers retain significant influence over institutional rules at the expense of other states (Drezner 2007; Koppel 2010) if they want (Slaughter 1997). Institutions therefore have the effect of amplifying the influence of great powers over other states rather than restraining them and balancing them out over time. Moreover, there is a robust literature on the use of global governance outside the EU and rules within it to reinforce the institutions, structures and rights of national governments within those institutions as they manage interdependence (Kapstein 1994). In these points, realist institutionalism therefore acknowledges the narrowing of the gap between realist and liberal research on institutionalization of international affairs, and leaves behind it the crude assumptions of autarky in an anarchic environment that still many still associate with the realist paradigm.

Alongside the first proposition on realist institutionalization of international order, there are two sub-propositions on the implications of that order for both international regimes and constituent member states.

Sub-proposition 1.1

> *Sovereignty, where it exists, is organized hypocrisy.*

There are two aspects to the argument that state power is relevant even when it is imperfect. Both are adopted directly from Krasner's insightful analysis of sovereignty as organized hypocrisy, in which he demonstrates how states may be formally recognized as legally sovereign entities but lack full autonomy or control within a specific territory (Krasner 1999, 2001). The first aspect speaks to the domestic control that states have over societal actors, whether they be social, political or economic, and whether they be domestic or foreign. The second speaks to the autonomy of states from outside interference and obligations. Neither of these are absolutes.

On the point of domestic control, the study of comparative government and the historical evolution of states reveals widely divergent degrees of control and modes of input (Mann 1984; Held 2006; Newman 2009) and modes of intervention (Hall 1986; Weiss 1998; Wade 1990) across time and space that any theory of international relations is bound to accept. However, the fact that state control is not total does not render the state irrelevant. The state is there, but often in the background. Private actors and disaggregated state actors may appear to have taken over the driver's seat from central state authorities (Slaughter 2009b; Djelic & Sahlin-Andersson 2006), and weakened the input of national parliaments when they act domestically and internationally (Greven & Pauly 2000) but they have home offices based in national territories and institutional environments that influence what they bring to the table of transnational governance (Zysman 1996; Doremus et al. 1998; Djelic & Quack 2003; Singer 2007; Grande & Pauly 2005). This becomes particularly apparent at critical decision points when the country in which commercial and other entities are headquartered flexes its otherwise resting muscle. Interdependence is in this way allowed to flourish and be managed across national borders without the necessity of state intervention. Commercial and other entities can through the same institutional environments (domestic and international) be held accountable and controlled where the state deems it necessary (Mann 1997). The control of the state is therefore incomplete, but so is the autonomy of those private actors and bureaucratic agencies acting on the global stage. To follow Cox's depiction, they depend on one another and penetrate one another (Cox 1981). The consequence is that the independence of private actors can be clawed back, as can international institutions, regimes and networks in which they operate. However, because the power to intervene directly is held by the states in which the most important entities are headquartered, only great powers that have the capacity to effectively veto common action or to effect a change in common course or policy with which others have to live (if a collectively binding position, whether legal and formal or informal) (Germain 2016). The others have few other realistic options (Pauwelyn, Wessel & Wouters 2012). The continuing power of the state therefore is highly unevenly dispersed within the international system. How unevenly depends on the nature of the international institutions, regimes and networks and how deeply they penetrate national policy-making structures. This is where the second half of sovereignty as organized hypocrisy becomes relevant.

The second aspect of the organized hypocrisy argument is that states lack perfect control over the outside environment: that they are normally constrained somehow by connections to the outside world. Those connections may be institutions of some kind that are directed at states as members of the international system, or they may be transnational in nature in the sense that they are beyond the direct control of national governments. Global institutions that exist to manage interdependence place demands on what states may legitimately do and not do without suffering penalties of some kind (Kahler 1992a, 1995),[4] even if the demands are modest enough to be compatible with the retention of both legal and control forms of sovereignty.

The establishment of transnational activity that places limits on state power in exchange for other gains is a political choice in the world of organized hypocrisy (Helleiner 1996; Agnew 2005) with asymmetric consequences – it restricts public policy preferences for non-great powers much more heavily than for great powers themselves. Other states may have some influence on rules and institutions through some form of club governance for great powers like the G7 (Kirton 1989; Mastanduno, Lake & Ikenberry 1989; Kahler 1992b) or through the direct impact they have on rule making and standard setting within the institutions the great powers set up (Drezner 2007).[5] Their acquiescence can also be instrumental in determining how strong the demands of international institutions on national sovereignty can be, should the hegemon have an interest in pursuing hard restrictions. However, this is not the same as setting out the institutions themselves, determining the degree of transnational activity or asserting state power when the great power or hegemon deems it necessary.

The choice for openness does not mean lack of control. In addition to the asymmetric freedom of manoeuvre that great powers enjoy to act unilaterally or promote their own standards to others, much of the global system of international standards and national commitments currently in place preserves formal sovereignty, public policy discretion and the capacity to experiment within the parameters of a programme to pursue particular goals.[6] Standards often work with the principle of responsible sovereignty – legal and bureaucratic responsibility to be a member in good standing of the international system by implementing agreed standards within the degrees of freedom provided by what are often principles-based standards at the international level (Brummer 2012).

Sub-proposition 1.2

> *International law, organizations and regimes are also organized hypocrisy. They reflect great power preferences over time rather than restraining them.*

Great powers reshape their institutional environments when they determine it is necessary and they have the capacity to do so. There are two sides to this argument. First, great power attempts to institutionalize their neighbours and provide order to the international system are unlikely to take place in a vacuum. There is an incumbent order and set of institutions with which one must contend. The issues at stake are not only specific rules and organizations, but what Streeck and Thelen refer to as the building blocks of social order – defining the rights and responsibilities of the actors in a system – which in turn significantly determine their nature (Streeck & Thelen 2005: 9). Where incumbent institutions have not already collapsed or been destroyed wholesale, great powers will have to contend with opposition to their plans. For this reason, economy drives an important component of institutional design: which is flexibility. Institutions that work from a realist institutionalist perspective focus on essentials only, leaving discretion to national governments unless that discretion undermines the institutions' key goals.

Second, a preponderance of resources allows great powers to push through change over the opposition of incumbent actors and institutions. Having said this, and borrowing from institutional theory, there is no single pattern to how the change takes place. The changes these great powers bring about may be either sweeping and disruptive (Baumgartner, Jones & Mortensen 2014), in which old institutions break down (Gowa 1983), or are broken down and replaced, or they may be incremental and transformative, taking bits and pieces of old institutions into the new order without making a hard break. Streeck and Thelen (2005) list displacement, layering, drift, conversion and exhaustion as key forms of gradual institutional change affecting the entire relationship between rule makers and rule takers. In the process of change, it is the powerful actors who have the capacity to act as rule makers, compelling others to act as rule takers within the overall regime architecture.

How then does one demonstrate whether institutions hold sway over great powers or not, if parts of incumbent institutions might persist in either case? The analytical key is in the *ordering principles* that determine the rights, obligations and status (Paul, Larson & Wohlforth 2014) of states in the system. If great powers refrain from demanding change due to inherited rules, treaties and principles and admit defeat within the incumbent rules of the game, then realist institutionalism is disproven. Similarly, if change only takes place within the existing rules and institutions, there is no positive proof to support the claim. However, if great powers engage in *bricolage* that evades incumbent institutions and their ordering principles, that exhibits freedom to choose the means to get to an intended outcome, there is support for sub-proposition 1.2. It is the discretion of great powers to compel others to accept obligations based on different rules of the game that they had not previously accepted that demonstrates this capacity. This may mean the broad rules and principles of the institutions involved (Strange 1983), or a re-interpretation that comes from the initiative of the great power involved (Grieco 1988).

Sub-proposition 1.2 contrasts with a number of theories regarding the potential impact of international institutions and organizations on great powers against which it can be tested. Liberal institutionalists and liberal intergovernmentalists contend that institutions are sticky because national governments have economic incentives to maintain and build on the interdependence that the institutions, rules and regimes make possible (Goldstein et al. 2000), Keohane & Martin 1995; Oye 1986). Complex interdependence theorists and neofunctionalists see national governments, central authorities in particular, overwhelmed, constrained, outmanoeuvred and outlearned by transnational networks, committees and agencies bent on transcending parochial national interests (Haas 1964: 9, 22, 35) and upgrading them beyond the reach of individual governments.

Proposition 2

> *States focus on distributional consequences (relative gains and the perception of them) in institutional design.*

Interest-based theories of international relations, whether realist or liberal, take commercial interests as the starting point for an aggregated national interest, at least where these are clear. Policy ideas are considered relevant where the commercial interests are diffuse or secondary. Although Moravcsik focusses on the relevant macroeconomic policy paradigms relevant to EMU (1998), the ideas may in principle by anything, though the entire spectrum is too large to consider here. Where commercial or broad, aggregated economic interests are present, which is the case in BU and EMU reform, ideas reflect those interests rather than deviating from them. In this analysis, policy ideas are considered relevant to the extent that they shape the great power's demands on other states (Barkin 2003; Blyth 2013). Great powers therefore seek to upload policy ideas into institutions that reflect and reinforce national economic interests to other actors in the international system, providing behavioural guidance around which expectations can converge.

Great powers will therefore seek to dominate outcomes through the demands that international institutions, from organizations to rules of the game, make on national governments. As with most public policy issues, great powers (with a preponderance of resources – production, trade, finance, knowledge, security) will seek to see particular policy paradigms, ideas and prescriptions institutionalized beyond simple rules of the game and output. These may be about specific policies, but are likely to include general principles about what states may legitimately do, what they must do and what they must not. The same applies to the status of international bodies and their relationship to states (Ruggie 1982; Schmidt 2008; Schmidt & Thatcher 2013) This phenomenon is recognized in European political analysis as well (Quaglia 2010; Verdun 2000). As with sub-proposition 1.1, there is a balance to be expected between demands that a great power has on others and providing enough room for manoeuvre to undercut political resistance.

For this proposition to have a lasting effect, great powers must be able to determine for themselves what principles, laws and regulations they want to follow, which speaks for a soft law approach based on general principles (Germain 2012, 2016); and they must spread those principles and further details to others through international institutions and the activity of professionals within them. Those principles define in some significant way who the relevant actors are and what they are there to legitimately do, either in broad or in policy-specific terms. On a day-to-day basis, policy professionals from great powers involved in international institutions make demands based primarily on their own national understandings of public policy priorities and the best way of tackling them. The test of whether this works lies in whether other states adjust to the preferences of the great power(s) involved.

Material resources therefore determine power most – but institutions give great powers the capacity to continually adapt and adjust the rules governing interdependence on the front lines – they can use knowledge dominance, national standards as a way to minimize own need for adjustment to others (they can adjust themselves on their own terms – see US on Basel Accords, leverage ratios and risk weighting). Their preferences, both broad and detailed, translate into the setup of world order (March & Olsen 1998; Ruggie 2002). This is separate from the issue of whether the state components of those interests are indistinguishable from private interests (Underhill & Zhang 2008; Underhill, Blom & Mugge 2010; Cox 2004; Strange 1996).

Proposition 3

> *Economy drives institutional strategy.*

This is a general proposition that has two separate implications outlined in sub-propositions 3.1 and 3.2, but which rests on a single logic. Great powers face strong incentives to eschew creating institutions from scratch or assuming major command and control functions over other states, due to the high costs of doing so (both economic and political, in terms of resistance from other states). Although great powers may choose otherwise, their chances of success decline as they do so. This proposition has two implications.

Sub-proposition 3.1

> *Economy favours incremental change in institutions and architectures.*

Incremental innovations that increase great power control of existing institutions and repurpose or redirect them, as tactics of nesting, bricolage and change within existing institutions, constitute economical go-to solutions for reshaping interdependence that great powers should attempt before more radical solutions. We owe this insight to the seminal literature on incremental institutional change that falls short of a punctuated equilibrium but is nevertheless cumulatively transformative in a significant way (Streeck & Thelen 2005). The five means of incremental institutional change posited are the exhaustion of old institutions, redirection of existing institutions from within, displacing old institutions with new ones that take over the old institution's functions, layering new institutions on top of old ones that redirect human behaviour in significant ways, and existing institutions may drift in a process of internal transformation.

What makes these incremental forms of institutional change so reliably commonplace is that they are economical. Powerful societal actors can seize opportunities to chip away at the established order in ways that would not be possible if a grand, disruptive re-institutionalization of interdependence were to take place. This tactic generates a minimum of social and political resistance and allows new patterns of behaviour to reinforce the institutional shift through daily practice.

This proposition allows for great powers to resort to other institutions when they are not getting results they want from existing ones. The principles reflecting distributional issues should be the same across the newly-developed institutions, even where the detailed rules and institutions are somewhat different and issue-specific. But by inserting new principles into those institutions, great power preferences can be built up over time, in one new institution after the other. This is particularly so if a new institution sets the conditions for acting collectively in other areas (i.e. if other institutions become effectively nested within).

As with most general principles, Proposition 3.1 does not suggest that a great power will never attempt to engage in wide-ranging, radical institutional change. However, there are strong costs associated with doing so. Incremental change provides an alternative to which great powers are more likely to go. The same applies to Proposition 3.2.

Sub-proposition 3.2

> *Economy favours influence and enforcement pyramids as a means of institutionalizing state and private behaviour rather than command and control.*

Great powers are likely to use instrumental power sparingly, relying on multiple, differently fungible resources to coerce, incite and persuade others to establish and maintain institutions and order. Imposition on other states remains an ultima ratio for directing state behaviour when other methods fail. Although a great power might be tempted to act more forcefully, the cost of doing so on a frequent basis would eventually overwhelm its capacity to do so for an extended period.

Realist institutionalism sees the power to coerce and impose as a real component of international relations (separating it from complex interdependence and liberal institutionalism) (Krasner 2000), but one that is rarely in the forefront (in contrast with classical realism). This means that there is an expected structure of power in the international system, in which great powers determine conditions for others and by which great powers are more sovereign than lesser ones. We owe this distinction to Stephen Krasner, who refined our knowledge of how the capacity for power could be used differentially to secure desired outcomes. One can add to this by linking the type of power play to the situation at hand, demonstrating why realist institutionalism makes sense to a great power, particularly a hegemon.

The role that coercion and force play in building and maintaining institutions is best thought of by taking a leaf from regulation theory, and describing the overall spectrum of tools and the situations in which they are most frequently and fruitfully used as an *influence and enforcement pyramid.* The logic behind the pyramid is that brute force and coercion, or even a command and control method of laying out rules and punishing non-compliance is counterproductive, generating evasion and defiance, and costly to monitor and enforce unless used sparingly. Before a state resorts to such measures, it gains better acceptance and compliance from others by giving them the opportunity to participate in the rule-making, implementation, monitoring, adjustment and enforcement processes (Ayres & Braithwaite 1995). Interaction starts with open dialogue between ostensibly independent actors, in which hierarchy is very much in the distance.

Ideally in an influence and enforcement pyramid, international relations can start by taking on an ostensibly open and communicative character about how to tackle a certain problem where international standards and institutions are concerned. This is typical of policy areas where there is a high degree of uncertainty or dispute about whether problems exist and what might be done about them. This stage forms the base of the pyramid, and can be used to revisit old items that have changed and require adjustment or simply a fresh look. Typical agreements that come out of this process are guidelines, codes of conduct and best practice benchmarks that are broad enough to encompass a considerable range of initiatives. It encompasses what some name experimental governance (Sabel & Zeitlin 2008), and in particularly robust forms, the open method of coordination. The networked governance of Kahler (2009), Cerny (2010), Prichard (2017), Slaughter (2009a), Slaughter (2009b), Drezner (2007), Koppel (2010), Posner (2009), Mattli and Büthe (2003) and others, albeit with different assumptions about the relative power of countries and private actors within those structures, also falls within this rubric.

The next stage on the pyramid reflects where an authority, in this case a great power, has attained clarity about its own preferences and the expectations it has on others, but still focusses on headline goals rather than the minutiae of what the expectation might mean for others. Typical for this stage are negotiations or demands, depending on the power relations involved, for firm commitments that actors behave according to institutionalized rules and standards. International institutions, international standard-setting bodies and even international treaties and conventions fall into this category. If the institutions and standards exist and behaviour evolves in a way that deviates from them, a friendly note (or at least a non-confrontational one) requesting clarification and correction would be the equivalent. However, there is no assumption at this stage that deviance is an imminent concern that should attract efforts to police or enforce behaviour. A priori institutional engineering may take place as a standard precaution against free riding or defection at some indeterminate point in the future, but not in a way that is specifically targeted.

The next stage of the pyramid is reached if the authority is confronted with disagreement and deviant behaviour from the others it wishes to control. Demands for specific behaviour, insisting on compliance with established rules and elaboration of and respect for new ones is typical of this stage. In an international relations context, a great power, in most cases a hegemon with the ability to cut through disagreements, insists on certain outcomes that others are expected to follow (whether that be direct state behaviour in matters of security or regulatory standard setting) voluntarily.

Should insistence fail to generate behavioural change, the hegemon can resort to coercion – escalating costs as non-compliance persists and worsens. Coercion is reflected in limited, specific sanctions from which the targeted actor can recover if it complies eventually. Imposition, the final stage and apex of the pyramid, applies to massive sanctions that place the existence of the actor in jeopardy (or in this case the government or its sovereignty).

This realist institutionalist view therefore shares elements with liberal literature on political leadership (Nye 1990; Young 1991; Brawley 1993), but goes beyond political, ideational and contractual forms of generating and maintaining order and institutions. Coercion and imposition (by force or otherwise) can play a role in getting states to accept the rules of the game (in addition to contract or conventions). Coercion includes economic sanctions targeted at domestic groups and institutions of another state. The demands can be detailed and extensive (Mann 1984). Imposition is where the target is so weak it has no option but to accept:

> Coercion occurs when rulers in one state threaten to impose sanctions unless their counterparts in another compromise their domestic autonomy. The target can acquiesce or resist. Imposition occurs when the rulers or would-be rulers of a target state have no choice; they are so weak that they must accept domestic structures, policies, or personnel preferred by more powerful actors or else be eliminated.
>
> (Krasner 2001: 30)

This applies to national vulnerability to shunning by financial markets as easily as it does to gunboat diplomacy and war (Rommerskirchen 2015). And yet, the economy of getting other states to behave works best and costs the least when incorporating formal independence of states and responsibility for interpreting and implementing international commitments and standards to manage interdependence voluntarily, and with some degree of freedom.

Table 2.1 summarizes these points and compares them to two alternative visions of international relations.

Having said all of this, these core assumptions are manifested and applied in historically specific ways. Elaborating how they have developed within the

Table 2.1 Contending theoretical principles

	Realist institutionalism	*Liberal intergovernmentalism/lib. Institutionalism*	*Neo-functionalism*	*New inter- governmentalism*
Order (Prop. 1)	Institutions backed by Great Powers to support interdependence Responsible Sovereignty	Institutions backed by states to support interdependence Responsible sovereignty plus delegated agency	Institutions, networks and Supranational governance Diffused power across levels Weak sovereignty	De novo institutions Strong sovereignty
Payoffs (Prop. 2)	States choose: relative gains (resources) Great powers push costs onto others	States Choose: Mix of absolute and relative gains	Actors choose: absolute gains (welfare)	Relative gains, absolute gains (welfare)
Institutional Change (Prop. 3.1)	Economy: incremental change	Punctuated change	Incremental and punctuated change	Punctuated change
Enforcement (Proposition 3.2)	Enforcement pyramids: Imposition and coercion where incentives and persuasion fail Nested, enforced commitments	Supranational supervision	Supranational supervision and enforcement Legal action (Commission and ECJ)	Open method of coordination in de novo bodies
Power (Proposition 3.2)	Power resources used with restraint to coerce, impose decisions on others	Power resources determine bargaining capacity on hard rules	Power resources diffused	Governments dominate supranatural bodies

international system since 1945 and how they have developed in Europe since 2008 requires a review of the literature which puts flesh on their bones. The two sections below demonstrate how the assumptions of great power exercise of power in establishing institutional mechanisms to manage interdependence, uploading policy ideas for other states in the system, and economy in the establishment and use of institutions leads to a specific form of state in international order: that of responsible sovereignty. Great powers have large incentives of economy to establish rules of the international game that allow other countries to retain their formal sovereignty and internal institutions while transforming them. Alternatives such as empire, while conceivable, remain second-best solutions that may not be sustainable.

Realist institutionalism and responsible sovereignty

The sections above outline *general* principles of how great powers are expected to shape their environments. This section looks at how they apply before the post-2010 changes in Europe, specifically how the United States organized the global institutions of financial stability in the post-Bretton Woods era, how national responsibility served as a defining ordering principal of the international system, how that principle survived the end of Bretton Woods and embedded liberalism globally, and how they formed the basis of European arrangements before the financial crisis of 2008. The purpose is to demonstrate how the propositions outlined above have worked in practice in the period preceding the cases studied in this book.

One of the key observations is that responsible sovereignty has been conceived in different ways, sometimes initiating misunderstanding about its meaning. Statism has been used as a proxy for ultimate legal and political responsibility for the state of finances, as has economic nationalism in the sense used by Helleiner and Pickel (2005). Germany's establishment of a new institutional order for Europe mirrors global norms and institutions of national responsibility for financial stability. This is remarkable primarily because of the overwhelming drive of European institutions and a coalition of international organizations and governments to push Europe toward federal institutions mirroring those of the United States. The German drive for a Europe of responsible sovereigns was intended to terminate a trajectory in which interdependence worked to the increasing detriment of German interests, and a strengthened political regime in which Germany had neither a veto nor the capacity to compel others to adopt its prescriptions on good policy. That trajectory had started with Germany's forcible entry into an EMU with a set of members that was suboptimal for advancing German interests. By insisting that national governments pay for their own problems, leaving them exposed and alone to the judgement of financial markets and establishing common institutions that acted as firewalls and coercive mechanisms rather than financial transfers, the reinforcement of national responsibility could be made compatible with financial stability in Europe – at the expense of other countries, not Germany.

Realist institutionalism's view on cooperation provides a different set of expectations that can be tested in the realm of plans for Banking Union. Unlike classical realism, realist institutionalism considers it entirely possible that states engage in institutionalized cooperation at the international level. Indeed, there are significant payoffs for a great power to organize international affairs in order to avoid chaos, and in the financial arena more specifically, to ensure that capital-rich states secure the basis of reliable and profitable international transactions. The starting points of a realist institutionalist view on cooperation are the provision of order between countries, but in a way that promotes the establishment of states as the responsible points of authority within that order. That is the skeleton of ultimate responsibility on which the sinews, flesh, nerves and organs of economic interdependence are built, and constitutes an ordering principle of the international system. There is no reason to believe that the premise of statist interdependence is eternal. Rather, it is historically contingent and relies on the determination of great powers to support it, and the absence of serious threats to security. In this it overlaps with neoliberal institutionalism, without sharing the expectation that the existing order stays when power relationships change.

Rule-making in international organizations is subject to conflict, but reflects the interests of the strongest participating states (Jervis 1999; Gruber 2000; Drezner 2007; Koppel 2010), who are in a position to pay attention to relative gains in setting global standards and other rules of international cooperation. Although they may choose to limit the sovereignty of others in a direct way (Krasner 1999), they often in practice place limits in an indirect way by establishing international rules through soft law (Brummer 2012), informal international law making (Pauwelyn, Wessel & Wouters 2012) and using loose networks (Kahler 2009) to advance their national interests (Slaughter 2009b). This form of reaching out to other states through soft law preserves national room to manoeuvre to the extent that international capital markets do not punish it greatly (Mosley 2000; Weiss 1998; Walter 2008). In doing so it narrows the room available to most countries for defection from the rules, norms and procedures preferred by financial great powers, and establishes responsible sovereignty as a basic organizing principle or practice for the international system (or subsystem). This set of practices is therefore not the result of a bottom-up process decided by transnational actors or equal national governments, but by one or a few great powers. This embedded/reinforced statism is the general practice for the international system, paralleled by a harder version for the EU, with higher degrees of compulsion than international norms, rules and practices allow, due to the special condition of one state coercing others. Although the solution provided benefits the great power(s) disproportionately, order and economic openness (to the degree that it is desired) performs better for most than a collapse into anarchic competition, or exclusion from the larger order on offer. In the EU case, the power of Germany relative to that of its neighbours increased significantly in the context of financial market pressure on the southern periphery of the Eurozone, but also on other countries outside the common currency, giving it options to coerce other EU member states in ways that would not be possible in the absence of such vulnerability. This means that German power is likely strongest here.

More broadly, informal international law making and standard setting allows strong states to establish rules that impose effective obligations on others, not by the power of international law, but by the prospect of being shunned by market actors as a non-member or non-compliant state with an inherently higher risk of being a poor investment location. While the rule makers technically have the same obligations to comply, they determine the rules themselves and reserve the right to explain their deviance from prescribed rules rather than comply. This leaves them free to implement global standards that suit them as rule makers, while other states accept them, willingly or not, as rule takers. Although this view shares much in common with neoliberal institutionalist views of a networked world order (Slaughter 2009b; Singer 2007; Hall 2008), it underlines the disparity between states, particularly in the relative ability to use power for national gain (Grieco 1988), and the ultimate reliance on state-centrism as the means by which standards are implemented, whether national or international (Kapstein 1994).

Furthermore, whereas neoliberal institutionalism would expect states to exit from demands that no longer serve them well, a realist institutionalist lens couples the impact that power disparities between states have on the power relations between them in a global governance (or regional governance) setting, with market discipline, which provides large incentives for other states to comply, regardless of their level of satisfaction with the rules imposed on them. It also provides a rationale for the powerful to impose constraints on weaker counterparts to preventing losses when cooperating with other states through enforcing commitments and preventing shirking (Fearon 1998: 288–9), what Jervis terms defensive realism (Jervis 1999: 44, 49; Glaser 1997). Targeted institutional development and maintenance is therefore explicitly compatible with realist institutionalism. If the expectations above are met in the European cases of Banking Union and EMU reform, it would have the added implication that attention to relative gains, the centrality of power in determining the central questions of international relations, and the salience of these factors in highly institutionalized environments can all take place even when security concerns between the affected states are absent (Powell 1994: 314, 327). If this is true, then the international politics of the EU are more rightly seen as reflecting what we know about international politics more broadly, rather than pointing toward an exception in which security concerns are suspended. It would also shed light on how power politics manages questions of intense institutionalized interaction in a regional setting, with implications for both other regions and global governance forums.

Responsible sovereignty as a principle of international governance (Moschella 2013) is predicated on national responsibility for the core regulation, protection and promotion of banks in the single market, regardless of functional incentives to transfer authority and pool resources at the international level, and regardless of demands made by the European Commission to respect the competition policy principles of the single market. This ordering principle is sometimes referred to as statism or economic nationalism, but confusingly, does not necessarily mean mercantilism (Gilpin 2001; Krasner 1978). It may mean state rights and responsibility to selectively and strategically manage and intervene in the economy that coexists with commitments to market liberalization (Helleiner & Pickel 2005). Responsible sovereignty shares the assessment of these concepts that states are not expected to transfer responsibilities to supranational institutions as a substitute for the nation, as economic patriotism contends (Clift & Woll 2013). As both of the latter literatures contend, however, economic nationalism embodies a ‘desire to shape market outcomes to privilege the position of certain actors’ (Clift & Woll 2012: 308), in this case, banks. As discussed below, and in contrast with traditional understandings of economic nationalism, those banks may either be domestic or foreign. If economic nationalism does exist, then we should see limits to the EU’s capacity to use the single European market to restrain intervention (as cases of negative integration) and to regulate banks directly (as positive integration). This position should continue until if and when a major credit event, such as a major sovereign default, breaks the ability of creditor states to survive without collective responsibility.

Beyond European rules, national responsibility for financial stability is also buttressed institutionally by international principles of banking regulation that form the basis for European arrangements. International agreements on banking regulation and financial stability underline the principle of home country control rather than collective or supranational supervision (Kapstein 1994), a principle that was largely taken over by both the FSB (Moschella 2013) and the European Banking Authority. Confirming the assertions of responsible sovereignty at both the international and global levels, Kapstein underlines that the purpose of national responsibility

> is to allow all countries to secure the benefits of an open economy while shielding their national financial institutions from systemic pressures. . . . In the European Community the concept is far more expansive, involving mutual recognition by each member state of the others’ home country regulations.
>
> (Kapstein 1994: 9)

The result is that individual countries retain responsibility for lender of last resort facilities to their own banks, but not foreign banks operating in their jurisdictions as branches;[7] that home country control forces countries to take responsibility for enforcing regulatory standards; and that central authorities retain control over the strategic asset of money (Kapstein 1994: 14–15). During the crisis, one country’s banks draining capital from subsidiaries established in other countries has been a serious threat to financial stability, one that German authorities clamped down on in 2011 when UniCredit began bleeding HypoVereinsBank, for example (Taylor 2012).

Although responsible sovereignty’s capacity to descend into mercantilism and economic nationalism is less visible during time of plenty, there are payoffs of support by national governments in international negotiations over trade, investment and market access during good times (Kapstein: 15). Conversely, protectionism and state intervention can be expected to rise in importance during hard times to ensure the joint good of bank survival in the private sector and economic stability in the public sector and continuing economic openness (Jabko & Massoc 2012).[8] For highly internationalized countries, radical openness to retain finance should be the preferred response while other countries will turn in more on themselves. Economic nationalism – an imperative to pursue the national interest within the parameters of responsible sovereignty, is therefore driven by the need to secure finance, while the form is influenced by national circumstances, and reinforced by the institutionally embedded norms of national responsibility that preceded the crisis and were amplified during the European debates of 2012. Those norms were used as a political weapon by creditor states to fight off calls for financial transfers to debtor states as part of a fiscal union, a Banking Union or both.

Story and Walter (1997) underline how home country control principles described by Kapstein and prevalent in international relations were adopted in the EU from the 1960s to the 1990s. To the extent that European Banking Union takes the governing principles of national responsibility and enforces them more broadly and strenuously, this constitutes more than simply responsible sovereignty, but enforced responsible sovereignty at the insistence of a financial great power that uses its leverage to shape the behaviour of others (see as follows).

The FSB exemplifies as well how this principle of responsible sovereignty has been instilled into early 21st-century international relations as a means of managing intense financial interdependence. The FSB has three broad functions with regard to regulatory standards: to promote better regulatory standards that promote financial stability; to promote state capacity to implement those standards; and to promote principles of cross-border cooperation between regulators when dealing with global systemically important banks.

A key point for the FSB to deal with regarding bank regulation, supervision and resolution was to set out that in in order for the principle of home country control for global banks to be effective and respected, considerable trust and confidence in the quality of regulation and its application would have to be ensured. Otherwise the preferred mode of regulation by both global systemically important banks and existing financial centres for bank resolution would not be possible. They would prefer what regulators call a single point of entry model for resolution, in which the parent bank and its subsidiaries are treated as a whole and subject to one regulator, regardless of where they do business, rather than a multiple point of entry model, in which host countries would take control of resolution for subsidiaries operating in their jurisdictions (Tonveronachi 2013: 377–8).

The model chosen in the exercise by great powers is to use international bodies and networks to establish a world of responsible sovereigns. Responsible sovereignty is organized hypocrisy for most states, in that it is embedded in and hence responsible to a new set of regimes and standards that make demands on national governments. States still retain a significant degree of latitude regarding how to comply and implement, however, so that international expectations are made compatible with the most fundamental of local laws, institutions and societal practice. This neither means that international demands are irrelevant if they should collide with domestic arrangements, nor does it mean that international obligations and expectations micromanage the manner in which countries perform certain functions that are expected of them in order to be members in good standing of the international community, as defined by international standard setters, which themselves are dominated by great powers. Responsible sovereignty has a similar, if not identical relationship between international obligations of states in good standing and domestic policy to the practice of embedded liberalism (Ruggie 1982). States are expected to expand their own capabilities in the context of international obligations. Where behaviour is non-compliant, aid may be provided on the basis of conditionality to ensure the change (Kahler 1992a). The difference is that the focus of obligations attempts to properly regulate markets rather than limit or counter them.

Responsible sovereignty is both built on (in great powers) and cultivates (in other states) the relative autonomy of the state with regard to society (more strongly for lesser powers than for great ones). State autonomy refers to the capacity of the state to establish priorities and act on them in cases where domestic support is lacking. In the context of responsible sovereignty, it means prioritizing international responsibilities over domestic concerns. The related concept of statism is a staple of realist international theory, which posits that the demands of international politics require the state to formulate foreign policy on the basis of the implications it has for the state's power in the international system. This may mean acting against the interests of powerful economic lobby groups (Krasner 1978; Doremus et al. 1998). Relative autonomy refers again to the state's capacity to take decisions that hurt domestic lobby groups, but based on skilful statecraft that allows the state to justify those decisions from time to time. This can happen if the state can call on alternative sources of domestic support to justify its actions, for example exploiting and cultivating gaps between public opinion and the interests of major producers. This would entail arguing that there is an enlightened self-interest in pursuing policies that do not maximize utility immediately but that have long-term benefits. It can also happen when the state acts to save domestic society from its own dysfunctionality so that it continues to survive. This is not only the case for individual examples of regulation that keep the economy functioning in spite of the tendencies of corporations (Jessop 2002, 2007), but for the entire system of economy itself (Helleiner 1996; Helleiner 2003; Schmidt & Thatcher 2013). But responsible sovereignty itself and the statism it implies within the rules of the game is a construct of post-1945 international political economy.

Statism, however, implies central control and direction of policy – a point on which there is a difference of opinion. Singer contends the autonomy of central banks and finance ministries is stronger than the rest of government due to their use of international networks to ensure its continuity in the face of policy challenges (Singer 2007). As Walter notes, this version of the transnational coalition is closer to Keohane's and Slaughter's notions of networks made up of autonomous disaggregated institutions of nation states, without central political control, and therefore not necessarily working in the broader national interest (Walter 2006: 10; Singer 2007). This is an important distinction between bureaucratic theories of international governance, which shares some features of neoliberal institutionalism and realist accounts. Walter refutes the idea that there is central control on the part of states, but that the G7 rests on complex, overlapping, interlocking relationships between disaggregated national bureaucracies. He sees steering taking place in the G7, based on political consensus, and backed by financial sector interests. While the United States must interact with others to achieve its ends, its engagement means that it has done far better in advancing its interests than those who looked at the country's declining material share of world GDP expected (Walter 2006: 11). Opposite the bureaucratic politics account and the related network account stands the view that governments, great powers in particular working through the G7, at times have ultimate say over whether to adopt the standards set out by these transnational bureaucratic actors. As in Proposition 2, statism in the classical realist sense is contingent and restricted by great power perceptions. We therefore have a means of testing whether statism and realist interdependence are real despite the involvement of national bureaucracies in international fora: on the basis of whether central government provides direction and oversight to the agencies involved, with the capacity to impose its will where that is required.

Overall, one can confirm a general trend toward ensuring financial stability on a national basis by imposing national regulations on all companies without exception (see the UK and the United States turn away from allowing foreign rules) and ringfences where required as a form of defence against contagion into the domestic banking system either from foreign banks or domestic banks with foreign business. In general this meant the end of tolerance for home country control, which had ultimately forced the UK government to compensate UK depositors after the bankruptcy of the Icelandic bank Icesave, to prevent a further run on its own financial system. It also meant what Tonveronachi describes as the de-globalization of G-SIBs, global systemically important banks, as they are forced to shed some of their foreign liabilities (Tonveronachi 2013).

Responsible sovereignty also plays a significant role in political economy analysis of reconfigured regulation of financial markets after the GFC. Capacity building at the national level has become a core strategy for stabilizing national economies and restoring them to health within a continuing paradigm of economic openness and reliance of financial markets. This constitutes a shift of neoliberalism's principle message that national governments should open their laws and institutions to the demands of international standard-setting bodies to one in which national governments should build up their states in response to new demands for reform. Gamble (2009, 2014), Schmidt and Walter (2013) argue that the core policy prescriptions of neoliberalism in response to the GFC borrowed the idea of failed states from geopolitics in the 1990s and 2000s and applied it to economic policy and regulation. The effect is a new focus on state building in a broader context of political consensus among the great powers that nation states, not international organizations, should constitute the primary seat of legitimacy, authority, and grand steering and compromise required to improve global economic governance. The 21st-century model of responsible sovereignty is designed to ensure that nation states all contribute to economic openness, growth and financial stability on the basis of national effort. This provides the best compromise between the need to enhance the quality of regulation, of macroprudential and microprudential regulation in particular, of macroeconomic management (with a particular focus on preventing macroeconomic imbalances), and the need of the great powers (not just the United States, but also other key groups, and including the larger emerging markets that have been admitted to those groups, including the FSB), to ensure that they retain sovereignty, and that formal international organizations and law are kept to a minimum, regardless of the demands and expectations of international organizations and the middle powers who typically promote them as a means of constraining more powerful members of the international system. This model reflects the active choice of states, but particularly the United States, to support that move by engaging networks (Slaughter 2009a) and using them to build states (Donnelly 2012). Again, responsible sovereignty and the role of the state is a political construct. In the EU, the proposals of the Commission, the IMF and the US government went in another direction, toward federal state and budget. Instead, Germany's self-chosen job of imposing responsible sovereignty as an alternative has been made easier (though not inevitable) by corresponding international norms, institutions and ordering principles of global economic and political governance.

This means of preserving state sovereignty and simultaneously moving countries in the same direction reflects the structure of an influence and enforcement pyramid, but without the enforcement. Open discussion about best practices and guidelines are main elements of interaction on global standards, as are actual standards that speak to public policy with a greater degree of precision (such as Basel capital adequacy standards, for example). The pyramid flattens out at the level where one country can insist that the others follow a demand within their own jurisdictions, much less impose a choice. Its main means of promoting standards is through market power – compelling foreign companies doing business in its own jurisdiction to behave according to its own preferences.

If it is true that great powers pursue such institutional strategies as a first choice, then we should expect the same trend toward cultivating responsible sovereigns in Europe, instead of a shift to greater supranationalism with powers to coerce all countries. The European cases of Banking Union and EMU reform that buttresses those agreements (or lack thereof) are potential examples of precisely that.

For great powers, which in most circumstances have to contend with the demands and expectations of other great powers when calculating their strategic interests, the relative autonomy of the state stems in the first instance from the capacity of government leaders to choose between two sources of domestic interest: from interest groups on the one hand and from voters on the other. For other countries, the need to adjust domestic policy in the context of international obligations and expectations gives them leverage in shaping reforms that would not have otherwise found themselves on the domestic political agenda. For great powers seeking to cultivate such relative autonomy, this goal can be achieved by establishing a political consensus on a regime that cultivates relative autonomy in return for status as a member in good standing (and in this case, as a place to do business safely and securely in accordance with generally accepted practices of good public policy as defined by the international regime). This is in contrast to a functional regime that binds the hands of states more thoroughly (Levy, Young & Zürn 1995; Pauwelyn, Wessel & Wouter 2012; Kahler 1995; Goldstein et al. 2000). The flipside is that lesser powers find themselves somewhat restricted by the lack of participation in club governance.

European financial stability

The Great Financial Crisis placed Europe at a crossroads. The supposed convergence of European governments on the norms and rules of EMU membership around German economic doctrine (Dyson & Featherstone 1999; Verdun 2000; NcNamara 1998) had proven weak under pressure (Chang 2004: 166), leading those institutions to fail and generating discord over the proper response to the crisis. Second, Europe provided for financial stability on the basis of German demands for national responsibility and economic orthodoxy rather than on demands for supranational institutions and fiscal solidarity that an international coalition, including EU institutions, had agreed on and advised. The IMF Report on Banking Union in February 2013 recommended three pillars, involving transfer of regulatory and lender of last resort functions to the European level (Goyal et al. 2013). That advice was repeated in October of that year as European negotiations stalled (Miedema 2013). Similarly, the OECD generated its own working paper on Banking Union and institutional reform in the EU which outlined why supranational powers and budget capacity would be good for everyone, not just those expected to receive payments in the short term (Wehinger 2013).

In this context, the limited success of supranational bodies inside and outside the EU to educate and convince Germany to establish EU bodies and fiscal powers underlines the limits they have in shaping outcomes that great powers don't already want. The ECB, European Systemic Risk Board, IMF, OECD and US government all underlined that financial stability and market integration in Europe had to be supplied at the same level. While these supranational bodies and outside actors pushed for a European Banking Union with strong regulatory powers and European funds and a public backstop to provide financial stability, the EU elected in favour of coordinating national systems and funding mechanisms, even as it extended the ECB a limited mandate as a bank supervisor. While France was willing to support such options, trading loyalty to France for loyalty for Europe (Clift & Woll 2012; Jabko & Massoc 2012), it merely represents the losing side of an intergovernmental contest between two camps that wanted very different outcomes for Europe (Quaglia 2010).

These outcomes suggest, in line with the propositions of realist institutionalism above, that ideas of how to use power and for what purpose matter for state behaviour (Morgenthau 1948; Scheuerman 2009, 2011; Jervis 1999), but primarily for the great powers that are intent on determining international order, not the ideas of weaker states or international coalitions, all of which pushed in the direction of federal European institutions and fiscal transfers.

One sees in the broad literature on constructivism and international relations that great powers tend to insist simultaneously, in the contemporary world at least, on a combination of national sovereignty, which keeps the hard obligations on national governments light, and international responsibility, which rests primarily on the weaker states of the international system.

As with Proposition 2, great power ideas imply consequences for other states. This overlap between realism and constructivism applies not only to specific policy issues and packages of issues that are bound together by the same paradigm (Radaelli & Borras 2011), but to the foundations of international politics regarding international order and the nature of states that governments protect and promote themselves. There are parallels to be found within the English School of international relations, which is broadly realist as a matter of analysis, but remains agnostic on the question of whether national governments consistently cultivate both Westphalian legal sovereignty and factual sovereignty (Bull 2002; Buzan 1993; Buzan 2004; Jackson 2000). The English School sees the commitment to national sovereignty as a primary institution for international relations on which all other institutions build. While there is some debate about whether those basic assumptions can be challenged and displaced (see R2P debate on human rights limits to sovereignty), the conclusion after much research is that challenging sovereignty as a primary institution is difficult and unlikely. A critical mass of powerful and lesser states must accept and live by the changed institutional understanding. This has not been forthcoming. The result is that national sovereignty, responsible as it might be, remains the foundation of international politics without being dogmatic about its eternal nature. Although less dramatic, students of international politics can turn the question around the other way and ask whether it is a fact that national governments accept the establishment of supranational authority to make decisions that national governments have to implement, whether regionally (EU, Phillips on Mercosur, ASEAN, globally (Pauwelyn, Wessel & Wouters 2012), or within a club of nations (Drezner 2007).

This debate about the nature of states, their relationship to one another and to the institutions of the EU was the centrepiece of talks over monetary and Banking Union in Europe. Proponents of supranational authority largely lost their bid to secure power at that level. Their view of enlightened self-interest as a means by which Germany could support EU powers and financial resources failed to win the day, even though it was clear to all that it would mean less integration of the EU's capital market. Instead what Germany secured were selected supranational rights to impose rules and standards already observed by strong countries on their weaker counterparts. The latter were countries that had lost the ability to borrow from financial markets, unlike the others. Germany in particular insisted on and protected a profound commitment to national sovereignty as the main building block of responsible membership within the Eurozone. At the same time it showed a willingness to suppress that sovereignty for what it saw as the own good of the member states and the community as a whole, over the objections of EU institutions and the reluctance of the debtor countries to restore national self-reliance, thereby strengthening the weak links/failed states of the system.[9]

This willingness to use coercion to impose responsible statehood and economic self-sufficiency on reluctant governments is a relevant factor that distinguishes what has happened in the EU from both international politics outside the EU, from neofunctionalist and neoliberal institutionalist expectations of EU development, but also from the voluntarist expectations of liberal intergovernmentalism. To underline this point of Europe being transformed on a non-consensual basis through the exercise of power, Habermas warned in 2013 that Germany was undermining the EU by pursuing its own national interest in a hegemonic fashion, coupled with an 'investor-friendly' approach causing suffering in the EU's periphery, a point raised also by Ulrich Beck (2013) (Scally 2014).

Research design

The rest of the book tests the competing expectations outlined above regarding the motivations and behaviour of the key actors, including which actors have proven to be most influential, as well as the institutional outcomes, in a series of interlocking case studies of the individual components. They are based on two large cases (EMU reform and Banking Union), each broken into smaller parts. Chapter 3 examines the reform of EMU, of national budget policy in particular as a core component of the Eurozone crisis that generated negative feedback loops across the single market, to which many actors reacted with proposals for change, including Germany. Chapter 4 covers the extension of new institutions to cover the impact of bank insolvencies, that also contributed to these negative feedback loops. Chapter 5 looks at the establishment of the ECB as the only federalized institution within the EU's financial stability architecture (and the only powerful institution not established outside the EU) as a means of enforcing good behaviour on the part of national bank regulators and banks throughout the Eurozone. Chapter 6 looks at the exemptions Germany established for itself, at the expense of undersupplying financial stability in Europe, in the provision of resolution powers (the power to wind down insolvent banks) and provide deposit insurance to failed institutions. It demonstrates, as in the case of monetary union, the establishment of new, coercive institutions with the capacity to impose behaviour, policy and institutions on weak states from outside the EU in the name of Europe.

Taken together, these are cases in which German demands for national consolidation in a new institutional and treaty environment were undertaken in the wake of the financial crisis. The ultimate interest of the study is on the character of the institutions and policies that are pursued and consummated in Europe, and the manner in which they are brought about, rather than the motivations of the actors. The method used is the congruence method of analysis. In-depth case studies will be conducted of intergovernmental negotiations over components of Banking Union and EMU reform. The cases will assess the degree of persuasion, insistence, coercion and imposition used. Attention will be paid to the formulation of national policy, particularly to the relative importance of state autonomy, domestic actors, external demands and the relevance of financial markets concerns in determining outcomes. The analysis will be applied to economic performance, national institutional capacity, policy ideas on the proper division of responsibility between EU and national authorities, and on the proper trajectory of economic policy, focussed either on demand management or fiscal austerity and structural adjustment programmes.

In the concrete cases to be researched, the following concrete hypotheses flow from the general hypotheses derived above:

H1: Germany, as a financial great power, will reshape European economic governance to manage interdependence in its own interest, including institutions outside the EU order.

These outcomes will differ noticeably from prevailing norms and expectations of international order in Europe. In practical terms, this means averting a further federalization of the EU in which German influence is reduced, and adopting principles from global economic governance that reinforce national responsibility in a rule-based context.

H2: Germany's demands will focus on distributional issues, although those demands may involve uploading economic policy and institutions on others. The demands of other states or international organizations about how interdependence should be managed will be discounted.

H2.1 An institutional manifestation of distributional concerns with institutional consequences is one in which Germany is not responsible for the bulk of costs for keeping interdependence operating. This can be seen if the ordering principle of Europe's reformed institutions will be based on national responsibility to act in accordance with new institutional commitments and subject to sanctions (whether automatic or at Germany's discretion). In practical terms, this means that national governments are the primary providers of financial stability, subject to the oversight and enforcement of institutions that enjoy German support.

H3: Germany will exercise economy in its institutional strategy. This means:

H3.1 It will promote incremental institutional changes that enhance its power over others by repurposing desired parts of the existing architecture rather than radical solutions. Layering institutions outside the EU as alternatives or controlling institutions; displacement, redirection or erosion of existing EU institutions and agreements are all means by which this can be achieved;

H3.2 It will seek to establish an enforcement pyramid in which the use of coercion and imposition on (other) states is possible, but sparingly used, and states are expected to enforce their own behaviour. The German government will show a willingness to coerce and impose the consequences of its institutional order on other states as a last resort, after exhausting other means of influence. Two outcomes that falsify this hypothesis are German self-restraint in the face of opposition or non-compliance, or the failure of German attempts to bear fruit (which disproves German capacity to act as a financial great power).

The rest of the book proceeds as follows in testing the hypotheses above. Chapter 3 examines changes to fiscal policy that led to the establishment of the TSCG. Chapter 4 looks at the establishment of a bailout mechanism for states and banks in the Eurozone. Chapters 5 and 6 examine the three pillars of Banking Union proper: supervision, resolution and deposit guarantee systems. Chapter 7 concludes.

Notes

1 There is no guarantee that a powerful state will succeed, but it is expected to try. The same principle can be extended during periods of imperialism to colonies. See Buzan and Lawson (2015).
2 This can range from the rules of accountancy and debt law relevant to loans to developing areas typical of the 19th century global economy to the plethora of contemporary international standard-setting bodies in which a small group of countries led by the United States dominates the process.
3 There may be trade-offs, such as the cost to the British Empire of maintaining formal colonies and a navy when the primary goal was to achieve economic gains through informal empire, which itself rested on the golden triangle of trade (profitable), colonies (potentially costly) and the navy (costly).
4 Cox's brand of historical materialism takes this finding further and suggests that because of this, that they thereby set out the requirements for survival and competition within the existing framework. This is said to shape their nature or threaten them with failure as states. See Cox (1981).
5 The possibility of establishing a new system of robust global institutions is not foreseen by the model here in the absence of a hegemon. Instead, one should expect regional orders with only thin arrangements between the great powers.
6 See mechanisms of the IMF and WB (FSAP), OECD principles of good corporate governance as an example of OMC and the peer review process of the FSB. Similar principles were used in the EU (Sabel & Zeitlin 2008).
7 Subsidiaries of foreign banks, which are fully-independent companies subject to host country control, reinforce the national bias. See Wade and Sigurgeirsdottir (2010).
8 See also Mervyn King's statement that 'global banks are global in life, but national in death'.
9 Based on the principle of sound public finance, as embodied in the Washington consensus, and implemented by the Troika of ECB, Commission and IMF in EU program countries. See Lütz and Kranke (2014).

References

Agnew, J. (2005) Sovereignty regimes: Territoriality and state authority in contemporary world politics. *Annals of the Association of American Geographers* 95, 2: 437–61.
Agnew, J., & Corbridge, S. (2002) *Mastering space: Hegemony, territory and international political economy*. London: Routledge.
Ayres, I., & Braithwaite, J. (1995) *Responsive regulation: Transcending the deregulation debate*. Oxford: Oxford University Press.
Barkin, J. S. (2003) Realist constructivism. *International Studies Review* 5, 3: 325–42.
Barnett, M., & Duvall, R. (eds.). (2004) *Power in global governance*. Cambridge University Press.
Baumgartner, F. R., Jones, B. D., & Mortensen, P. B. (2014) Punctuated equilibrium theory: Explaining stability and change in public policymaking. In Sabatier, P. A. ed., *Theories of the policy process*. Boulder, CO: Westview, 59–103.
Beck, U. (2013) *German Europe*. Cambridge: Polity Press.

Bickerton, C. J., Hodson, D. & Puetter, U. (2015) The new intergovernmentalism: European integration in the post-Maastricht era. *Journal of Common Market Studies* 53, 4: 703–22.

Blyth, M. (2013) *Austerity: The history of a dangerous idea*. Oxford: Oxford University Press.

Brawley, M. (1993) *Liberal leadership: Great powers and their challengers in peace and war*. Ithaca: Cornell University Press.

Brummer, C. (2012) *Soft law and the global financial system: Rule making in the 21st century*. New York: Cambridge University Press.

Büthe, T., & Mattli, W. (2011) *The new global rulers: The privatization of regulation in the world economy*. Princeton University Press.

Bull, H. (2002) *The anarchical society* (3rd ed.). New York: Columbia University Press.

Buzan, B. (1993) From international system to international society: Structural realism and regime theory meet the English School. *International Organization* 47, 3: 327–52.

Buzan, B. (2004) *From international to world society? English school theory and the social structure of globalisation*. Cambridge: Cambridge University Press.

Buzan, B., & Lawson, G. (2015) *The global transformation: History, modernity and the making of international relations* (Vol. 135). Cambridge: Cambridge University Press.

Carstensen, M. B. (2013) Global in life, still national in death? Special bank resolution regimes after the crisis. In Moschella, M. & Tsingou, E., eds., *Great expectations, slow transformations: incremental change in post-crisis regulation*. Colchester: ECPR Press: 77–124.

Cerny, P. G. (2010) *Rethinking world politics: A theory of transnational neopluralism*. Oxford: Oxford University Press.

Cerny, P. G., & Prichard, A. (2017) The new anarchy: Globalisation and fragmentation in world politics. *Journal of International Political Theory* 13, 3: 378–94.

Chang, M. (2004) *Realigning interests: Crisis and credibility in European monetary integration*. Basingstoke: Palgrave MacMillan.

Clift, B., & Woll, C. (2012) Economic patriotism: Reinventing control over open markets. *Journal of European Public Policy* 19, 3: 307–23.

Clift, B., & Woll, C. (eds.) (2013) *Economic patriotism in open economies*. London: Routledge.

Cox, R. W. (1981) Social forces, states and world orders: Beyond international relations theory. *Millennium-Journal of International Studies* 10, 2: 126–55.

Cox, R. W. (1987) *Production, power, and world order: Social forces in the making of history*. New York: Columbia University Press.

Cox, R. W. (2004) Beyond empire and terror: Critical reflections on the political economy of world order. *New Political Economy* 9, 3: 307–23.

Djelic, M. L., & Quack, S. (2003) *Globalization and institutions*. Edward Elgar Publishing.

Djelic, M. L., & Sahlin-Andersson, K. (eds.) (2006) *Transnational governance: Institutional dynamics of regulation*. Cambridge: Cambridge University Press.

Donnelly, S. (2012) Institutional change at the top: From the financial stability forum to the financial stability board. In Mayntz, R. ed., *Crisis and control: Institutional change in financial market regulation. Frankfurt am Main: Campus Verlag*: 261–75.

Doremus, P., Keller, W., Pauly, L., & Reich, S. (1998) *The myth of the global corporation*. Princeton: Princeton University Press.

Drezner, D. (2007) *All politics is global: Explaining international regulatory regimes*. Princeton: Princeton University Press.

Dyson, K. H., & Featherstone, K. (1999) *The road to Maastricht: Negotiating economic and monetary union*. Oxford: Oxford University Press.

Eichengreen, B. (1987) *Hegemonic stability theories of the international monetary system.* National Bureau of Economic Research (No. w2193).

Eichengreen, B. (1997) Saving Europe's automatic stabilisers. *National Institute Economic Review* 159, 1: 92–8.

Eichengreen, B., & Frieden, J. (eds.) (1994) *The political economy of European monetary unification.* Boulder, CO: Westview Press.

Eichengreen, B., & Wyplosz, C. (1998) Stability pact. *Economic Policy* 26.

Fearon, J. D. (1998) Domestic politics, foreign policy, and theories of international relations. *Annual Review of Political Science* 1, 1: 289–313.

Gamble, A. (2009) *The spectre at the feast: Capitalist crisis and the politics of recession.* Basingstoke: Palgrave Macmillan.

Gamble, A. (2014) Neo-liberalism and fiscal conservatism. In Schmidt, V. & Thatcher, M. eds., *Resilient liberalism, political economy through boom and bust.* Cambridge: Cambridge University Press: 53–76.

Germain, R. (1997) *The International organization of credit: States and global finance in the world-economy.* Cambridge: Cambridge University Press.

Germain, R. (2012) Governing global finance and banking. *Review of International Political Economy* 19, 4: 530–5.

Germain, R. (2016) Locating authority: Resolution regimes, SIFIs and the enduring significance of financial great powers. *Journal of Banking Regulation* 17, 1: 34–45.

Gilpin, R. (2001) *Global political economy.* Princeton: Princeton University Press.

Glaser, C. L. (1997) The security dilemma revisited. *World politics, 50,* 1: 171–201.

Goldstein, J., Kahler, M., Keohane, R. O., & Slaughter, A. M. (2000) Introduction: Legalization and world politics. *International Organization* 54, 3: 385–99.

Gowa, J. S. (1983) *Closing the gold window: Domestic politics and the end of Bretton Woods.* Ithaca: Cornell University Press.

Gowa, J. S. (1989) Rational hegemons, excludable goods, and small groups: An epitaph for hegemonic stability theory? *World Politics* 41, 3: 307–24.

Goyal, R. et al. (2013) *A banking Union for the Euro area*, IMF Staff Discussion Note SDN 13/01, Washington, DC: International Monetary Fund.

Grande, E., & Pauly, L. W. (eds.) (2005) *Complex sovereignty: Reconstituting political authority in the twenty-first century.* Toronto: University of Toronto Press.

Gray, C. S. (2013) *War, peace and international relations: An introduction to strategic history.* London: Routledge.

Greven, M. T., & Pauly, L. W. (2000) *Democracy beyond the State? The European dilemma and the emerging global order.* Rowman & Littlefield.

Grieco, J. M. (1988) Anarchy and the limits of cooperation: A realist critique of the newest liberal institutionalism. *International Organization* 42, 3: 485–507.

Grieco, J. M. (1995) The Maastricht treaty, economic and monetary union and the neo-realist research programme. *Review of International Studies* 21, 1: 21–40.

Gruber, Lloyd. (2000) *Ruling the World: Power politics and the rise of supranational institutions.* Princeton: Princeton University Press.

Haas, Ernst. (1964) *Beyond the nation-state.* Stanford: Stanford University Press.

Hall, P. A. (1986) *Governing the economy: The politics of state intervention in Britain and France.* Oxford: Oxford University Press.

Hall, R. B. (2008) *Central banking as global governance: Constructing financial credibility.* Cambridge: Cambridge University Press.

Hall, R. B., & Biersteker, T. J. (2002) *The emergence of private authority in global governance.* Cambridge: Cambridge University Press.

Hasenclever, A., Mayer, P., & Rittberger, V. (1997) *Theories of international regimes* (Vol. 55). Cambridge: Cambridge University Press.

Held, D. (2006) *Models of democracy*. Stanford: Stanford University Press.

Helleiner, E. (1996) *States and the reemergence of global finance: From Bretton Woods to the 1990s*. Ithaca: Cornell University Press.

Helleiner, E. (2003) *The making of national money: Territorial currencies in historical perspective*. Ithaca: Cornell University Press.

Helleiner, E., & A. Pickel. (eds.) (2005) *Economic nationalism in a globalizing world*. Ithaca: Cornell University Press.

Hooghe, L., & Marks, G. (2009) A postfunctionalist theory of European integration: From permissive consensus to restraining dissensus. *British Journal of Political Science* 39, 1: 1–23.

Jabko, N., & Massoc, E. (2012) French capitalism under stress: How Nicolas Sarkozy saved the French banks. *Review of International Political Economy* 19, 4: 562–85.

Jackson, Robert. (2000) *The global covenant: Human conduct in a world of states*. Oxford: Oxford University Press.

Jervis, R. (1999) Realism, neoliberalism and cooperation: Understanding the debate. *International Security* 24, 2: 42–63.

Jessop, B. (2002) *The future of the capitalist state*. Cambridge: Polity Press.

Jessop, B. (2007) *State power*. Cambridge: Polity Press.

Kahler, M. (1992a) External influence, conditionality and the politics of adjustment. In Haggard, S. & Kaufman, R. eds., *The politics of economic adjustment: International constraints, distributive conflicts and the state*. Princeton: Princeton University Press: 89–136.

Kahler, M. (1992b) Multilateralism with small and large numbers. *International Organization* 46, 3: 681–708.

Kahler, M. (1995) *International institutions and the political economy of integration*. Washington, DC: Brookings Institution.

Kahler, M. (ed.) (2009) *Networked politics: Agency, power and governance*. Ithaca: Cornell University Press.

Kapstein, E. (1994) *Governing the global economy: International finance and the state*. Cambridge, MA: Harvard University Press.

Keohane, R. O., & Martin, L. L. (1995) The promise of institutionalist theory. *International Security* 20, 1: 39–51.

Keohane, R. O., & Nye, J. S. (1984) *After hegemony: Cooperation and discord in the world political economy*. Princeton: Princeton University Press.

Kindleberger, C. P. (1986) *The world in depression, 1929–1939*. Berkeley: University of California Press.

Kindleberger, C. P. (2005) *Manias, panics and crashes* (5th ed.). New York: Wiley-Blackwell.

Kirton, J. J. (1989) Contemporary concert diplomacy: The seven-power summit and the management of international order. *International Studies Association*, 29.

Koppel, J. (2010) *World rule: Accountability, legitimacy and the design of world governance*. Chicago: University of Chicago Press.

Krasner, S. D. (1976) State power and the structure of international trade. *World Politics* 28, 3: 317–47.

Krasner, S. D. (1978) *Defending the national interest: Raw materials investments and U.S. foreign policy*. Princeton: Princeton University Press.

Krasner, S. D. (1982) Structural causes and regime consequences: Regimes as intervening variables. *International Organization* 36, 2: 185–205.

Krasner, S. D. (1983a) *International regimes*. Ithaca: Cornell University Press.

Krasner, S. D. (1983b) Regimes and the limits of realism: Regimes as autonomous variables. In Krasner, S. D. ed., *International regimes*. Ithaca: Cornell University Press: 355–68.

Krasner, S. D. (1991) Global communications and national power: Life on the Pareto frontier. *World Politics* 43, 3: 336–66.

Krasner, S. D. (1999) *Sovereignty: Organized hypocrisy*. Ithaca: Cornell University Press.

Krasner, S. D. (2000) International law and international relations: Together, apart, together. *Chicago Journal of International Law* 1: 93.

Krasner, S. D. (2001) Rethinking the sovereign state model. *Review of International Studies* 27, 5: 17–42.

Levy, M., Young, O., & Zürn, M. (1995) The study of international regimes. *European Journal of International Relations* 1, 3: 267–330.

Lütz, S., & Kranke, M. (2014) The European rescue of the Washington consensus? EU and IMF lending to central and eastern European countries. *Review of International Political Economy* 21, 2: 310–38.

Mann, M. (1984) The autonomous power of the state: Its origins, mechanisms and results. *European Journal of Sociology* 25, 2: 185–213.

Mann, M. (1997) Has globalization ended the rise and rise of the nation-state? *Review of International Political Economy* 4, 3: 472–96.

March, J. G., & Olsen, J. P. (1998) The institutional dynamics of international political orders. *International Organization* 52, 4: 943–69.

Mastanduno, M., Lake, D. A., & Ikenberry, J. (1989) Toward a realist theory of state action. *International Studies Quarterly* 33, 4: 457–74.

Mattli, W., & Büthe, T. (2003) Setting international standards: Technological rationality or primacy of power? *World Politics* 56, 1: 1–42.

Mattli, W., & Woods, N. (2009) *The politics of global regulation*. Princeton: Princeton University Press.

McNamara, K. (1998) *The currency of ideas: Monetary politics in the European Union*. Ithaca: Cornell University Press.

Miedema, D. (2013) EU must speed up Banking Union to gain trust, IMF says. *Reuters*, 9 October.

Milner, H. V., & Keohane, R. O. (1996) Internationalization and domestic politics: An introduction. In Keohane, R. O. & Milner, H. V. eds., *Internationalization and domestic politics*. Cambridge: Cambridge University Press: 3–24.

Moravcsik, A. (1993) Preferences and power in the European community: A liberal intergovernmentalist approach. *Journal of Common Market Studies* 31: 473–.

Morgenthau, H. (1948) *Politics among nations: The struggle for power and peace*. New York: Alfred A. Knopf.

Moschella, M. (2013) Designing the Financial Stability Board: a theoretical investigation of mandate, discretion, and membership. *Journal of International Relations and Development*, 16, 3: 380–405.

Mosley, L. (2000) Room to move? International financial markets and national welfare states. *International Organization* 54, 4: 737–73.

Newman, E. (2009) Failed states and international order: Constructing a post-Westphalian world. *Contemporary Security Policy* 30, 3: 421–43.

Nye. J. S. (1990) *Bound to lead: the changing nature of American power*. New York: Basic Books.

Oye, K. A. (1986) *Cooperation under Anarchy*. Princeton: Princeton University Press.

Paul, T. V., Larson, D. W., & Wohlforth, W. C. (eds.) (2014) *Status in world politics*. Cambridge: Cambridge University Press.

Pauwelyn, J., Wessel, R., & Wouters, J. (eds.) (2012) *Informal international law-making*. Oxford: Oxford University Press.

Pollack, Mark A. (2003) *The engines of European integration: Delegation, agency and agenda-setting in the EU*. Oxford: Oxford University Press.

Posner, E. (2009) Making rules for global finance: Transatlantic regulatory cooperation at the turn of the millennium. *International Organization* 63, 4: 665–99.

Powell, Robert. (1994) Anarchy in international relations theory: The neorealist-neoliberal debate. *International Organization* 48, 2: 313–44.

Quaglia, L. (2007) The politics of financial services regulation and supervision reform in the European Union. *European Journal of Political Research* 46, 2: 269–90.

Quaglia, L. (2010) *Governing financial services in the European Union: Banking, securities and post-trading*. London: Routledge.

Radaelli, C., & Borras, S. (2011) The politics of governance architectures: Creation, change and effects of the EU Lisbon strategy. *Journal of European Public Policy* 18, 4: 463–84.

Rommerskirchen, C. (2015) Fiscal rules, fiscal outcomes and financial market behaviour. *European Journal of Political Research* 54, 4: 836–47.

Rosenau, J., & Czempiel, O. (1992) *Governance without Government: Order and change in world politics*. Cambridge: Cambridge University Press. Ruggie, J. G. (1982) International regimes, transactions, and change: Embedded liberalism in the postwar economic order. *International Organization* 36, 2: 379–415.

Ruggie, J. G. (2002) *Constructing the world polity: Essays on international institutionalisation*. Abingdon: Routledge.

Sabel, C. F., & Zeitlin, J. (2008) Learning from difference: The new architecture of experimentalist governance in the EU. *European Law Journal* 14, 3: 271–327.

Scally, D. (2014) Habermas warns Germany risks undermining EU. *Irish Times*, 4 February.

Scheuerman, W. E. (2009) *Morgenthau*. Cambridge: Polity Press.

Scheuerman, W. E. (2011) *The realist case for global reform*. Cambridge: Polity Press.

Schmidt, V. A. (2008) Discursive institutionalism: The explanatory power of ideas and discourse. *Annual Review of Political Science* 11: 303–26.

Schmidt, V. A., & Thatcher, M. (eds.) (2014) *Resilient liberalism in Europe's political economy*. Cambridge: Cambridge University Press.

Singer, D. A. (2007) *Regulating capital: Setting standards for the international financial system*. Ithaca: Cornell University Press.

Slaughter, A. M. (1997) The real new world order. *Foreign Affairs* 76: 183–97.

Slaughter, A-M. (2009a) America's edge: Power in a networked century. *Foreign Affairs* 88.

Slaughter, A-M. (2009b) *A new world order*. Princeton: Princeton University Press.

Snidal, D. (1985) The limits of hegemonic stability theory. *International Organization* 39, 4: 579–614.

Stopford, J. M., Strange, S., & Henley, J. S. (1991) *Rival states, rival firms: Competition for world market shares*. Cambridge: Cambridge University Press.

Story, J., & Walter, I. (1997) *The political economy of financial integration in Europe: The battle of the systems*. Cambridge, MA: MIT Press.

Strange, S. (1983) "Cave, Hic dragones!", in Krasner, S. ed. International regimes. Ithaca: Cornell University Press: 337–54.

Strange, S. (1996) *The retreat of the state: The diffusion of power in the world economy*. Cambridge: Cambridge University Press.

Streeck, W., & Thelen, K. (2005) *Beyond continuity: Institutional change in advanced political economies*. Oxford: Oxford University Press.

Tonveronachi, M. (2013) De-globalising bank regulation. *PSL Quarterly Review* 66, 267: 371–85.

Underhill, G. R., Blom, J., & Mügge, D. (eds.) (2010) *Global financial integration thirty years on: From reform to crisis*. Cambridge: Cambridge University Press.

Underhill, G. R., & Zhang, X. (2008) Setting the rules: Private power, political underpinnings, and legitimacy in global monetary and financial governance. *International Affairs* 84, 3: 535–54.

Verdun, A. (2000) *European responses to globalization and financial market integration: perceptions of economic and monetary integration in Britain, France and Germany*. Basingstoke: Palgrave Macmillan.

Wade, R. (1990) *Governing the market: Economic theory and the role of government in East Asian industrialization*. Princeton: Princeton University Press.

Wade, R., & Sigurgeirsdottir, S. (2010) Lessons from Iceland. *New Left Review* 65: 5–29.

Walter, A. (2008) *Governing finance: East Asia's adoption of international standards*. Ithaca: Cornell University Press.

Wehinger, G. (2013) Banking reform: A new year's resolution. *OECD Observer* 297, Q4.

Weiss, L. (1998) *The myth of the powerless state: Governing the economy in a global era*. Cambridge: Polity Press.

Young, O. R. (1991) Political leadership and regime formation: On the development of institutions in international society. *International Organization* 45, 3: 281–308.

Zürn, M. (1998) *Regieren jenseits des Nationalstaates: Globalisierung und Denationalisierung als Chance*. Berlin: Suhrkamp.

Zysman, J. (1996) The myth of a 'global' economy: Enduring national foundations and emerging regional realities. *New Political Economy* 1, 2: 157–84.

3 The TSCG and EMU reform

Establishing responsible sovereignty

This chapter examines the establishment of an international treaty outside the structure of the EU that imposes obligations on EU member states, forces a reshaping of the Eurozone's rules and policy architecture, and does so at the initiation and ultimately discretion of one state: Germany. Europe's sovereign debt crisis, at least in the southern periphery of the Eurozone, underlined the inherent weaknesses of a monetary union without a fiscal union – that is, without automatic transfers between the member states of the union. As early as 1994, an American analysis of EMU underlined that as the membership became more diverse, fiscal transfers would be necessary to even out disparities across regions and moderate cyclical highs and lows in the Eurozone economy (Eichengreen & Frieden 1994; Hagen & Eichengreen 1996; Bayoumi & Masson 1995). Without the moderating effect of such transfers, and in the absence of an optimal currency area in which all countries were highly alike, periodic strains on the national economies within the Eurozone would naturally lead to suboptimal policies over an extended period, as well as political tensions between countries over growth, employment and stability levels that could tear the Eurozone apart (Eichengreen 1997). Either countries with low inflation rates would find themselves permanently disadvantaged by interest rates that were too high for their economies, or countries with high inflation rates would find themselves in a boom-bust cycle in which interest rates were too low, provoking economic bubbles that would burst with catastrophic consequences.

Although most analysts promoting fiscal union did not explicitly foresee banking crises developing in boom-bust countries (except Eichengreen & Wyplosz 1998, who expected that the sovereign would default first), they did see the overall macroeconomic trends that would dominate the first decade of EMU and contribute to making banking crises possible. They also expected that the existence of a fiscal union would lessen the likelihood of banking crises by lessening the strain on national economies when necessary. The means to restrain inflation and public sector borrowing in inflation-prone countries, i.e. centralized controls on national fiscal policy, was considered a critical counterweight to automatic transfers to prevent moral hazard – fiscal profligacy and irresponsibility by the financially weak in particular, but also for politicians in general. This was the purpose

DOI: 10.4324/9780203702130-3

behind the Stability and Growth Pact (SGP) and the Excessive Deficit Procedure (EDP) that were adopted prior to EMU's launch, but which remained ineffective and unused, in part due to compromises that prevented automatic sanctions on governments, and in part due to a 2004 relaxation of rule application at the behest of Germany and France. It is for these reasons that literature on EMU concurs that the monetary union is characterized by a centralization of monetary policy at the EU, but a decentralization of fiscal policy in the hands of the member states. Neither EU fiscal transfers nor EU fiscal controls were worth mentioning, at least until the point when the TSCG was signed in 2012. And while the SGP and EDP placed limits on national fiscal policy on paper, those powers were effectively re-nationalized in the reform of 2005 that relaxed the definition of when a state had an excessive deficit, at the behest of the EU's largest and most powerful member states (Blavoukos & Pagoulatos 2008; Chang 2006; Howarth 2007). While coordination increased nationally in the related area of the Broad Economic Policy Guidelines, EU powers themselves did not increase (Hodson 2009; Enderlein & Verdun 2009).

The absence of fiscal transfers was deliberate, however. Although the original membership of EMU did not constitute an optimal currency area, the countries of the so-called deutschmark zone did, and had no need for such transfers. Southern Europe, in contrast, was the most likely set of countries that would draw on such transfers at the expense of the north. The lack of fiscal policy was not only an issue of proper governance, but of political economy, in which the main beneficiaries and payers were clear, and in which it was easy for commentators, economists, voters and politicians to frame the situation as anything other than a zero sum game in which deutschmark zone countries would pay for other countries. There was very little consideration for the benefits that would also accrue to all Eurozone countries if Southern Europe could be relied on as a consumer of high value-added goods from Northern Europe. The result is that EMU was deliberately under-institutionalized, with a centralized monetary authority and decentralized, national authority over fiscal policy.

In negotiations over Banking Union, as well as much commentary on the process, the lack of a fiscal union would come back to haunt the EU, due to the lack of a European taxpayer-funded public backstop to ensure the safety of banks when all other measures had failed. Given the extremely high levels of leverage across the European banking sector compared to counterparts in the United States and Canada, the magnitude of the public backstop required to provide for financial stability was also correspondingly large. The gap between what was required and what national governments could provide was therefore considerable across the board, and extremely so in those countries like Spain and Ireland, where banks borrowed even more heavily than others to fuel lending based on interest rates that were too cheap for the economy. On functional grounds, the inability of some countries to provide public backstops on their own, and the resulting financial instability beyond those countries, was sufficient to put the issue back on the negotiating table of European heads of government.

However, the same distributional conflict that stood in the way of EMU developing a fiscal union proved to dominate discussions on Banking Union as well. Not only did northern European countries repeat their rejection of fiscal transfers across national borders (or mutualized debt that all EU member states would be liable for), they placed the blame for the Eurozone crisis firmly with Southern European countries (and to a lesser extent Ireland) and pushed through measures inside and outside the EU to force them to exercise fiscal restraint and self-reliance. That constituted a push for responsible sovereignty as the organizing principle of international relations instead of a European federation. This chapter focusses on the nature and intent of the TSCG and reforms to tighten EU oversight of national fiscal policy as the centrepiece of that push, and the role that it plays in the broader plans for Banking Union. The TSCG constituted a reshaping of European economic governance outside the EU that Germany could not achieve within it (H1) for distribution issues (H2) by layering institutional commitment to price stability and harnessing and pushing control and sanction institutions within the EU (H3). It demonstrates that the TSCG aims to provide financial stability based on sound public finance and national public backstops. The consequence of this in principle is that countries with weaker public borrowing capacity must have smaller banking systems, so that that they can credibly support the smaller banks with lender of last resort facilities. The consequence in practice is that the banking sector in Southern Europe must shrink from its mid-crisis levels more than it would have to do if more extensive fiscal transfers were in place. In the medium-term, this means economic contraction in Southern Europe as both the public sectors and banking systems shrink.

This chapter aims to test the premise that the establishment of the TSCG in particular reflects the premises of realist institutionalism more than those of (liberal) intergovernmentalism or neofunctionalism, and that it is directly linked to the business of establishing monetary union. The link of premise, to reiterate, is that the TSCG increases pressure on national governments in the Eurozone to stabilize their public finances without assistance from other member states in the EU. This expectation cannot help or ameliorate weak links, however. In the overall architecture of financial stability in the Eurozone, the TSCG is a buttress against Southern European claims on northern Europe for enhanced public assistance, while other measures discussed in this book are a buttress against claims for private assistance to banks directly. It is part of a larger firewall between north and south.

This chapter is structured as follows. Section 2 provides background into the link between bank debt and sovereign debt, the mechanisms by which national instability translates into international contagion, and ends with an assessment of the limits of national borrowing capacity as a problem with which European leaders and officials must deal. Section 3 provides an outline of the various reforms to address those issues. Section 4 examines the degree of voluntarism and coercion in ratifying reforms of the EU treaties and institutions, and of the TSCG. The specific issue of extraordinary bailouts of states is a separate topic handled in the next chapter. Section 5 concludes.

The bank-sovereign link

The most pressing aspect of the financial and economic crisis from 2010 onward for EU countries and especially for the Eurozone as a whole was the inability of some member states to act as lenders of last resort to their own banking systems in time of financial stress. This was something of a surprise to the Europeans for more than one reason. First, very few politicians and analysts had thought about a bank collapsing with systemic implications for the Eurozone or about the reverse scenario in which the Eurozone's declining economy brought banks – in plural – into increasing jeopardy. This meant that it was not an issue of EU responsibility and was simply not considered. Those who were genuinely concerned about economic decline leading to default within the Eurozone focussed primarily on sovereigns rather than banks as actors attempting to manage the economy, and as the High Contracting Parties of the Maastricht Treaty, which outlined EMU's architecture. This focus on macroeconomics, with its background in optimal currency area theory, is why Germany, Austria and the Netherlands in particular invested so much attention and effort at the moments when EMU's rules were being drafted, and members being selected, into preventing the member *states* of the Eurozone from borrowing too much for too long. There was no indication in the period between the drafting of EMU and the outside of the Eurozone crisis that that thinking had changed or been subject to serious review.

Second, thinking in the EU about the implication of monetary unions for financial stability, for banks in particular, had failed to keep pace with commonly accepted knowledge and practice. The received wisdom on bankruptcy of either individual banks or the solvency and liquidity of the entire banking system since the 1880s is that central banks must perform the function of a lender of last resort. Otherwise, bank collapses, whether real or imagined, will spread from one bank to the next until the all of them fall, or become a self-fulfilling prophesy that incites depositors and investors to flee one bank after another, causing all of them to collapse. Whereas national central banks could purchase corporate and sovereign debt in the event of an emergency and save both banks and sovereigns from collapse before the launch of EMU, they could not afterward. Meanwhile, the ECB was legally prohibited from taking over that role from its national counterparts. In the thinking of the time, this provision in the Maastricht Treaty was intended to erect a barricade around the ECB against an expected onslaught of (southern) EMU member states demanding that the new central bank monetize their debt – purchase it from them in virtually unlimited quantities at low rates of interest for which all EMU member states would ultimately become liable. The insistence by Germany, Austria and the Netherlands on national responsibility for national public finances was so ruthlessly entrenched into the Maastricht Treaty that it sacrificed the ECB's legal capacity to fulfil the role of lender of last resort. Although the ECB would unilaterally undermine these restraints as the crisis unfolded, fierce and relentless German resistance in the face of unparalleled financial collapse underlined that not only did EMU deviate from the principle that central banks should serve as the lender of last resort, but that this function was barred deliberately.

Third, banks and states successfully supported each other in the first few years of the crisis (Donnelly 2011), which encouraged the view that they could sustain each other's financial viability for as long as was required. When states injected banks with fresh capital in 2008 and 2009, they did so with borrowed money that the banks themselves then purchased and held on their balance sheets. As interest rates started to rise, banks benefited from the combination of receiving higher interest rate income from government, and the assumption (until the Greek crisis) that sovereign debt had a virtually zero risk of default. This meant that they did not have to set aside capital against the risk of default (Gros 2013). In this way, banks enjoyed increasing rates of return from investments in sovereign debt – for as long as the sovereigns could pay the interest rates. That capacity started to erode in 2010, when Greece and Portugal found themselves cut off from financial markets and came to a full stop in 2012, when Spain and Italy were forced to pay interest rates that were unsustainable.

The eruption of the Eurozone crisis in 2010 represented the point at which financial markets increasingly shunned Southern European governments, after two years of financial and economic crisis. Interest rates for treasury bills rose significantly from the historic lows that had prevailed since the countries entered monetary union to 6% and higher, roughly 4% above German bunds, and effectively more than doubling the interest paid on a portion of the national debt. That portion would also grow faster than the country's immediate borrowing needs, since the government would have to periodically repay old bonds coming due at a lower rate of interest with new bonds at a higher rate. Under these conditions, and with Southern European countries entering a third year of recession with fragile and deteriorating public finances, shunning by financial markets brought Greece and Portugal to the point of collapse, while Spain and Italy managed to stay away from the brink. Greece's default, and Portugal's need for financial assistance, coupled with Ireland's, generated the real threat that sovereigns would not repay their debts, unleashing a chain of bank collapses throughout Europe. The innovations of 2010 and 2012, described below, reflect an attempt to avoid disaster in this situation.

The reason why the ECB was not granted authority to act as the lender of last resort for situations like these is that Germany and its allies were obsessed during the negotiations with the prospect of moral hazard by individual member states and ensuring that institutional rules and procedures minimized that likelihood. The roots of responsible sovereignty were not only visible in the lack of an EU fiscal policy, but in the limited mandate of the ECB. Germany and its allies concluded that a fully functional ECB with powers to buy corporate and sovereign debt would encourage moral hazard in the Eurozone's weaker member states and force the stronger member states to bail them out in the event of a crisis. This is why the rules were set up to ensure national responsibility for national finances, to punish those who transgressed their obligations (regardless of the fact that the rules were loosened later on and never truly enforced). This aversion to solidarity on the part of EMU's stronger member states, coupled with a certain aversion to fiscal responsibility on the part of EMU's weaker member states (whereby strong and weak refers to the capacity to live comfortably within EMU membership criteria on government borrowing, rather than the size of the economy) ensured that no burden-sharing would be possible, either in the direct form of a fiscal union with cross-border transfers and the capacity to issue Eurozone debt, or in the indirect form of ECB purchases of national bonds for which the EU member states would eventually be liable.

The undersupply of financial stability in the Eurozone therefore does not stop at the absence of a fiscal union, but extends to Germany's attempt to undermine the role of the central bank in a time of emergency. The result is that the absence of a central lender of last resort in the Eurozone was reinforced. Such pressure was the only way in the eyes of Germany (and a few others) to instil extreme caution on the part of the Eurozone's weaker member states in public finances. But it also meant that the capacity of those states to support the national banking systems would also be limited. This was certainly deliberate, and of such critical importance to the founders of EMU that it must be considered constitutional in nature – a principle so important that breaching it directly or through any other measure would be a deal breaker for those countries that had insisted on it in the first place. That was Germany and the Netherlands in 1992 when the Maastricht Treaty was signed. Finland and Austria joined the group of hardliners in 1995 when they joined the European Union. The banking issue may not have been consciously in the minds of the contracting parties that set up EMU, but the collective capacity of states to borrow was a core issue. When the Eurozone crisis erupted, the inability of some countries to act as lenders of last resort therefore re-politicized the original principles of the single currency. It would either retrench its fundamentally intergovernmental nature in fiscal policy, strengthening the states within their collective responsibilities, or establish supranational institutions and fiscal capacities that would take EU integration to a truly supranational level.

From the perspective of the ECB, this position was untenable, as it threatened complete financial collapse on the continent, leading to controversial innovations. The ECB's Securities and Markets Program (SMP) and Outright Monetary Transactions (OMT) provided monetary accommodation for a cash-strapped financial sector with no other source of liquidity. While the SMP bought corporate and public debt on secondary markets in limited quantities, the OMT announcement indicated the ECB's willingness to buy as much as was needed for as long as was necessary to supply both the private and public sectors with cash during an investment strike. While the OMT announcement stabilized financial markets and allowed some governments to resume normal borrowing, it also was designed to be temporary until the political actors could come up with a solution. It therefore bought policy entrepreneurs time rather than doing away with the problem of financial instability emanating from the Eurozone's southern periphery. These institutional developments are discussed in more detail in the next chapter, as they are highly relevant on the topic of bailouts, which is treated there in detail.

The SMP and OMT generated tremendous critique from nearly all corners of society and government in Germany, and more than one resignation of a German official from the Executive Board of the ECB. The reasoning was that the ECB had overstepped its authority in purchasing treasury bills from Southern European countries and undermined the incentive for Eurozone member states to prudently restrain their borrowing by purchasing those bills in significant quantities (SMP), and then in unlimited quantities (OMT), thereby postponing the day of reckoning and damaging the integrity and stability of the single currency in the process. That confrontation between the ECB and Germany remains to the present day, with the ECB maintaining that its measures are temporary and necessary in the absence of a political solution by the rest of the EU and its member states.

Nevertheless, the construction of EMU's rules continues to mean that the member states of the Eurozone have to guarantee financial stability through national fiscal mechanisms – taxpayer guarantees and cash infusions for banks or the whole banking sector – as happened in 2008 throughout Europe. The uneven capacity of governments to support such a burden then became apparent. The ECB stepped in with emergency measures to relieve the pressure on the weakest links in Southern Europe, in the form of purchasing government debt on secondary markets. This meant banks and other financial institutions would purchase the bonds first and then sell them to the ECB, which had agreed in advance to purchase them. This ruse deliberately circumvented the legal prohibition on the ECB monetizing (purchasing) government debt, but staved off a collapse of both public and private finance that the Maastricht Treaty would have ensured had it been respected to the letter. Despite this, the temporary nature of the measure, and the requirement for treaty changes to sort out the question of how that debt would be repaid and by whom, re-opened the arena for new agreements on (1) whether the ECB would be allowed to continue purchasing debt; (2) whether there would be some kind of EU bailout mechanism to come to the aid of weak member states in distress; or (3) whether the responsibility would continue to rest on the shoulders of the member states themselves, with the attendant undersupply of financial stability in the Eurozone (Donnelly 2014a, 2014b). The effect multiplies the number of weak links in the European financial system.

The efforts of Germany, together with the Netherlands and Finland were crucial in ensuring that Europe responded to the question of who should bear the burden of adjustment through the third path, despite overwhelming pressure from other actors to follow the second. What is more, the fiscal retrenchment goals laid out in the Treaty on Stability, Coordination and Governance, which reinforced and imposed these responsibilities on the member states even more insistently than before, could only be achieved by circumventing EU institutions that favoured more solidarity between the member states, plus EU powers and financial resources to regulate financial crises. The intergovernmental agreements, or IGAs as they came to be known, initiated a new form of executive intergovernmentalism outside the EU that imposed the will of the German led coalition on both EU institutions and on Southern European countries who would suffer the wrath of financial markets, and therefore financial collapse if they failed to agree to the German bloc's terms. But unlike the New Intergovernmentalist interpretation, layering outside the EU was crucial to this happening.

This chapter walks the reader through that development to strengthen the case that the motivations of Germany to demand the TSCG are directly related to the other institutions of EMU and Banking Union in the pursuit of distributive gains, and that the motives and methods reflect a realist mode of politics, and are therefore power- and interest-based rather than institutionally constrained or influenced in a significant manner. The acid test of institutionalist theory, as the reader recalls, is whether existing institutions of cooperation restrain and exact respect from the member states and generate path dependence, even when this works against their interests, or whether institutions are subject to attack and abandonment when they no longer serve their purpose.

On the other hand, a failure to achieve further cooperation and even supranationalism on the basis of the existing institutions and principles of conduct do not disprove the institutional or liberal intergovernmentalist viewpoint. Nor would a simple shift in power from the more supranational organs of the EU – the European Commission, Court and Central Bank, to the member states represented in the Council (Bickerton, Hodson & Puetter 2015) – fundamentally disprove neofunctionalism. It would show a change in the character of supranational governance, but not a change in its fundamental nature. The use of relative power to shape the outcome of a negotiation only underpins the expectations of intergovernmentalism, however. Only the abandonment of old institutions, the unilateral imposition of new rules against an unwilling group of followers, and the use of coercion would confirm the realist institutionalist thesis. Showing it is therefore not an easy task. The rest of the chapter examines whether these criteria are met to a sufficient degree to make a confident observation on the links to Banking Union, whether or not realist power politics are a determining factor in these institutional changes, and most importantly, what factors have made such a change possible. A useful account must shed light on the fungible power resources that powerful states possess, that weak states lack, under what conditions (to determine the scope of validity that the findings of this chapter have), and how the incentives line up to make a realist expression of power politics possible. To the extent that it is confirmed to exist, support for a realist account can be found.

As the Eurozone crisis gained momentum, pressure grew on European governments to prop up their banking sectors with lender of last resort facilities as the US government had done, with the assistance of an accommodating monetary policy from the Federal Reserve. In the absence of central banks capable of doing the same thing, national governments found themselves on the front line, advancing credit to banks, providing outright cash injections (grants) to them, guaranteeing their creditworthiness by standing up for losses incurred by non-performing loans and financial derivatives without any current market value (toxic assets). While this provided temporary relief from market pressures, the deficit and debt levels of the Maastricht Treaty then served as constraint on the Eurozone's more financially fragile members – to the extent that the Commission and Council used them to pressure those governments to refrain from bailing out banks.

Proposed responses

The dilemma in which Europe found itself in 2010 posed the question of who would adjust in dealing with the situation. Assuming that the ECB would not be able to monetize debt indefinitely, dealing with it meant bringing government debt and deficits down to a manageable level so that financial markets would not shun the country, and that enough room would be left for governments to borrow in a bank crisis. The first option, promoted by fiscal conservatives, was that individual countries would adjust downward, ratcheting down borrowing in the public sector and in the banking sector, and suppressing domestic consumption. This is the path that was eventually chosen, meaning macroeconomic deflation and successive rounds of fiscal austerity in Southern Europe, Ireland and France, coupled with pressures to deleverage banks, so that national fiscal backstops would be capable of borrowing to support the banking system. The second option was that individual countries with the capacity would adjust upward. Under this scenario, Germany would have reduced its current account surplus through higher rates of consumption, acting effectively as the export market for other European economies, and serving in that additional way as Europe's economic motor. The US government was still arguing for this option in various forms throughout the construction of Banking Union and the reform of EMU, individually and in coordination with the French government and the European Commission, seeking to balance austerity with measures to promote growth and jobs. Particular forceful American proposals were for Germany to reduce its large current account surplus by increasing demand and imports, which would benefit its European trading partners (Carnegy 2014). This would lead to less need for southern retrenchment or deleveraging as southern economies used the opportunity to establish a more robust export sector. The third option was a fiscal union, in which Germany would adjust downward through fiscal transfers, thereby diminishing pressure on Southern European countries to deflate and deleverage. That option would be tabled by the American government in 2014, and again during the Greek crisis of 2015. The IMF supported the goal of balancing adjustments and softening demands for austerity as well. In June 2014, it announced support for allowing national governments to make investments in infrastructure that would not count toward the yearly deficit for the purposes of the EU's fiscal rules. During the Greek crisis of 2015, the IMF's appeals became more urgent, arguing that Europe either had to institute a fiscal union to relieve pressure on the public budgets of the weaker states in the euro area, or cut the debt loads that had built up in the context of Europe's preceding imbalanced decade (Moghadam 2014).

Remedies inside and outside the EU

This section deals with the linkage between the provision of a public backstop to the Eurozone in response to the onset and continuation of the Eurozone crisis from 2010 onward and reforms to the fiscal policy architecture of EMU. It outlines the functional demand for a common backstop, the political demand for a common backstop from France and a number of Southern European countries, and the alternative demands for responsible national fiscal management that came from the German-led coalition of conservative member states.

The most prevalent functionalist response to the Eurozone crisis was calls for the European Union to move in a federal direction, specifically by adopting a fiscal union. It was not the only proposal, but the one that was central to most functional plans for dealing with the spectre of financial contagion across Europe's borders. The advocates included the US government, the IMF and OECD, a number of think tanks (Henning & Kessler 2012) and a number of European governments, of which France as one. These calls were for (1) solidarity between the member states in light of (2) speculation by international financial markets, which were seen to be at the root of the Eurozone's troubles, in addition to (3) the need for the Eurozone to develop policies and mechanisms of sound countercyclical macroeconomic management, and (4) an assumption that macroeconomic differences across regions within a currency area are natural but must be compensated through a common fiscal mechanism to steer against regional disparities (rather than cyclical ones).

In practice this meant advocating a fiscal union in which money would flow from countries with strong tax revenues to countries with weak revenues. They also pushed for euro bonds to buy time and leverage for domestic restructuring, managed by an EU Treasury Department and headed by a European Secretary of the Treasury or Finance Minister (Matthijs & McNamara 2015). The primary intent of these proposals was to create the political and financial power necessary to counter the threat of depression with a financial 'bazooka', as US Treasury Secretary Geithner put it. Such measures would not only empower the EU to act quickly, decisively and with great force in a crisis, but to manage the Eurozone economy in a countercyclical and symmetric way. Ideally, and with prudent management, the EU would thereby acquire the standard tools of macroeconomic management that all modern governments had had since the 1930s – to lesser or greater degrees. It would also allow capital to flow to Southern Europe without depressing German demand. In that light, it is worthy of note that American calls were equally strong for Germany to boost domestic consumption and reduce its current account surplus with the rest of Europe so that other countries had the possibility to earn their way out of their predicament.

Although these proposals had functional foundations, numerous member state proponents had direct material incentives to advocate them and did. Most importantly, they were vulnerable to the decisions of financial markets regarding whether or not to roll over their debt, to buy new debt, and at what interest rate. These were the proponents of fiscal union. France does not fall into the direct fire of financial markets, with the exception of Goldman Sachs' announcement that the ultimate target of the Eurozone crisis would be France, but the heavy investment of French banks in the Eurozone's southern periphery meant that without a fiscal union, the French banking sector would suffer enormous losses.

The Eurozone agreed to a partial provision of cross-border transfers as a temporary measure in May 2010, then as a permanent measure in 2010 as it became apparent that financial markets would continue to not only speculate against Southern European countries, but against large Southern European countries in which creditor countries had invested more heavily than elsewhere. The European Financial Stability Facility (EFSF) and the European Stability Mechanism (ESM), agreed in May and October of 2010 respectively, provided cross-border financial transfers in the form of loans to stave off collapse. Spain's inability to raise funds in June 2012 in particular raised the possibility of default, which in turn would introduce financial contagion in the financial sectors of France, Germany, the Netherlands and the UK, among others.

The counterproposal by Germany, the Netherlands and Finland sought to reaffirm national responsibility for national public finances, and for macroeconomic steering within the context of a single monetary policy. Countries that found themselves in difficulty and had to be bailed out due to severe economic circumstances were not the victims of misfortune and malevolent financial markets, but of home-made macroeconomic imbalances that could be prevented in the future by restraining borrowing in both the public and private sectors. Rather than working with the assumption that catch-up countries, those with a lower standard of development and standard of living, could borrow quite a lot and experience higher than average rates of growth and inflation without serious negative side-effects on the economy as a whole, the German-led coalition's assumption was that national consumption could only be sustained by money earned from exports to the rest of the world. In other words, consumption-based borrowing of all kinds, including borrowing from banks for housing and government borrowing for income transfers and other forms of social spending should be suppressed as much as possible. To the extent that catch-up countries caught up to GDP per capita levels of Europe's core, they would have to do it more slowly and on the basis of international competitiveness in goods and services, which in turn would keep income and price levels lower than catch-up countries would experience under a leveraged model of economic growth. Note that this black and white, either-or juxtaposition ignored Germany's own middle way, entrenched in its own constitution, that public sector borrowing was justifiable to the extent that the proceeds flowed into investment in infrastructure, which held the possibility of contributing to future gains in productivity, and therefore improved international competitiveness. It also failed to recognize that the German model of low domestic consumption was not attainable for all, and therefore unrealistic as a means of allowing poorer countries in the Eurozone to catch up with their neighbours. Nevertheless, the narrative and the standpoint served as the basis for proposals to reform the existing budget rules for the Eurozone member states to reinforce national responsibility for borrowing decisions, and for avoiding macroeconomic imbalances, largely without the assistance of the other EU states.

From the perspective of the German-led coalition, fiscal union as proposed by most of its EU counterparts would have the negative impact of encouraging moral hazard by enticing member states to over-borrow, or allowing their banks to over-borrow, knowing that fiscal transfers would transfer responsibility for repayment to taxpayers from other countries. That threat created the need for a counterproposal on fiscal union. That package consisted of reforms within the EU, and increasingly, outside the EU, where Germany was able to secure agreement under coercion to impose stronger changes on EU member states than the EU itself would have allowed. Those innovations: the Six-Pack, the Two-Pack and the TSCG, are discussed below.

Reforms within the EU

Reforms within the EU demonstrate incremental changes to EMU architecture (H3) that underline national responsibility coupled with sanctions as an enforcement pyramid (H3) with clear distributional issues (H2). They can be divided into two categories: those which apply to the Eurozone only and those apply to the entire EU. The European Semester and the Six Pack apply to all EU member states, although in practice, it is most relevant to the Eurozone. The Two Pack applies in practice only to those countries within the Eurozone. The Euro Plus Pact applies to both the Eurozone and selected countries that have opted to join. These multiple reforms attempt to increase the responsibility of member states for retrenching their own finances and managing their own economies in a sustainable way. They attempt to do so by installing one layer of increased pressure after another to demonstrate their commitment to a pre-set list of performance criteria, and subjecting performance to higher Commission supervision and peer pressure in the Council.

The first of these innovations was the European Semester, which was launched in 2011 after its adoption in 2010 (European Commission 2010). It intended to strengthen the peer review and political commitment of individual member states to develop and implement National Stability Plans (NSPs – for Eurozone members) or National Convergence Plans (NCPs – for other EU member states) and National Reform Plans on an annual basis to the Commission and the Council. Those NRPs, NCPs and NSPs would be drafted in the context of an Annual Growth Survey (AGS) published by the Commission for the entire EU the preceding November, and discussed in March. It would then be up to the Council to approve of any country-specific recommendations (CSRs) made by the Commission. Member states present NCPs/NSPs for budgetary policy and National Reform Plans for structural adjustment policy, competitiveness and employment in April, for review. The European Semester itself had no sanctions attached to it if countries chose to deviate from the advice given, however (Heinen 2010). Program countries receiving assistance from the EFSF/ESM are subject to a separate Adjustment Program with a higher degree of obligation and are not included in the European Semester. The EP consults on employment policy.

Discussions and country-specific recommendations in Brussels during the first half of the year (the European Semester) would be followed by the National Semester, from July to December, in which implementation would take priority. While the Council communication on the European Semester stressed that the EU intended to improve coordination for the purpose of improving EU competitiveness (European Council 2011), the practical emphasis of the Semester was to put increased pressure on member states to introduce structural reforms and restrain their public borrowing. This is underlined by the innovation of introducing ex ante coordination of national policies with European goals instead of ex post review (European Council 2011), and the appointment of European Semester officers who would serve to oversee the national budget process during the National Semester.

The Euro Plus Pact was adopted in March 2011 on the heels of the decision to introduce the European Semester. Like the Semester, the Pact takes place within the context of enhanced cooperation within the EU, using the open method of coordination on a broad range of economic policy goals that are considered important for improving economic performance, with the ultimate goal of contributing to competitiveness and the sustainability of public finances. The Council declaration announcing the Pact states that signatories add additional components to their National Convergence or National Stability Plans, so that the EPP adds a layer on to the previously existing Broad Economic Policy Guidelines. The headline goals of the EPP are international competitiveness, employment, sustainability of public finances, financial stability and EU tax policy. Each of these categories in turn commits the signatories to pursue improved performance in key components of the headline goals. The competitiveness category requires reporting and improvement on productivity, with special attention to unit labour costs, meaning that wages should only increase to the extent that they have already generated more economic value in goods and services sold by companies than they cost. This ensures both improvements in international trade competitiveness and low inflation. The employment category focusses primarily on structural reforms, retraining and tax incentives that push people back into the work force who would otherwise have remained unemployed, and direct them into the most competitive sectors possible. The public finance category not only includes overall budget balances, but also long-term challenges to public finance that are well-known in policy circles but sometimes get little attention by politicians – particularly pension payments for baby boomers that are due to undermine the solidity of public finances in the first and second quarters of the 21st century. The financial stability category commits the participants to push forward on installing and improving on national resolution mechanisms for failing banks and installing and carrying out regular stress tests on their banking sectors to ensure a national basis for financial stability (European Commission 2011). Finally, the tax issue reflected a desire by several countries to close tax havens within the EU – Austria and Luxembourg – by ending bank secrecy and thereby improving tax revenue to national governments once hidden accounts were revealed.

The Euro Plus Pact effectively hardens the aspects of the Europe 2020 program that apply to sustainable finances and economic management for the countries that participate. One reasoning is that Europe 2020, like the Lisbon Agenda that preceded it, provided too much latitude for national governments to commit themselves to concrete plans for improving particular policy areas. Another is that like Lisbon I, from 2000 to 2004, the set of goals in Europe 2020 were too broad and sometimes post-materialist in nature to provide a clear focus on improving public governance and economic performance.

Despite the increased pressure on the EPP signatories to follow through on their commitments, they were bound only by political agreement rather than legal obligation, and the Pact lacked sanctions for non-compliance. It also lacked specific mechanisms for dealing with what Germany perceived as the root of financial instability: macroeconomic imbalances. Those issues would be brought up in EU negotiations over the course of 2011, and given form in the Six Pack and the Two Pack in time to be launched in early 2012. The Six Pack and Two Pack, with its enhanced set of preventive and corrective tools, would then be merged with the European Semester.

Six Pack, Two Pack and reform of the SGP and EDP

In contrast to demands for a fiscal union based on increased EU borrowing capacity and a pooling of repayment (Salines et al. 2011), Germany, the Netherlands and Finland pushed a mirror image of that fiscal union to ensure that national governments would be increasingly compelled to manage their public finances in a prudent fashion. This meant not only observing the debt and deficit criteria for membership in the single currency, but also committing to fairly narrowly conceived policies of economic sustainability. The most important of these was avoiding macroeconomic imbalances that might create economic fragility and unsustainable debt levels without violating the formal criteria of Eurozone membership. In practice, this meant that Europe developed new treaties and mechanisms in the attempt to prevent crises from happening before they could start. This would not only apply to countries like Greece and Portugal, with their propensity to run high public sector deficits, but also countries like Ireland and Spain, which had floated their economies on mountains of private rather than public debt, and could not repay once the economy showed signs of sustained weakness.

The ethos of the demands that these three countries supported was to force responsibility on national governments so that Europe as a whole would not be called on to step in with resources to prevent a systemic crisis. However, forcing national governments to change their constitutions, their finance ministries and their concrete economic management policies was going to be difficult to pass by the member states. The result is that some reforms were carried out within the EU, while others were established outside the EU, where more forceful demands could be made on Eurozone member states. Those demands, once made, would be difficult for weaker states to refuse without the risk of unleashing a negative reaction by financial markets, who might surmise that the country would be left behind in the modest efforts to stabilize the Eurozone (the EFSF and ESM), or fail to perform, or both.

In terms of substantial policy goals, the Six Pack, which came into force in December 2011 for all EU member states except the UK, builds on the Eurozone's SGP and the EU's Broad Economic Policy Guidelines while the Two Pack builds on the EDP. The Six Pack is therefore intended to prevent the likelihood of excessive debt and deficit levels, and to punish non-compliance. It generated the following innovations to more strongly instil what the Commission saw as practices of responsible statehood within and outside the Eurozone:

1 *Quantitative indicators for medium-term budget objectives* (MTOs), as well as indicators for 'significant deviations' (Bouwen 2013: 6) designed to end the high degree of latitude national governments continued to exploit in laying out plans for fiscal consolidation.
2 *Applying the Excessive Deficit Procedure to debt as well as the deficit benchmarks for sound finances*, with the intent of compelling countries to run budgetary surpluses, so as to bring down debt-to-GDP levels that had moved beyond the 60% threshold in most countries over the course of the crisis.
3 *Constitutionalizing EU fiscal policy obligations* or embedding them in laws identified as having a 'durable' status.
4 *New Macroeconomic Imbalances Procedure* (prevention and correction).

In addition to the AGS introduced with the European Semester, the Six Pack introduced a Macroeconomic Imbalances Procedure that replicates reporting and peer review on deficit and debt levels into the area of macroeconomic imbalances. This expands the scope of the EU's surveillance and recommendations to include key issues of wage levels, housing prices and private-sector borrowing. It also introduced an Alert Mechanism Report (AMR) highlighting problems within specific countries for national governments and the Council as a whole to incorporate into their March deliberations. It also tasks the Commission with generating In-Depth Reviews (IDRs) of selected problems in particular countries, which would be issued ahead of the March Council meeting.

5 *Gradual financial sanctions up to 0.5% of GDP for SGP violations for Eurozone member states.* First round is interest-bearing deposit than converts to fine after continued intransigence.
6 *Gradual financial sanctions for MIP violations (failing to take the advice)* (Bouwen 2013: 6)

The most attention-grabbing innovation, however, was the introduction of Reverse Qualified Majority Voting (RQMV) in the Council, which means that warnings and sanctions issued by the Commission would have automatic validity unless the Council blocked the decision with a Qualified Majority Vote. This reversed the previous mechanism, one that France had long insisted on since the beginning of EMU, that only a positive decision by the Council could lead to warnings and sanctions. The Six Pack is also an important innovation over the Euro Plus Pact in that it has the binding force of EU law behind it rather than a simple political agreement facilitated by the Open Method of Cooperation.

Overall, the Six-Pack therefore builds up pressure on the member states that goes beyond what was originally agreed on for the European Semester, partially on the basis of what Germany and its close allies had managed to construct in the EP. It therefore appears that the German strategy of constructing political agreements that lack the status of EU law and fail to include some member states indeed help generate legal changes within the EU at a later date. The results are significant: national finances and broader economic and social policy are reviewed by the Commission and by the member states collectively in the Council. A harder line on macroeconomic orthodoxy is made possible by the institution of RQMV, the scope of demands is increased through the development of the MIP, and an enforcement mechanism is instituted for the Eurozone member states outside the legal limits of the EU. The developments are compatible with sovereignty, however, until a national government runs so far behind that it is forced to apply for a bailout under the European Stability Mechanism. Indeed, both the EPP and the Six Pack were considered prerequisites by Germany, Finland and the Netherlands for agreeing to financial contributions to the ESM. The Six Pack attempts to prevent a country from needing such assistance. The Two Pack, on the other hand, strengthens the legal mechanisms for controlling a country that must turn to the ESM for help.

The Two Pack, which came into force in May 2013, was designed specifically for countries falling under 'enhanced surveillance' within the EDP, and when a country has received financial assistance through the ESM: (1) a form of enhanced surveillance is not specified in the regulation, but the purpose is to prevent contagion of financial stability to the rest of Europe. In this light, specific steps are to be developed to guide the member states to 'timely and durable' reduction of deficits; recommendations are made by the Commission and decided by the Council. Because the demands may vary from the normal content of the BEPG, the Council has explicit freedom to make different demands of the state in need of assistance. (2) Probation: specific steps are to be taken to review national government policies until 75% or more of the aid disbursed to a Eurozone member state has been repaid, to ensure they stick with their reform plans. It is therefore designed to sort out the conditions under which the member states of the Eurozone would be prepared to grant and disburse aid (Bouwen 2013: 7).

An additional goal of the Two Pack was to try to make surveillance and demands from the ESM process consistent with EU law. Whether that was successful is dubious, given the fact that the ESM process and the TSCG make use of EU institutions as agents to perform some of the key functions, but were established deliberately outside the EU to prevent opponents in the Council and in the Parliament from blocking their establishment.

Reforms outside the EU

The changes within EMU were conditioned by changes effected outside the EU that could not be achieved within (H1). The TSCG was proposed by Germany in May 2010, agreed in principle in the European Council on 9 December 2011 and signed on 2 March 2012 by 25 EU member states (the UK and Czech Republic rejected the treaty). It entered into force in December 2012 after Finland ratified it as the 12th signatory, in accordance with the terms of the treaty. The main engineers were Merkel and Sarkozy.

The TSCG commits signatories to move toward a public budget which is in balance or in surplus (Article 1). A structural deficit of no more than 0.5% GDP is permitted, which is close to requiring a balanced budget (unless debt is below 60%). In that case, a deficit of 1% of GDP is permitted. This in itself sets the bar far higher than is the case in the SGP, and poses a problem for countercyclical macroeconomic steering or crisis. Budget deficits in the United States and UK after the onset of the financial crisis exceeded 12% of GDP, for example.

What is more striking is the obligation of the signatory states to embed that budget commitment in their constitutions (Article 2). This takes economic policy out of the hands of democratically elected governments, and constitutes one of the elements of German demands that would have proven unacceptable in the context of the EU. That is also one reason why one might reasonably be sceptical that German ambitions to merge the TSCG and ESM treaties with the EU are unlikely to find approval. Another is that non-members of the Eurozone who stand to lose by signing are not under the same kind of pressure to do so. They may suffer at the hands of financial markets for a time, but have more flexibility and chances to rebound.

In addition to constitutional amendments mandating a balanced budget, the Treaty also mandates the establishment of independent budget offices at the national level to supervise compliance and progress, reinforced surveillance of national budget policies through the other member states of the Eurozone, and ex ante coordination of debt issuance, which means seeking permission to borrow. For those countries subject to the EDP, the Treaty also gives the other Eurozone member states a role in determining the conditions that countries under enhanced surveillance must meet, including structural and other reforms, with wide-reaching consequences. Moreover, those decisions are based on recommendations from the European Commission, and subject to reverse qualified majority decisions on all stages of the EDP, rather than just sanctions, as in the Six Pack. The EDP and sanction mechanisms are therefore as automatic as possible without doing away with the involvement of the Council entirely (Ioannou, Leblond & Niemann 2015). On top of these obligations, the TSCG brings in the Commission to report on and the European Court of Justice to rule on whether a signatory is in breach of its obligations, and the ECJ to authorize a fine up to 0.1% of GDP for failure to implement its obligations. Funds flow into the ESM. To date, because the ECJ has not yet been asked to do such a thing, it is not yet clear whether it would accept this role. It is clear, however, that there are certain legal problems with asking an EU institution to perform a task that is requested of it by members of an outside treaty, particularly if it involves the use of coercion against a state.

The Commission was generally positive about the TSCG with the reasoning that it was granted a role, and that the problem of illegality will be resolved if the signatories are successful in having that treaty and the ESM merged with the EU in the medium term. The Parliament, on the other hand, was been deeply critical of both the policies and the method of attaining them (Stavridis & Irrera 2015).

The innovations of the TSCG and the ESM were not the end of changes that Germany planned, however. Linkages between the TSCG's focus on national finance and the other aspects of Banking Union, particularly resolution and bail-out of failed banks, led German Finance Minister Wolfgang Schäuble to suggest in March 2014 that the Eurozone could not provide financial stability without the appointment of a Eurozone finance minister empowered to supervise and direct key fiscal and banking matters, primarily in the event of an emergency, but also in cases where it became clear to that person that national economic and financial policy was coming off the rails, at least by the financial benchmarks of the TSCG. At the same time, he clarified in Davos that the members of the Eurozone were sovereign nations with the right to take their own decisions, and that they would remain so in principle (Schäuble 2014). This combination of benchmarks, independence for financially prudent member states and tutelage for the rest confirms the suspicion that in at least this area of finance, that responsible sovereignty was the model of relationship between the Eurozone (rather than the EU) and its member states that the Germans were trying to instil and institutionalize. These proposals, which in Germany were known as Protocol 14, after a corresponding protocol in the 2009 Lisbon Treaty, received the support of the Council President, but not from a significant number of EU member states. In Germany's view, the demands made sense that in exchange for the multi-billion German contribution to the ESM's budget, the EU would establish a European Finance Minister to oversee stronger, quantified budget controls on the member states (Der Spiegel 2013). Schäuble suggested after the underwhelming reaction a renewal of the proposals after the May 2014 European Parliament elections, and the election of a new Commission later that year.

A key defining feature of the TSCG is its status as an international treaty outside the framework of the other EU treaties. This point was a bone of contention at the time of its negotiation, its ratification and has been since then, as it makes reference to EU treaties and makes use of EU institutions, but is not itself an EU treaty. Had that been the case, then all EU member states would have had to agree to a change of existing EU treaties in accordance with Article 48 of the TFEU, which sets out procedures for amending the Treaties. However, faced with UK opposition to a treaty change, Council President van Rompuy proposed that the Council be able to agree instead on an amendment of Protocol 12 of the TFEU, after consultation with the European Parliament and the ECB. Protocol 12 details the obligations of the signatories on fiscal policy, whether member states of the Eurozone or not. This would allow the EU to effect a common political commitment over the objections of the UK veto.[1] But since the changes to Protocol 12 were not in themselves a treaty with legally binding obligations on national governments, the German government insisted on a separate treaty outside the framework of the EU's treaties, so that obligations could have far greater force than what could be achieved in the compromise-laden context of EU negotiations. The fact that the TSCG makes use of EU institutions and procedures to impose far more stringent budgetary conditions than EU treaties themselves allow for is the principal reason why the treaty has been attacked as illegal (Fischer-Lescano 2014). Another reason is that it effectively splits the EU into signatories and others. From the German perspective, however, the procedures of the Six Pack and the Two Pack, the involvement of European institutions and the application of peer pressure were required to add applied pressure to the legal obligations of a treaty. The fact that Germany was prepared to make such dubious legal demands on the other member states of the EU in the face of UK resistance to treaty change demonstrates the keenness with which the German government intended to impose austerity on other EU member states. The main expectation is that the strongest incentive to sign and ratify is by countries that need credibility in the face of financial markets, and that need access to the ESM (Closa 2012).

The German position on the legal dubiousness of the TSCG was mitigated in its own view, and accepted by the Commission, by virtue of Article 16, which requires the signatories to attempt to merge the treaty with the EU Treaties within 5 years. It is therefore presented as a temporary measure. However, it would then have to deal with Article 48, requiring unanimity of all EU member states, and initiating a UK referendum by virtue of the European Union Act 2011.

German proposals for even more specific policy prescriptions led the Netherlands to walk away as a key ally. Micromanagement of national finance was only acceptable to the Dutch if applied to programme countries, but not countries that managed their economies within the demands of the TSCG as it already stood (Escritt 2014). This demonstrates that while German demands led the charge to establish the foundations of a new European financial order, going it entirely alone was not considered feasible. The failure of the German Finance Ministry's proposal underlines that although Germany can be considered to have great power status, much more so than any other state, its powers are not extensive enough to be considered hegemonic.

How voluntary is the choice for retrenchment?

The economic implications of the TSCG are very compelling indeed. They have such a negative view on public debt that they effectively force states trying to improve economic growth and development to suppress consumption, prices and wages and earn money from international trade instead, regardless of what other claims are made in the context of the EU's Annual Growth Survey and Country-Specific Recommendations. While the policy prescription has worked well for Germany, Japan, China and a selected number of East Asian countries, there are reasonable questions about the capacity of other states to follow this model. If not, then the TSCG has the effect of making some countries very much poorer than they were. Some of that adjustment toward sounder public finance is certainly healthy and reasonable, but it is also reasonable to ask whether there were conditions surrounding the negotiation of the treaty that amounted to coercion on countries that have little immediate material interest in signing on to such obligations. In other words, is competitive deflation a mercantilist strategy that also involves coercion against other countries to follow and to accept institutional demands of the strongest country doing so?

The starting point of those conditions lies in the German practice of competitive deflation (Lapavitsas 2012; Cesaratto 2011). This is a typical German approach to economic competitiveness which was relaxed briefly in the mid-2000s before being resumed from 2005 onward. The German effort involved multiple components that may or may not be suitable for other countries, depending on the production and consumption profile. Export-led economic growth allows the economy to depress wages and prices without a catastrophic loss of employment and income. In this context, unemployment insurance benefits can be reduced to increase the supply of low-cost labour at the margins, deals with unions can be made to pay new hires at a lower wage than standard employees and foreign labour can be imported in non-unionized companies to perform a variety of tasks previously carried out by more expensive domestic personnel. As a national economy, Germany also spent less on goods and services from abroad than it sold, running a strong current account surplus. Where the economy lacks the same level of export-related income and employment and the ability to run large surpluses, however, i.e. where the economy relies more heavily on domestic consumption, wage and price declines generally lead to economic contraction as a whole. This means that the German model cannot be replicated for Europe (Dullien 2013).

Competitive deflation eventually generates vulnerabilities for the countries that have not kept pace in pushing down prices and wages. Goldman Sachs' Chief European Economist Huw Pill calculated in 2012 that in order to catch up with the competitive deflation with which they were confronted and restore price competitiveness, program countries like Greece and Portugal would have to reduce prices by 50%, and direct competitors like France and Spain by 30% in the absence of significant structural reforms. Those reforms would have to focus on diverting investment and employment away from housing and domestic consumption (including public sector employment, which he noted in France was still too large) and toward export markets, as Germany had done. Pill argued that for financial markets, the key indicator of whether a country's bonds should be bought or sold was whether it had good prospects of turning current account deficits into surpluses, based on such reforms, increased price competitiveness and suppressed domestic demand. France benefits from the fact that investors see the country as having a similarly low risk default profile to German bonds, but with bonds offering a higher rate of interest. That sets it apart from the southern periphery, which offers higher interest rates, but with a higher risk of default (Pill 2012).

The key to delineating whether the intent of coercion is present is whether the related demands embedded in the TSCG demonstrate concern for consequences for others, and for the general economic health of Europe, or not. The German choice views inflation as an evil that should be not only controlled, but in the context of inflation since the launch of monetary union, reversed with deflation as a necessary evil to restoring competitiveness. This is explicitly targeted against the member states that Germany pushed to sign at a moment when saying no would have unleashed an investment strike on financial markets. This can hardly be considered voluntary.

As a consequence, the TSCG is strongly tuned to the practices of Germany and its few allies, with strong exports relative to GDP and low domestic consumption relative to GDP, in a highly competitive environment. Other countries are not able to generate the external sources of employment and economic activity, leading to a downward spiral. That downward spiral is not ameliorated by the national base of European fiscal policy, but intensified. This has the effect that the TSCG deliberately induces deflation in Southern Europe and other catch-up economies of the Eurozone, and relies primarily on export-led growth, development and employment rather than home-grown economic activity. Given the limited capacity of all EU countries to base their economies on the German model, this points to a system of governance that extends strong advantages to Germany and a few other countries with a similar economic profile at the expense of the others. In this context, there is no utility for consumption-focussed economies in abiding by the rules voluntarily.

Coercion, order and ratification

The method of Germany getting ratification of moving outside the EU can be clearly shown to be the result of power politics, imposing commitments against the will of the other signatories (H1, H3). The TSCG, for all of the restrictive measures that it forces national governments to impose upon themselves and their legislatures, allows some room for counter-steering during economic downturns. It therefore provides them with a significant room for manoeuvre and economic management. The condition is that it requires them to build up significant reserves during times of plenty that are then released during downturns. In this way, budgets remain balanced and fiscal demand stimulus remains intact in principle. But the manner in which demand stimulus is permitted ensures that public borrowing is not a significant part of the equation. If enforced, the TSCG therefore generates long-term incentives to not only balance the budget on an annual basis, but to bring gross public debt significantly below the 60% threshold of the Maastricht Treaty as a second pillar of fiscal responsibility, and to build a rainy day fund as the third pillar. This expectation is harder for some countries to meet than others.

The TSCG's rules put the EU's weaker economies at a significant disadvantage as they try to manage their economies on a yearly basis, and as those with significant, chronic budget deficits and debt levels attempt to bring them down to meet the Treaty's performance targets. While that requires effort of most EU governments, it is difficult to see why most of them might agree to such a treaty. This section outlines the logic that accompanied negotiation and/or ratification in selected EU member states. It shows that credibility of the country to financial markets was key to putting pressure on government and parliament to say yes to the treaty and to ratify it.

Critical, however, is the fact that Germany made access to the ESM's emergency management funds contingent on signing the TSCG. Markets, in turn, do not evaluate the creditworthiness and borrowing capacity of a country based on access to the ESM entirely, but national governments certainly acted as if they would, based presumably on the strength of commitment to sound finances. We turn now to demonstrating the strength of the compulsion that governments felt, including countries not under direct pressure from financial markets.

France

France negotiated and ratified the TSCG under two presidents respectively from opposite sides of the political spectrum, employing different approaches to dealing with German demands, and seeking out different allies in the process. Nicolas Sarkozy, the conservative President who negotiated for France, officially took the stance that Germany's ambitions ought to be broadly supported so that France could win critical details. These details did not amount to much, however. Thomas Klau of the European Council on Foreign Relations indicates that Sarkozy, known for his close stance with German Chancellor Angela Merkel 'often suppressed his real personal anger over German positions because of the fear that markets would treat France as being part of the European south' (Carnegy & Peel 2012). This reinforces a statement by Goldman Sachs' CEO during the ratification process that France might be as much a worthy target of speculation as any other Southern European country.

Sarkozy was equally swayed by an overarching matter of viewing the TSCG at the time it was negotiated in an all-night session of the Heads of State and Government as an opportunity to force the UK out of Europe by putting a transfer of sovereignty on the table that was known to be unacceptable (Stephens 2014).

Ratification demonstrated strong, uniform support from the main parties. Although the conservative Sarkozy government and National Assembly lost power shortly after the TSCG had been concluded, the successor Socialist government under Francois Hollande submitted the TSCG to the National Assembly for ratification on 19 September 2012 (Assemblée Nationale 2012). Instead of a constitutional amendment mandating a balanced budget, the bill proposed a legal amendment introducing automatic budget cuts where required to meet the commitments of the treaty, much as budget sequestration functions in the United States in the absence of political agreement on how to cut spending or raise the debt limit. This choice proved important in defusing critique from Hollande's own party that the TSCG violated that right of a democratically elected government and national assembly to manage fiscal policy (Carnegy & Peel 2012; Assemblée Nationale 2012: 72–9). Similarly, the method by which the TSCG and European Semester requirements are incorporated into national law would remain national questions (Assemblée Nationale 2012b: C2).[2]

France ratified the TSCG on 9 October 2012 under a socialist National Assembly, with a large majority: 477 to 70 (Lafilliâitre 2012). Prime Minister Marc Ayrault spoke of the need to ratify the treaty to instil confidence of others in France. The Foreign Minister, who also conducted the report on why France should sign, emphasized that the Treaty mostly repeated EU agreements in light of the Eurozone crisis (European Semester, Six Pack, Two Pack), that had been negotiated with EU institutions and aimed to fulfil France's other EU commitments, but that since the President of the European Council had been unable to get all member states to sign, the extra measures had to be established by international treaty. The government would define a separate law to reduce budget deficits automatically which violate the criteria. The only proposed amendment came from the extremist Front Nationale, which suggested that only a referendum could decide on such constraints on the budgetary power of the National Assembly (Assemblée Nationale 2012a).

The National Assembly's basis for voting was established by Representative Guigou, who chaired a parliamentary review of the treaty (Assemblée Nationale 2012a). The Guigou report starts with the observation that EMU budget rules had been flouted since 2000, and that macroeconomic imbalances were allowed to grow out of control in Greece, Ireland, Portugal, Spain and Italy. In addition, France had performed poorly on public finances, increasing its debt by 45% over the previous decade. This faster rate of debt growth (other countries had averaged 30%) threatened to damage France's credibility with financial markets. The treaty would therefore contribute to financial stability through fiscal stability through harder commitments to budget reform than previously undertaken. Nevertheless, the report concludes that the Treaty respects national sovereignty and the right of national parliaments to determine fiscal policy, with the exception of ensuring a structurally balanced budget.

However, much of the report underlined that the scrutiny of financial markets and France's credibility had been made salient and pressing by German demands for action. In the context German demands for the TSCG, France had to comply with those demands and ratify or lose the confidence of financial markets about the country's creditworthiness (Assemblée Nationale 2012a: 50–4). In return, Germany would support plans for Banking Union (ibid.: 82–7), and would be open to the prospect of economic government at the European level (ibid.: 92–6), in itself a political mantra of the French political establishment for infusing European economic policy with more socially-minded objectives and criteria (Assemblée Nationale 2012c, 2012d, 2012e). The Guigou report saw in this regard an opportunity to reform European economic governance, which faced the reality of uncoordinated competitive deflation on the part of Germany, which was estimated at 20% in the 2000s, and then effectively imposed it on other states, including France.

The most immediate trade between Germany and France that was underlined in the conclusions of the Guigou report was that Germany had imposed the TSCG on other countries as a precondition for making progress in the ESM. In the context of reaching a broader compromise political package on the TSCG, the European Semester and other elements of European economic governance, France had gotten Germany to support talks on introducing a financial transaction tax, bank supervision and (as yet undetermined) measures for tackling unemployment, particularly youth unemployment in the midst of a crisis (Assemblée Nationale 2012a). The opposition conservatives (UMP) unsurprisingly supported ratification the TSCG, and the budget law change, as their own president had negotiated it, and indicated they would have gone even further to introduce a constitutional amendment rather than implement by normal law. The same is true for the liberal (UDF) allies of the UMP under Charles de Courson. The bill was only opposed by the Green party and the far left.

There were consequent debates about what would be included in a structural deficit and what would not. The debates show that this was not clear at the time of ratification. The timing of the TSCG's hold on French finances was also an important consideration in review. The French Senate calculated that in the medium term, France would have to reduce its deficit to 1% of GDP by 2017 (Sénat 2012). The Senate underlined that failure to ratify would weaken France in the context of the Eurozone crisis, particularly as market expectations of a country's difficulty tend to become self-fulfilling, which would result in dramatic hikes in interest rates, coupled with difficulty securing assistance from the ECB and the ESM (Sénat 2012: IIIB). The Senate noted that in the case of the ESM and the EFSF, France had to be involved so that Germany was not expected to bear the main financial cost alone. While the TSCG could function without France, the cost of not signing could be catastrophic. In addition to the general negative costs above, France would suffer damage to its reputation as a country that holds its commitments (Sénat 2012: IIIB). The Senate urged the government to push ahead with the TSCG's envisaged Interparliamentary Conference, in which the European Parliament and National Parliaments would vote on resolutions of EU decisions, in a format for the Eurogroup as well, and supported by a reinforced COSAC (Sénat 2012: II).

The government's commitment to budget retrenchment in accordance with the TSCG proved short-lived, however. The Socialist Party was routed in 2014 municipal elections based on poor economic performance, leading to the appointment of a new Prime Minister at a time when Brussels expressed reluctance to grant extensions beyond the two years the country had already been given (Horobin 2014). The new Prime Minister Valls announced challenges to budget rules in a speech to the Assemblée Nationale on 8 April 2014 (Lichfield 2014), and a rejection of austerity. The UMP warned that the price would be France's humiliation once it was subjected to controls by Brussels for failing to reach its targets (Gomes Ferreira 2014).

Portugal

Portugal was the first country to ratify the TSCG after one day of debate in the Portuguese legislature on 12 April 2012. The Government, which tabled the bill, and the President of the Assembly underlined that accepting the golden rule for balanced budgets and the other demands of Germany was necessary to secure sorely needed financial assistance from the EU. Three parties voted in favour (PSD, CDS, PS), and three against, demanding a referendum (PCP, BE, PEV, Greens) which was rejected (Sic Noticias 2012). The Government added that not only was the political commitment to balanced budgets required to secure financial aid for Portugal, but to convince financial markets that there would be no need to engage in speculation against any country in the Eurozone (Government of Portugal 2012). Ratification of the TSCG in Portugal was therefore much quicker than in other countries: almost immediately after the last adjustments were made to the Treaty in March 2012 (European Parliament 2013). The payoff for Portugal was confidence of financial market participants, leading to lower interest rates on government bonds than the 7% that had to be paid during the crisis of 2012. By

April 2014, interest rates on 10-year bonds had dropped to pre-crisis levels, at 3.7% (Nascimento Rodriguez 2014).

Ireland

The Irish government ratified later than Portugal, despite its precarious position with financial markets, due to the requirement of holding a referendum. On 31 May 2012, the public approved the TSCG by 60%. That approval was in turn begrudgingly linked in the referendum campaign to access to bailout funds from the ESM. In political discourse, that clause had been referred to in Ireland as Germany's 'blackmail clause'. In addition to strengthening conditionality of loans for access to the ESM, the terms also disappointed much of the Irish political landscape, which would have preferred to see an end to the austerity imposed on it by the IMF and the EU after the onset of the financial crisis in 2008. The terms of the TSCG made that austerity permanent, becoming known in local parlance as the Austerity Treaty, and therefore unpopular. In Ireland, the perception was also strong that the clause had been inserted specifically to coerce Irish voters in a referendum to vote in favour (Waterfield 2012a). The Yes campaign for signing the ESM treaty warned that if Ireland voted no, the country would be faced with 'a Greek-style banking run, a tripling of Ireland's borrowing costs and would plunge the country into bankruptcy by 2014' (Waterfield 2012b).

The Irish government refused some of the demands made on it by the IMF and EU in 2013 before it exited its assistance program. Finance minister Michael Noonan decided that spending cuts would be taken at a more moderate pace than demanded, citing that Ireland could and would not impose more austerity. In doing so, he cited to Parliament a 1916 Yeats poem recalling the reasons why Ireland finally broke from the UK and fought for its independence (Evans-Pritchard 2012).

Spain

Rumours abounded on the day of the Irish referendum that the IMF had prepared a contingency plan for a Spanish bailout, a rumour that the Spanish government vigorously denied for a short time until applying for aid (Paris 2012). The Spanish government tabled the Treaty on 24 May, at the same time it turned to the IMF. It underlines that it was in Spain's interest to ratify the agreement quickly, even accepting the powers of EU institutions because the country had suffered significantly from a persistent lack of confidence (by financial markets) since May 2010 in the context of the Eurozone crisis (Congreso de los Diputados 2012a).

In the Spanish case, the legal dubiousness of the TSCG actually facilitated ratification. Article 93 of the Spanish Constitution permits the government and Congreso to ratify a treaty by regular law if powers are delegated to an international organization or institution. Since Articles 4 and 5 of the TSCG delegate oversight tasks to the Commission and Council, the Spanish government claimed that ratification could proceed by normal law. Had the TSCG remained a purely international treaty, this would not have been possible.

As with Ireland and Portugal, Spanish ratification took place in the midst of an interest rate crisis and negotiations with the EU for a bailout. Spain needed to adopt first, and then ask for more time in principle from the Council. After agreement with the Council in July 2012, interest rates started to decline slightly from the 7% that most considered the breaking point (Shellock 2012). The Congreso ratified the Treaty on 21 June 2012 with a very large majority, which also opposed all tabled amendments (Congreso de los Diputados 2012b).

Italy

Italy negotiated the TSCG under the leadership of the technocrat Mario Monti, acting as both Prime Minister and Finance Minister, who succeeded Berlusconi in November 2011. Sweeping austerity measures were introduced in December 2011 as a response to rising interest rates that were overwhelmingly adopted by both houses of parliament. Monti then announced his intention in July 2012 to leave Italian politics once the TSCG had been ratified. Although the anti-TSCG and austerity movement found support in the ad hoc candidacy of Beppe Grillo, serious contenders like left-of-centre Democrat Pier Luigi Bersani to replace Monti went to great lengths to identify with the 'responsibility and confidence' that Monti embodied in the February 2013 elections (Dinmore & Segreti 2012). While many of Monti's austerity measures were politically unpopular, they also helped Italy to avert even worse disaster in the wake of an investment strike by financial markets, in which interest rates for government bonds hit 6% and more. Bersani won a minority government in the election on this platform, but had to make way in talks with various parties of a grand coalition of left and right for party comrade Enrico Letta. Although Letta chafed against the TSCG and the other new instruments of European economic governance which had already been ratified, he proved powerless to dismantle it until he was ousted by the left wing of his party on 13 February 2014. The new government of Matteo Renzi, although more populist in tone, focussed on the kind of structural reforms made necessary by the TSCG's restrictions on government borrowing.

Czech elections in early 2014 led to a change of government from the Eurosceptic conservatives to Europhile social democrats who are prepared to sign the TSCG as part of a larger strategy to join the euro by 2020. Only an act of Parliament was required to ratify (Oliver 2014). After the Czech Republic's accession, the UK remained the only country outside the TSCG.

Of the countries that originally signed, **German** ratification took the longest. Ratification was subject to a constitutional challenge against the ESM to which the TSCG was tied. The issue of the court case was whether the German government had the legal right to commit German funds to the ESM. The Constitutional Court ruled on 27 September 2012 that the government had the right to make a tentative agreement, but that it had to be approved by the upper and lower houses of the German parliament, and that the German exposure had to be limited to the capital subscription of 190 billion euros to which it had already signed on. Since passage in the Bundestag and Bundesrat had already been secured, the full package could be considered ratified the same day.

Conclusions

The TSCG was designed to pressure the EU national governments to accept responsible sovereignty as an ordering principle of European politics (H1). It was established for distributional issues (H2) and was the start of incremental EMU reform (H3) that included tougher sanctions on defectors and termination of sovereignty for repeat offenders (H3.2). The European Union's economic governance framework, and the demands it makes on national economic policy cannot be properly analyzed in the absence of the TSCG, the manner in which it raises the fiscal policy bar for member states, and the degree to which the treaty and its terms were effectively imposed on national parliaments and electorates. Whereas observers outside the EU process and from Southern Europe promoted the establishment of a fiscal union early on in the Eurozone crisis, the multitude of measures introduced inside and outside the EU establishes a control union instead. The lack of a fiscal union and EU own resources in this context reinforces the centrality of national government within Europe, but also its responsibility for ensuring sound finances at all costs. In the context of the Eurozone crisis, this not only places individual countries in an effectively permanent state of vulnerability to pressure from financial markets to meet the TSCG's targets, it keeps that vulnerability at a fairly high level for as long as uncertainty about the crisis's resolution persists. To the extent that analysis of the European Semester suggests otherwise, it needs to take the more demanding standards of the TSCG and the EPP into account.

The intergovernmental nature of reforms surrounding the TSCG, European Semester is revolutionary, to the extent that the reforms collectively represent realist institutionalism, generating important institutional innovations that sideline the EU institutions or use them 'on a secondary level'. The legal basis was taken from the Schengen Treaty, which is an IGA to further cooperation in an area which other countries reject. The German position on economic reforms, defined by Angela Merkel in 2010 in Bruges, was not to generate additional legal powers for EU institutions where they did not exist, but to cooperate as Eurozone member states where collective action was required (Buras 2013). In the absence of opportunities to work with EU institutions, they have been circumvented, and by virtue of the harder demands of the TSCG, effectively hollowed out. Whether Commission attempts to soften the demands of the European Semester (Zeitlin & Vanhercke 2014) will be successful remain to be seen.

The contrast between Merkel's Bruges speech and that of Margaret Thatcher in 1988, and the implications that follow from it, help to differentiate between the two types of intergovernmentalism harboured by the two leaders, and see the implications that should be drawn for EU or international relations theory.

Whereas Thatcher stood on the principle of absolute sovereignty, in which the UK, like all member states, should have the right to retain ultimate responsibility for public policy, and to choose freely to which European policies the UK subscribes, Merkel's project subscribes to the principles of responsible sovereignty, and divided sovereignty (compatible with the principle of subsidiarity), in which states enjoy autonomy, but have responsibilities to conduct their public policy within prescribed limits that are set out in the IGAs and the attendant international treaties, both within the TFEU and outside it. Whereas Thatcher's principle of absolute sovereignty is intended to maximize the insistence that states choose voluntarily to enter into agreements to their mutual benefit without giving into coercion (a philosophy not incompatible with Brexit later on), Merkel's principle of responsible sovereignty opens the exact opposite possibility. A state that fails to govern itself responsibly, as set out in the principles of self-sufficiency (over financial solidarity), sound public finance (over borrowing to catch up) and sound private finance (over borrowing to catch up) will be subject to outside management by its official creditors once financial markets have turned their backs on them. And in the case of the macroeconomic imbalances procedure, perhaps even before. Although Germany found itself confronted with a monetary union that was not to its liking and could not easily extract itself from it or expel those it wanted out, it did have the capacity to exacerbate an existing crisis and exploit the weaknesses of other EU member states.

Overall, the case of the TSCG and Eurozone reform generates no evidence of classical realist collapse under pressure, or neofunctional institution-building that responds to functional demand and politicized transnational coalitions. Nor do we see (voluntary) intergovernmental agreement or de novo institutions within the EU framework. We see instead a German attempt to reconfigure the architecture of EMU within the context of EU rules, to upload its preferences to others, even among a subset of like-minded actors (enhanced cooperation) before abandoning the attempt. It is telling that even a smaller set of countries could not find agreement with Germany on a *voluntary* basis, and that an opportunistic construction of a Shadow EU through bricolage and coercion was what Germany reached for instead.

Intergovernmental distribution plays a key role in national positions, but also entrenched German ideas. The other actors clearly felt coerced into supporting German demands once the German government discarded the path of compromise and consensus that is central to how the EU was designed to work. Implementation has been weak, however, suggesting that the practical implications of signing the TSCG will depend on German discretion.

There are also visible limits to German power. The EU itself could not really be hijacked as much as Germany wanted. It required allies that may have agreed with responsible sovereignty within the EU, but disagreed with the methods – at least within the EU. Those allies with reservations could then only be coerced as well by moving outside the EU. What has not happened, however, is that those governments agreed to transpose Shadow EU agreements into the EU itself. It is therefore unlikely that the EU will simply absorb those non-EU developments as the German government would like, and as neofunctionalists speculate.

Notes

1 The European Union Act 2011 (UK) would have forced the UK to hold a referendum in the event that the government signed a treaty transferring sovereignty to the EU.

2 In France, the Assemblée Nationale's European Affairs Committee engages with parliamentarians in March, followed by a vote in May on the government's annual stability program. In the National Semester, the Finance Committee engages with the European Affairs Committee in setting out the rest of the year's work.

References

Assemblée Nationale. (2012b) *Amendement N°2 présenté par M. Collard et Mme Maréchal-Le Pen*. Paris, 28 September.

Assemblée Nationale. (2012a) *Compte rendu integral: Première séance du mercredi 3 octobre 2012*. Paris, 3 October.

Assemblée Nationale. (2012b) *Compte rendu integral: Deuxième séance du mercredi 3 octobre 2012*. Paris, 3 October.

Assemblée Nationale. (2012c) *Compte rendu integral: Première séance du mardi 9 octobre 2012*. Paris, 9 October.

Assemblée Nationale. (2012d) *Rapport fait au nom de la Commission des Affaires Étrangères sur le Projet de Loi n° 197 (Procédure accélérée), autorisant la ratification du traité sur la stabilité, la coordination et la gouvernance au sein de l'Union économique et monétaire par Mme Elisabeth Guigou, Députée*. Paris, 4 October.

Assemblée Nationale. (2012e) *Union européenne: traité sur la stabilité, la coordination et la gouvernance au sein de l'UEM: Loi n° 2012–1171 du 22 octobre 2012 autorisant la ratification du traité sur la stabilité, la coordination et la gouvernance au sein de l'Union économique et monétaire*. Paris, 22 October.

Bayoumi, T., & Masson, P. R. (1995) Fiscal flows in the United States and Canada: Lessons for monetary union in Europe. *European Economic Review* 39, 2: 253–74.

Bickerton, C. J., Hodson, D. & Puetter, U. (2015) The new intergovernmentalism: European integration in the post-Maastricht era. *Journal of Common Market Studies* 53, 4: 703–22.

Blavoukos, S., & Pagoulatos, G. (2008) Negotiating in stages: National positions and the reform of the Stability and Growth Pact. *European Journal of Political Research* 47, 2: 247–67.

Bouwen, P. (2013) *The two-pack on economic governance: establishing an EU framework for dealing with threats to financial stability in euro area member states*. Brussels: European Commission Occasional Papers, May.

Buras, P. (2013) *The EU's Silent Revolution*. ECFR/87. London: European Council on Foreign Relations, September.

Carnegy, H. (2014) US Treasury secretary Jack Lew calls on Germany to boost growth. *Financial Times*, 19 February.

Carnegy, H., & Peel, Q. (2012) Crisis strains ties between German and French leaders. *Financial Times*, 20 October.

Cesaratto, S. (2011) 13 Notes on Europe, German mercantilism and the current crisis. In Emiliano Brancaccio, E. & Fontana, G. eds., *The global economic crisis: New perspectives on the critique of economic theory and policy*. Abington: Routledge: 246.

Chang, M. (2006) Reforming the stability and growth pact: Size and influence in EMU policymaking. *Journal of European Integration* 28, 1: 107–20.

Closa, C. (2012) *Jugando a ratificar: las reglas de entrada en vigor del nuevo Tratado de Estabilidad, Coordinación y Gobernanza del euro (ARI)*. Madrid: Real Instituto Elcano, 7 March.

Congreso de los Diputados. (2012a) *Proyecto de Ley 121/000010.*

Congreso de los Diputados. (2012b) *El Congreso autoriza la ratificación del Tratado de Estabilidad, Coordinación y Gobernanza en la Unión Económica y Monetaria*. Madrid, 21 June.

Der Spiegel. (2013) Mehr Rechte für Europäische Kommission: Merkel will Europäische-Verträge ändern. *Spiegel Online*, 19 October.

Dinmore, G., & Segreti, G. (2012) Italy's democrats pledge responsibility in post-Monti era. *Financial Times*, 12 July.

Donnelly, S. (2011) The public interest and the economy in Europe in the wake of the financial crisis. *European Political Science, 10*, 3: 384–92.

Donnelly, S. (2014a) Power politics and the undersupply of financial stability in Europe. *Review of International Political Economy, 21*, 4: 980–1005.

Donnelly, S. (2014) Banking Union in Europe and implications for financial stability. *Studia Diplomatica. LXVII, 2*: 21–34.

Dullien, S. (2013) *A German model for Europe?* London: European Council on Foreign Relations. Policy Brief ECFR/83.

Eichengreen, B. (1997) Saving Europe's automatic stabilisers. *National Institute Economic Review* 159, 1: 92–8.

Eichengreen, B., & Frieden, J. (eds.) (1994) *The political economy of European monetary unification*. Boulder, CO: Westview Press.

Eichengreen, B., & Wyplosz, C. (1998) Stability pact. *Economic Policy* 26: 67–113.

Enderlein, H., & Verdun, A. (2009) EMU's teenage challenge: What have we learned and can we predict from political science? *Journal of European Public Policy* 16, 4: 490–507.Escritt 2014.

European Commission (2010) A new EU economic governance - a comprehensive Commission package of proposals. Brussels, 29 September.

European Council. (2011) *European semester: Special report.*

European Parliament. (2013) DG Internal Policies (Constitutional Affairs) *Article 136 TFEU, ESM, Fiscal Stability Treaty: Ratification requirements and present situation in the Member States*, 12 December.

Evans-Pritchard, A. (2012) Europe's debt crisis credibility hangs on thin Irish thread. *Telegraph*, 16 October.

Fischer-Lescano, A. (2014) *Human rights in times of austerity policy*. Nomos.

Gomes Ferreira, Ana. (2014) Não haverá austeridade em França, garante Manuel Valls. *Publico*, 8 April.

Government of Portugal (2012) *Intervenção do Primeiro-Ministro no debate parlamentar sobre ratificação dos Tratados que cria o Mecanismo Europeu de Estabilidade e sobre Estabilidade, Coordenação e Governação na União Económica e Monetária*. Lisbon, 12 April.

Gros, D. (2013) Banking Union with a sovereign virus: The self-serving treatment of sovereign debt. *Intereconomics* 48, 2: 93–7.

Hagen, J. von, & Eichengreen, B. (1996) Federalism, fiscal restraints, and European monetary union. *The American Economic Review*, 134–8.

Heinen, N. (2010) The European semester: What does it mean? *Euractiv*, 6 October.

Henning, C. R., & Kessler, M. (2012) Fiscal federalism: US history for architects of Europe's fiscal union. *Peterson Institute for International Economics Working Paper* 2012–1.

Hodson, D. (2009) EMU and political union: What, if anything, have we learned from the euro's first decade? *Journal of European Public Policy* 16, 4: 508–26.

Horobin, W. (2014) French Prime Minister manuel valls faces confidence vote. *Wall Street Journal*, 8 April 2014.

Howarth, D. (2007) Making and breaking the rules: French policy on EU 'gouvernement économique'. *Journal of Common Market Studies* 14, 7: 1061–78.

Ioannou, D., Leblond, P., & Niemann, A. (2015) European integration and the crisis: Practice and theory. *Journal of European Public Policy* 22, 2: 155–76.

Lafilliâitre, J. (2012) Vote du traité européen de stabilité budgétaire (TSCG): Définition et mode d'emploi pour la France. *Challenges*, 10 October.

Lapavitsas, C. (2012) *Crisis in the Eurozone*. London: Verso.

Lichfield, J. (2014) New French Prime Minister manuel valls rallies liberal values as he squares up to Brussels. *The Independent*, 8 April.

Matthijs, M., & McNamara, K. (2015) The euro crisis' theory effect: Northern saints, southern sinners, and the demise of the eurobond. *Journal of European Integration* 37, 2: 229–45.

Moghadam, R. (2014) Sustaining the recovery: Strategies and policies for growth and stability. Speech to the Brussels Economic Forum. Brussels: 10 June.

Nascimento Rodriguez, J. (2014) Juros da dívida portuguesa lideraram descida em abril. *Expresso*, 30 April.

Oliver, C. (2014) New Czech PM vows to ratify EU fiscal compact. *Financial Times*, 21 February.

Paris, C. (2012) IMF Begins talk on Spain contingency plans – sources. *Wall Street Journal*, 31 May.

Pill, H. (2012). Eurozone will continue to muddle through. *Telegraph*, 8 December.

Salines, M., Glöckler, G., Truchlewski, Z., & del Favero, P. (2011). *Beyond the economics of the Euro: Analysing the institutional evolution of EMU 1999–2010*. ECB Occasional Paper No. 127.

Schäuble, W. (2014) *Round table interview at world economic forum*. Davos.

Sénat. (2012) *Projet de loi autorisant la ratification du traité sur la stabilité, la coordination et la gouvernance au sein de l'Union économique et monétaire. Rapport n° 22 (2012–2013) de M. François MARC*. Finance Committee, 9 October.

Shellock, D. (2012) Spanish bonds rally but euro fears remain. *Financial Times*, 11 July.

Sic Noticias (2012) Portugal é o primeiro país a ratificar Tratado Orçamental Europeu, 13 April.

Stavridis, S., & Irrera, D. (eds.) (2015) *The European parliament and its international relations*. Abingdon: Routledge.

Stephens, P. (2014) Britain and France are in the same (sinking) boat. *Financial Times*, 24 January.

Waterfield, B. (2012a) Ireland says yes to EU fiscal pact. *Telegraph*, 1 June.

Waterfield, B. (2012b) Irish referendum: Secret polls predict Yes vote despite low turnout. *Telegraph*, 31 April.

Zeitlin, J., & Vanhercke, B. (2014) *Socializing the European semester? Economic governance and social policy coordination in Europe 2020*. SIEPS Report No. 7.

4 The ESM

Stabilizing the Eurozone without a fiscal union

To what extent did the EU respond with further integration in response to the EZ crisis? There was a clear lack of funds in Southern Europe to stabilize banks and governments. Neofunctionalism would expect more EU institutions and resources to maintain interdependence. Liberal intergovernmentalism would expect governments to support new institutions underlining national obligations and creating package deals of mutually beneficial, but not conflicting interests. Realist institutionalism predicts a more radical restructuring of the European institutional order to better reflect great power interests. In 2011–2012, the key impetus behind change was the fiscal cliff that cut off Southern sovereigns from financial markets, coupled with bank insolvencies they could not afford to bail out. Temporary help from the Eurogroup became permanent in 2012, but focussed on reinforcing responsible sovereignty rather than instituting a fiscal union or any meaningful financial transfers. Ultimate control and the overall ordering principles were kept outside the EU legal order to protect it from legal and political tampering.

This chapter focusses on the ESM as a mechanism established to provide enforcement of German demands on countries that had been cut off from international financial markets, in other words to provide the command and control elements of an enforcement pyramid (H3). It then acquired special rights and standing within the structure of EMU while remaining deliberately outside the reach of EU law and institutions and under the effective control of Germany (H1). The demand for the ESM in broad terms came from the need to ensure a lender of last resort function for the Eurozone in some form – an innovation with distributional consequences. In the context of a missing fiscal union, national governments found themselves confronted with the question once the financial crisis struck of whether to subsidize national banks in order to keep them in business, or outright nationalize them. Given the limits on national capacity in some countries, however, concrete proposals were made from a number of quarters to introduce a common EU fund for bailouts in one form or another. In the absence of a fiscal union, a European stability fund of some kind could be established to fight fires in emergencies. But it became clear to the participants early in the game that the cost of providing an effective bailout fund would be enormous – perhaps exceeding a trillion euros – and therefore require the financial equivalent of a fiscal union for

DOI: 10.4324/9780203702130-4

all countries involved. The potential beneficiaries and paymasters were clear, in a repeat of the divisions over fiscal union in EMU.

In the contest of the Eurozone crisis, the same distributional conflict played itself out. The main goal of Southern Europe, and of France, was to secure generous European financial capacity to (1) fight off speculation and self-fulfilling prophesies about national insolvency, (2) provide a financial shock absorber during times of crisis, (3) contribute to orderly resolution of crises with additional financial firepower and (4) keep the membership of the Eurozone and the degree of financial interdependence intact. Beyond this, the Commission wanted to (5) lay the foundation for a restructuring of the European banking market through increased competition, supervision, mergers and takeovers to proceed with a suitable public backstop. This meant a full public backstop in the form of a European budget and treasury bills backed by European taxpayers that would disburse money as required even before a crisis had erupted, and without international negotiation. This would alleviate unsustainable burdens for national governments in the Eurozone unable to provide backstops of their own.

The main goal of Germany and its allies was to (1) prevent contagion and meltdown from uncontrolled collapses of either banks or sovereigns or both, (2) limit financial liability for Germany in doing so, (3) simultaneously prevent moral hazard as a result in the banking sector, and (4) address the related issue of what it viewed as moral hazard in Ireland and Southern European countries, which generated unsustainable bubbles with cheap money that required significant public backstops when the bubbles burst. This meant a firewall controlled by creditors and reinforcing responsible sovereignty rather than a transfer system.

These two camps represented therefore on the one hand a US-style move toward European bailout mechanisms and fiscal backstops required for them to work which would engineer international politics out of decision making and operations, and on the other hand, a reinforcement of national responsibility for public finances and bank solvency, both as a matter of general principle, and in the exercise of conditionality by those who would provide the financial assistance to the recipients.

The implications of the German-led coalition reinforce asymmetries of power and the reliance of European economic governance within Banking Union on responsible sovereignty. The previous chapter underlined the difficulties for national governments in acting as the lender of last resort for their banking systems. In light of the financial instability caused by a default of a sovereign, this placed the question of whether to bail out countries and their banks onto the European Agenda. As with fiscal policy, the key issue at stake in European talks over bailing out sovereigns, and then banks, was who would adjust when states could no longer foot the bill, and what could be done to sever the negative feedback loop between states and sovereigns.

This chapter walks the reader through the following options and initiatives, as well as the outcome of EU negotiations, coupled with an assessment of how actors shaped events. It then draws conclusions about how closely the findings reflect the hypotheses regarding responsible sovereignty outlined in Chapter 2. Based on those hypotheses, we might expect one of three outcomes at the European level: no solution (in which national bank collapses fall entirely in the hands of national governments, regardless of their capacity to bear the burden) (possible under intergovernmentalism); supranationalism designed to adjust by using a relatively accommodating monetary and fiscal policy (a European bailout fund serving as a public backstop to national governments) (under neofunctionalism), or reinforced national sovereignty that adjusts to crises by providing minimal European assistance in combination with deleveraging (shrinking banking sectors) and deflation (budget retrenchment) (realist institutionalism).

National bailouts

The European Commission accepted national bailouts and state aid as a lender of last resort function at the beginning of the GFC. It released proposals afterward for supranational powers and funds, supported by other international and European actors, which failed to materialize due to German, Dutch and Finnish opposition. In 2008, as the financial crisis hit the UK and Ireland and then the rest of the European Union, public backstops for insolvent banks were national in nature. Without any sizeable budget at the European level, and without any European powers to become involved in the support of banks, the only available mechanism was for national governments to serve as the lender of last resort for their own national banks. European Competition Commissioner Nellie Kroes supported calls from national governments to provide such aid by issuing a Block Exemption, a general permission for state intervention. They do not discriminate between banks on the basis of nationality and would have to be repaid quickly enough to avoid market distortions. They also could not be used for interbank takeovers, but otherwise the Commission viewed financial assistance to banks as a necessary evil in the interest of financial stability.

The block exemption also required national governments to seek permission from the European Commission, but provided a high degree of legal certainty that approval would be forthcoming, allowing governments to act quickly. In some cases, the Commission attached conditions to the aid that could be followed up on afterward, such as the sale of a bank's business unit, if it were involved in providing other financial services, but this did not put the provision of state aid for banks into question.

Concerns were present that without all countries withdrawing state aid at the same time, or on the same schedule, that an uneven playing field would be established in which state-owned or supported banks from one country would be able to buy up banking units from other countries that had bitten the bullet and re-privatized or repaid their borrowed capital. This fear was particularly strong amongst the developed, capital-rich countries of Western Europe, as evidenced in the orchestrated takeover of ABN AMRO by a consortium of banks. Kroes accordingly reminded national authorities that they would have to draw up an exit strategy for ensuring that banks paid back the state aid they received. In practice, this meant waiting for the moment when the economy had sufficiently recovered from the effects of the financial crisis to ensure that banks were capable of paying back the aid without collapsing. The first review was scheduled for 2011, and as the European economy continued to not only stagnate but worsen in the context of the Eurozone crisis, the Commission found it had no choice but to delay the demand for an exit and to review again in 2013. In 2013, although the intensity of the period between 2010 and 2012 for the Eurozone had subsided, both economy and banking system experienced such downward movement and instability that neither national governments nor the Commission were actively drawing up a separation of banks from sovereigns. That job would require the establishment of resolution systems to handle collapses once the state stood back, and the introduction of some sort of European banking supervision which would hopefully generate some clarity about how much financial assistance Europe's zombie banks still required.

At the moment of the 2013 review, those political deals and legal packages had not yet been made, so that national governments remained responsible for providing the public backstop for their own banking sectors. This effectively froze the banking market, promoting a long-term renationalization of banking, as banks adjusted to the reality that they would have to rely on national, not European resources in their final hour of need (Epstein 2017). This calculus prevailed after the ESM had been established, underlining that the ESM as a bailout mechanism reinforced national responsibility for financial stability.

The result of continued national responsibility for financial stability in banking and for the Eurozone is the undersupply of a public backstop in some countries more than others. Countries with stronger borrowing capacity on financial markets could avoid financial distress and calls to share resources, while those with more fragile economies and weak borrowing capacity faced an inability to shore up their financial systems. The assets of national banks soon became liabilities (Epstein 2014) that could no longer be borne. However, in terms of the most important limits on borrowing for sovereigns, the most important restrictions proved not to be public governance rules, but the judgement of financial markets. Whereas the Southern European coalition sought a bailout mechanism that would break this reliance on financial markets for the weakest members of the Eurozone, the German-led coalition sought precisely the opposite, reinforcing Southern vulnerability. National governments would be forced into responsibility to the greatest extent possible, along with private actors – a pattern that is discussed at length as follows. It was then followed up in steps that led to the ESM's establishment. The first precedent for this line of attack was established with Ireland. In 2008 the ECB and Ireland's fellow member states, led by Germany, forced Ireland to issue state aid on its own to take on 60 billion euros of bank liabilities in order to prevent a Eurozone-wide financial collapse (Evans-Pritchard 2012).

Stability bonds and the bazooka

Given Ireland's enormous exposure, it is unsurprising that it strongly favoured the establishment of a European bailout mechanism that would provide assistance to both banks and sovereigns in distress. Those same hopes and expectations were shared by other states in Southern Europe, who found themselves subject to the strongest economic declines in the EU, and then to the strongest pressure on the solvency of their banking systems.

With broad Southern and Irish support, the Commission floated the notion of common debt to pay for a larger stability fund in 2011. It issued a Green Paper on Stability Bonds in 2011 (European Commission 2011). The proposal went nowhere and the consultation website was taken down. Italy and France also tried unsuccessfully to lobby Germany together to provide more financial firepower in the fund in mid-2012 (Elliott & Smith 2012). While Germany remained restrictive on overall funding levels, it did not take the extreme position within its coalition. The Netherlands and Finland opposed any provisions allowing the ESM to purchase government debt on either primary or secondary markets (Armitstead 2012).

France, meanwhile, found itself so vulnerable to the prospect of speculation at the hands of financial markets that it sided with its southern neighbours and enlisted international help in the attempt to make its case to Germany. Italy had been subject to financial market speculation in the fall and winter of 2011 that had seen interest rates rise to unsustainable levels. Although part of the response had to come from the Italian government itself, the IMF underlined that it could only be part of the solution, since deterrent capacity of a firewall capable of keeping all of the Eurozone's member states inside would remain a necessity if the currency bloc were to protect itself from the prospect of speculation ripping it apart.

In that light the IMF (Lagarde) urged the establishment of a firewall in January 2012 that went significantly beyond 500 billion euros, and for the introduction of Eurobonds or mutualized debt. The size would be required to not only provide support for small countries like Greece, which was in acute distress at the time, but larger countries like Spain and Italy (Traynor 2012). The United States followed up on that suggestion promptly in February 2012, and at regular intervals afterward. In February, US Secretary of the Treasury Timothy Geithner, seeking to move Europeans to sort out their crisis, argued that Europe's agreement to establish a small emergency bailout fund in 2010 was insufficient, and that the interest rate speculation running rampant in Southern Europe in late 2011 and 2012 required a bazooka in order to deter financial markets from speculating on national default (Blackden 2012).

After the IMF and the US came the OECD in March through May 2012, OECD Chief Economist Pier Carlo Padoan referred to funds as a firewall and urged a significant increase (Deen & Sterns 2012). General Secretary Angel Gurria pressed further that the fund should have 1 trillion euros, to constitute 'The mother of all firewalls' (Emmott 2012). Meanwhile, Germany insisted that a fund could not exceed half that amount. In that context, the European Commissioner Olli Rehn refused to comment on Gurria's proposal, citing that talks were under way with the member states (Kanter & Eddy 2012). But as Europe failed to deliver on these expectations, the World Bank weighed in as well, underlining that failure to do so could unleash a new global financial crisis, a 'Lehman moment' (Elliott, Smith & Kollewe 2012) for which Europe would be responsible. In 2014, the

United States government repeated concerns that the public backstops in place were woefully insufficient, taking into account the resources available to the Eurozone's weaker links. This political advocacy came after lobbying by a group of leading EU economists, which had argued as early as 2009 for such measures in an open letter calling for public measures to restore liquidity to financial markets, restoring securitization and reducing leverage in the EU banking sector simultaneously (Alesina et al. 2008). A common financial facility would help achieve the first goal.

EFSF and ESM

The EFSF and ESM are innovations outside the EU to uphold interdependence on German terms (H1, 2) and to augment German leverage over others in making and enforcing demands on others through the Eurogroup (H3). The EFSF was established by the Eurozone member states in May 2010 as the Eurozone crisis gathered steam. It was intended in the first instance to provide assistance to the governments of Ireland and of Greece in the context of the European economic downturn. It was then later extended to cover Portugal as well.

From the beginning, the potential recipient states and the donor states harboured differing views regarding the terms of financial assistance, and whether the EFSF ought to be an open-ended arrangement with an indefinite mandate. The EFSF was established outside the European Union as a private company registered in Luxembourg and owned and operated for the member states that supplied its capital. On the insistence of the German government and parliament (European Parliament Research Service 2014), the EFSF was depicted as a special purpose vehicle that would be wound up once the crisis for the Eurozone had been contained. In practice, this meant reaching a point where program countries receiving financial assistance could borrow money on capital markets again at reasonable interest rates.

The EFSF was established quickly after the May 2010 Council decision, on 7 June 2010. It provided for direct assistance to national governments, precautionary facilities and facilities to purchase bonds of sovereigns. Purchases on primary markets were to take place in conjunction with direct intervention, and on secondary markets on the basis of ECB advice (EFSF 2011). The EFSF modus operandi was first to have negotiations among the countries paying into the fund. Then on the request of a country for assistance, the EFSF signs a Financial Assistance Facility Agreement with the country involved that sets out the terms and conditions of the assistance. These terms and conditions can be amended.

Germany's reluctant decision to support a permanent ESM to replace the EFSF came at the end of 2010, after it had become apparent that financial markets expected the program countries to collapse again once the assistance had been withdrawn (Dyson 2016). This could be seen in persistently high interest rates demanded for loans to those countries in private markets, which the governments could not afford. The political agreement in December 2010 left terms and conditions unclear beyond the expectation that assistance would come in the form of loans, and that conditionality would be demanded in exchange, with a focus on overhauling public finances of the recipient countries.

In practice, both the ESM Treaty itself, and the political circumstances of ratifying it changed several times afterward, putting the substance of the treaty and conditions on assistance into doubt, as well as whether the most powerful country in the arrangement would allow it to go ahead at all. It is important to review those developments in the context of describing the ESM, for they determined the shape. What one sees is that Germany agreed to the ESM as a measure of political and economic necessity, but rejected measures that would see the fund transformed into an unofficial fiscal union. That would have happened if aid were made available as transfers rather than loans, if the terms of repayment were relaxed sufficiently that repayment was called into question or if the quantity was increased so strongly that potential recipients viewed high levels of borrowing as politically feasible, regardless of the capacity to repay. One element that could have led to this was the capacity of the ESM to issue bonds for which the member states would be collectively liable.

The ESM Treaty was signed on 11 July 2011, and then again in a new form on 2 February 2012, incorporating new political agreements and technical improvements decided up to and including December 2011. ESM treaty terms were that it would enter into force when 12 countries had ratified.

In the words of the European Parliament:

> Those decisions aimed at improving the effectiveness and flexibility of the mechanism, providing for new financing tools similar to those of the EFSF, more flexible pricing of financial aid, timing of the capital contributions, urgency decision-making procedures and finally, a conditionality link to the Treaty on Stability Coordination and Governance.
>
> (European Parliament 2013)

The events of October and December 2011 leading to a revision of the ESM Treaty revolved around the question of how much aid could be provided and under what conditions. Whereas the earlier agreements had been made to deal with the relatively small economies of Ireland, Greece and Portugal, Italy had come under direct pressure by financial markets in the fall of 2011. This changed the scenario for the ESM from having to deal with small bailouts to the prospect of dealing with large ones. This again raised the question of whether the member states were willing to provide enough capital to combat the prospect of a sovereign default in a large country – a fund of money with which the Eurozone could either prevent a country from going bankrupt, or prevent a bankrupt country from initiating a domino effect that would bring down the rest of Europe with it. The options available for such a large fund acquired various names according to the details of the option: a bailout mechanism, Eurobonds, a bazooka and a firewall.

These negotiations took place between the governments of Germany, France, the United States and Greece, which had been granted financial assistance in 2010 from the Eurogroup through the EFSF. It also involved to a lesser degree the member states of the Eurozone as actors who would have to accept whatever arrangements were made, plus the Presidents of the European Council and the European Commission, who played more direct supporting roles in the negotiations.

By the end of 2010, the reality of interest rate hikes in Europe had already convinced Germany along with the rest of the member states that some form of financial assistance would be required to prevent financial contagion in an interdependent Europe, and that it would have to be in place indefinitely. The option of doing nothing was therefore already off the table in 2011. Negotiations in 2011 revolved around two issues: the level of money that would be made available and the extent of conditions that would be delivered on in return.

The most pressing distributional disagreement over the ESM revolved around the level of assistance. Three countries – Germany, backed by Finland and the Netherlands – remained adamant that the level should remain as low as possible and that conditionality should be high to ensure that recipients would bear the greatest possible cost of adjustment to debt and deficit levels (Martin & O'Donnell 2013). In this context, German finance minister Wolfgang Schäuble opened up the possibility of forcing Greece out of the euro (Salmon 2012), with the implication that EFSF/ESM funds and deterrent capacity could be devoted to protecting other countries more likely to survive an onslaught by financial markets. At the same time, the level of funds provided by the ESM could be kept relatively small. Although Greece could not legally be forced out of the Eurozone, the terms of assistance, if any were forthcoming at all, could easily make membership feasible or not. During the Cannes summit, Greece was already undergoing an economic and political meltdown. A bank run was underway in Greece that had only been contained by the ECB shipping cash into the country on a daily basis, in an effort to prevent panic. This took place in the context of Greek parliamentary elections in which Eurosceptic parties were expected to win significant support and scuttle the existing EFSF bailout deal from the EU and IMF. While the parties wanted to remain in the euro and receive transfers, they rejected the conditionality and the deflationary consequences that came with them.

France, Ireland, Southern Europe, the United States and a host of international organizations took the opposite tack – that only a massive fund could contain the true nature of the problem –which was not only about national economic management, but about fending off speculation by financial markets on sovereign debt (Evans-Pritchard 2014). Accordingly, all of them had lower expectations on conditionality for funds, if they had any at all. They also viewed pushing Greece out of the Eurozone as undesirable, even though France was willing to support the idea of a Grexit with Germany, to push Greece to rescind its demands on the terms of EFSF assistance.

In the absence of German willingness to foot the bill for such transfers or entertain Eurobonds, however, the contingency plan if Greece rejected the terms of its bailout was to prepare for the country to leave the Eurozone, willingly or unwillingly. Peter Spiegel (2014b) reports that the European Commission, the ECB, IMF and the Euro Working Group started on Plan Z in January 2012, which would set out the details for such an exit. In this process, it became clear to the ECB that a transition would be very difficult.

Germany also showed a willingness to use coercion to enforce demands. Greek elections on 6 May 2012 saw gains for Eurosceptic parties that rejected conditionality and repayment (New Dawn on the fascist right and Syriza on the left). This was already apparent before the election happened, leading France and Germany to warn political parties that they expected any government to respect conditions attached to loans. In the aftermath of the election, that pressure was repeated, but Greece remained divided. Germany split internally between what Spiegel (2014b) reports was called the infected leg camp, which advocated responding to Greek intransigence by ejecting it from the Eurozone thereby encouraging other countries to redouble their commitment to conditionality; and the domino camp that advocated supporting Greece financially lest it descend into uncontrolled default and unleash a chain reaction of sovereign defaults and national economic collapses. Merkel eventually chose in October 2012 after months of deliberation not to push Greece out due to uncertainty over the consequences, though this was not communicated to Greece, lest it reduce the leverage of the ESM (Spiegel 2014b).

Nevertheless, securing Greek commitment to ESM/Eurogroup conditionality proved extremely difficult. Problematic for the ESM was also the fact that one of its key recipients proved to be able to commit to the conditionality terms with great difficulty. Commission President Barroso finally convinced Samaras (Greece) not to ask for new concessions in November 2012, a full 6 months after the election. With that agreement in place, German concerns about moral hazard could be put to rest, and a new disbursement of Greece's bailout paid (Spiegel 2014). However, details of the plan later showed that the Eurogroup had indeed made concessions to Greece in the form of partially suspended interest payments for 10 years, giving more time to repay. In return they accepted a highly conditional slicing up of assistance into tranches that would effectively bind future governments to Troika oversight (Neuger, Bodoni & Stearns 2012). As part of a pattern of negotiations between the Eurogroup and Greece that would extend through 2015, the Eurogroup apparently sought both signs and mechanisms of control over the Greek government before relaxing conditions. It was an important political point for Germany, Finland and the Netherlands that the debt restructuring neither amounted to debt relief nor new loans beyond what had already been made, but simply an alteration of the conditions. This is both different from other cases in that it offered more concessions to Greece and imposed more control.

With this, the ESM could proceed in practice with Greece as part of the euro. However, it raised new questions over the level of funding that the ESM required. That was visible in German ratification, discussed as follows, and in devising bank resolution mechanisms (discussed in Chapter 6) that kept bailout sums and ESM funds required low.

Bank recapitalization

Direct negotiations to amend the ESM started even before it had been inaugurated, however. As before, the size of the fund was the most important issue. A secondary issue was whether ESM funds could be used to directly recapitalize banks rather than sovereigns. This latter issue was raised in June 2012 by

Spain, which needed money to prop up its banks but could no longer borrow from financial markets, and otherwise feared the stigma of requesting assistance from the ESM. The Spanish government emphasized that banks, not the government, needed loans. In this context, in which a large country faced economic collapse, and then public insolvency as a consequence, Germany and the other ESM members approved using funds to recapitalize banks, provided that the guarantor was the Spanish state, or state agency (European Parliamentary Research Service 2014). This allowed both sides to stick to their principles.

The compromise demonstrated again that within the German-led camp, Germany had a clear capacity to get what it wanted based on its own calculations, which underlines the power of the single government rather than a collection of countries. Two German allies, the Netherlands and Finland, were unhappy with German willingness to make ESM funds available for bank recapitalization. Dutch MP Madelaar underlined that those terms had been inserted after the Council agreement, while the Dutch parliament was still considering ratification. In this context, however, Council President Herman van Rompuy pointed out that individual countries like the Netherlands could do nothing to stop the development (Lynch 2012).

However, these countries fully supported Germany's intention to use the ESM as a firewall rather than a public backstop. Eurogroup President Dijsselbloem of the Netherlands underlined that banks, then investors, and then national governments would have to deal with the risk of bank failure without calling on the ESM:

> Strengthen your banks, fix your balance sheets and realise that if a bank gets in trouble, the response will no longer automatically be that we'll come and take away your problem. We're going to push them back. . . . You deal with them.
> (Baker 2013)

This position was tested to the breaking point during the Greek crisis of 2015, when the Greek Finance Minister Varoufakis attempted to convince his Eurogroup colleagues to alleviate the country's public sector debt burden by extending bond maturities and reducing interest rates by transferring EFSF loans to the ESM at better conditions (Alderman 2015). Instead, Germany effectively defended responsible sovereignty by raising Greece's forced departure from the Eurozone as an alternative (Spiegel Online 2015).

Size

The Spanish compromise left the question of the ESM's resources unanswered, however. Renewed debate ensued regarding whether Eurobonds should be issued or not. For all practical purposes, Germany, the Netherlands and Finland successfully won their position against the pressure of the other Eurozone member states. The ESM can issue bonds of its own (EFSF 2014), but these are not the same as Eurobonds, which are mutualized debt that falls back directly on the treasuries of the Eurozone member states as the Commission had proposed, and French

President Macron would propose and German Chancellor Merkel would reject anew in 2017 (Karnitschnig 2017).

The issue proved to be the main object of disagreement again from September 2013 onward during intergovernmental talks on resolution, which led proponents of Eurobonds to bring up a re-opening of the ESM Treaty. Germany opposed changes that would allow the ESM to be expanded with Eurobonds. German domestic party opposition was strong on both sides of the political spectrum, and secured in advance before talks (Cermak 2013a).

Speaking at a Bundesbank symposium on financial stability in February 2014, Schäuble underlined that Germany opposed any move to amend the ESM treaty so that Eurobonds could be issued. Doing so would reduce the pressure on national governments to balance their budgets on the basis of their own efforts and resources, and was therefore out of the question. Nor should the ECB be looked at to restore growth. Instead structural reforms and international competitiveness would have to be the focus of national economic policy (Market News International 2014; Bundesministerium der Finanzen 2014).

Similarly, Germany opposed the retroactive use of ESM funds to help Ireland reduce the cost of its own bailout in 2008, by lowering the interest payments and extending the payment schedule of its debt portfolio. An Irish negotiator for the treaty claims that the June 2012 negotiations over ESM provided a commitment to use some of the money to clear up the state guarantees for Irish banks, in recognition of the burden of guarantee that Ireland had been forced into assuming in 2008, but that the promises were reneged on when Germany insisted later that it would assume no responsibility for legacy assets, i.e. that existed before the ESM's launch (Evans-Pritchard 2012). This turn-around on the part of Germany ensured that restrictions on further financial commitments, both legal and in public opinion, discussed as follows, were respected.

The consequences of establishing the ESM as a firewall rather than a bailout mechanism can be seen in the case of Ireland, which was forced to redouble financial self-reliance. The country increased capital buffers of about 25 billion euros in 2013 (managed by the National Treasury Management Agency) as the way to provide for ongoing financial stability after exiting the internationally organized bailout. In doing so, it not only distanced itself from the ESM but from eligibility for support from the ECB's OMT (outright monetary transactions) program (Telegraph 2013). In this way, Ireland largely replicates the behaviour of more successful East Asian countries after the 1997 financial crisis.

Finally, the manner in which the ESM was employed to deal with the meltdown of Cyprus demonstrated that the limits in size are robust enough to withstand enormous political pressure in a crisis. Bailouts are not automatic, and not calibrated to the needs of keeping banks or existing public sector borrowing requirements afloat. As the Cyprus case showed, they may also be insufficient to prevent a meltdown of the financial system. The consequences are significant evidence of the strong intention of the German-led coalition to limit costs, regardless of the negative circumstances for financial stability. In the Cyprus case, it was necessary to suspend capital mobility (Grabel 2015) and ration the supply of money being disbursed from banks. Money rationing, by which depositors were limited to withdrawals of 300 euros per day, were introduced during the Cypriot bank crisis and only lifted at the beginning of April 2014. The prohibition on exporting euros from Cyprus was instituted to prevent Cypriots and other depositors from bleeding the banking system and the national economy dry simultaneously. This is a serious intervention that effectively creates two separate euros with an increasing potential for differing exchange rates the longer the capital barriers are upheld. Those capital barriers remained in place until April 2015.

In preparation for buttressing the finances of Greece and other countries, the ESM was inaugurated on 8 October 2012 with a capital base of 700 billion euros, of which 80 billion euros were paid up front, and a total of 500 from the EU and 200 from the IMF. ESM capital subscriptions are greatest for Germany and France, with 27 and 20% of the ESM's capital respectively, followed by 18 and 12% for Italy and Spain, nearly 6% for the Netherlands, and 3% or less for all other Eurozone member states. The ESM is set up so that binding decisions are taken by the Board using weighted votes. As a 25% blocking minority is in place, only Germany has a veto on disbursement. Curious is that Luxembourg, Cyprus and Austria, three countries with large banking systems (at the time Cyprus had not yet undergone its crisis), have low contributions at 0.2, 0.1 and 2.7% respectively. Drawing on assistance from the ESM requires that the applicant country is a signatory of the TSCG as of 1 March 2013. This reinforces the intent to ensure that national responsibility for public finances is both accepted and delivered on for recipients.

Conditionality and control: enhanced surveillance for countries with EFSF/ESM assistance

ESM initiated changes to EMU that incorporated a full enforcement pyramid, complete with procedures to manage deviant states, known as program countries (H3.2). Budget retrenchment was a general quid pro quo for creditor countries to provide financial assistance through the EFSF and the ESM. This is the background for the TSCG, which was concluded within a month of the ESM Treaty and which the ESM Treaty demands a country ratify before it qualifies for consideration of ESM financial assistance, whether real or provisional stand-by arrangements. That treaty obligation to balance the budget places limits on the capacity of government to act as a lender of last resort for banks, and makes it likely that a country will fall very early under stewardship of the Two Pack if it attempts to do so.

A consequence over the medium term is that banks, particularly in the Eurozone's southern periphery, will eventually have to deleverage, probably by reducing their balance sheets, to the extent that national borrowing capacity is sufficient to handle lender of last resort functions without help from other EU member states. Sarcinelli (2012) underlines the link between the size of the banking sector as a percentage of GDP and the likelihood of catastrophic financial crisis – as seen in Iceland and Cyprus (and Ireland).

Whereas collective action at the European level on Banking Union provides financial stability that is superior to that provided by national governments, EMU reform in 2012 is designed to restrict the liability of creditor states for the debts of debtor states, and to minimize any room for what creditor countries see as moral hazard. Consequently, the ESM's involvement in the Bankia bailout of 2012 in Spain was constructed deliberately to reinforce the Spanish state's responsibility to repay, because otherwise, it would have been fiscal union through the back door. This was still insufficient to prevent revolt in the scientific, legal, economic (Dettmer et al. 2012) and political communities in Germany. The creditor countries rejected fiscal union from the early 1990s onward, and the fiscal compact of 2012 reinforces that demand.

The terms of ESM reforms to funnel funds into bank guarantees placed further controls by creditor countries on the use of those funds, and underlined an intergovernmental logic outside EU structures. The EFSF and the ESM, which took over from the EFSF in July 2013, remain outside the EU treaties and function and take decisions in the same way that the IMF does, according to international law. Care was taken to ensure that the funds only purchase assets on secondary markets, (thereby preserving Article 123 TFEU's prohibition on the monetization of debt), and to provide legal security for extraordinary measures to ensure the stability of the Eurozone (amendments to Article 136) (*Milano Finanza* 2012).

The capacity of Germany to impose conditionality on target countries depends on whether they need financial assistance, however. While conditionality was central to the relationship between program countries and the Eurozone, it remained much more controversial for other member states. Otherwise more than willing to support the German position on economic reform, the Netherlands reportedly threatened to leave the euro rather than accept German demands for contractual obligations on the member states to not only balance budgets, but undertake specific economic policy reforms (Escritt 2014). It was certainly not the only country that might have had difficulties with the proposal. On this matter, unlike for the issue of using ESM funds for bank recapitalization, the German government backed off.

In exchange for allowing ESM funds to go to banks rather than governments, Germany demanded that EU decisions to release those funds be subject to a threefold form of security that would ensure the ESM would very rarely be used. It also wanted the fund to remain as small as possible while remaining sufficient to avoid disaster. Loans would be extended by individual member states, who would then hold debt seniority (to be paid first in the event of liquidation instead of other, particularly private creditors), and a double unanimous vote of the member states would be required to release money from the fund. Even then, the budget committee of the German Parliament announced it would question the terms in ratification, and the opposition would challenge it (Deutscher Bundestag 2012). Regarding to quantity of input, EFSF/ESM loans are not intended to reduce debt primarily, but to stabilize markets, allowing countries to weather herd behavior in a storm. In the end, the moneys agreed were not even sufficient to cover German holdings in Spanish debt that had lost all market value (Gore & Roy 2012).

By 'sufficient to avoid disaster', the above paragraph only refers to the capacity to avoid disaster provided national governments remain conservative and prudent in their financial obligations, and that national banking sectors also voluntarily reduce their activities, to ensure that they are not severely exposed to risks of non-performing loans. In this sense, Ireland again shows by its behavior that following the East Asian model of self-reliance is not only the intent of keeping the ESM so small, but the long-term consequence for banks and governments of such a small fund.

Given the unrelenting position of Germany, the Netherlands and Finland, countries in need of financial assistance had little choice but to accept German demands and sign the treaty without achieving any of their core demands. They did so to prevent speculative attacks by financial markets on rogue debtor states, but also sought (unsuccessfully) relaxed conditionality.

The key factor reinforcing national responses is therefore material incentives – the question of who pays – further buttressed by German attempts to further entrench the principle of national responsibilities that are already present in the EMU architecture. Banking Union and the TSCG therefore do not do away with distributional conflicts or reduce the transaction costs of restructuring and recapitalization for the weakest links in the European economy. Assuming that national governments and the EU 'collectively' continue to save banks rather than euthanize (some of) them (and there is no stomach within the Commission for allowing the latter to happen), a Banking Union with a backstop would cost enormous amounts of cash up front and bank guarantees later that might/probably will become real liabilities. Creditor countries that reject fiscal union and Eurobonds would be saddled with new financial demands, which they also reject.

Ratification

The ECJ

The agreement on the ESM displays strong elements of extra-EU international agreement outlined above that were accepted and confirmed by the ECJ on 27 November 2012. Until that moment, the ability of the EU to make use and reference to the ESM in the context of European legislation was cast in doubt. The first point of observation regarding the ESM's intergovernmental nature deals with the fast-tack treaty change to the TFEU in which the Council, and the Council alone, declared the ESM in conformity with EU law, to protect it against legal challenges. The amendment of the TFEU as a core EU treaty was the first to be undertaken under new provisions made possible in the Lisbon Treaty, which allows clarifications that do not create new powers. In the *Pringle* case, initiated by an Irish national and Member of Parliament who wanted to have the ESM declared illegal for both violating EU treaty provisions and evading democratic control that would take place within the EU, the ECJ found that this was the case and upheld thereby the legality of involving the ESM in bailout and resolution matters. In a double rarity, the ECJ accelerated the processing of the *Pringle* case and met as a full court of 27 judges (Kingston 2013). The ECJ confirmed that national governments had the right to establish their own treaty and mechanism to ensure financial stability in Europe (De Witte & Beukers 2013). It ruled further that because the ESM applied strict conditionality to financial assistance, that it did not violate the no bailout clause of the articles governing EMU. The ECJ also approved of the Council's action to amend Article 136(3) via the simplified procedure to reflect that agreement in Council Decision 2011/199. Because the ESM treaty was outside the EU, it conferred no powers on the Union. Had it done so, it would indeed have constituted a major change for which the simplified procedure was not appropriate (Van Malleghem 2013). This leaves discretion with the ESM, which in turn leaves discretion to Germany.

Germany

The most important national challenge to ESM survival was within Germany itself, where the German Constitutional Court had to rule on a challenge to the legality of the ESM treaty, both in substance and procedure of adoption (Schmidt 2013). Its first ruling on 19 June 2012 found the German government guilty of not sufficiently consulting the German parliament during its talks regarding anything involving the European Union, as required by Article 23 of the German constitution. It bound the government to comply with demands regarding the supply of information, and its timeliness, so as to grant parliamentarians a reasonable opportunity for review on any matter involving the European Union. The government's position had been that because the ESM treaty was outside the EU, that it had no obligation to consult parliamentarians. The Court rejected this, noting that the ESM supported EU functions, particularly within monetary union, and that Council decision 2011/199 amending the TFEU confirmed this connection (Bundesverfassungsgericht 2012b). The treaty was nevertheless debated in both Bundestag and Bundesrat and passed both houses on 29 June, only to be subject to a new set of six legal challenges that were decided partially by preliminary ruling on 12 September 2012, and then finalized on 18 March 2014. During the summer, the German finance minister stated that if the Court found against the treaty, or took too long, that there could be negative consequences for financial stability in Europe (Scally 2012). The September 2012 ruling permitted Germany to ratify the ESM treaty subject to strict conditions that Germany's involvement would not exceed 190 billion euros, and both houses of the German legislature, the Bundestag and Bundesrat, would have 'comprehensive involvement' in ESM and Euro Plus Pact/TSCG affairs that touched on the powers of the legislature (Bundesverfassungsgericht 2012a). In the end, only the domestic demands of Germany affected the content, structure, modus operandi and overall architecture of bailouts in the context of the ESM. Numerous actors pushing for a larger fund with less conditionality did not move the German position.

Greece

Greek attention on the ESM in 2010 and onward was focussed on dealing with its own financial crisis and on the conditionality placed on aid rather than on ratifying the ESM specifically. Considerable resistance was offered from both the political establishment and from government bureaucracies to Troika demands for policy change. Greece continued to be plagued by chronic instability, coupled with question of whether the country would remain in the euro or not, punctuated by negotiations to reduce the country's debt in March, and elections in May and in June 2012. Greece tried to divert bailout money meant for banks to other purposes in its second bailout, and was stopped by the Troika (Jenkins 2014).

Greece asked again in January 2014, from its position as the EU Presidency, for lower interest rates and a longer repayment schedule for aid disbursed through the ESM instead of haircuts. Athens also warned it could not accept further austerity measures being demanded by the Troika. Finance minister Stournaras: 'This is out of the question. There will be no new fiscal conditionality because it is already too tough' (Spiegel 2014a). But Greece confronted a French government that would not help persuade Germany, even as it argued for more leniency for other countries (Guardian 2012).

Greece, although it ratified the ESM, can therefore be seen as not compliant, or at least not voluntarily so. Greece therefore gives a taste as to the limits and conditions of the new international order in Europe as they try to constrain domestic politics in the member states. As a program country, it is not so much dealing with the EU, but with the Troika of ECB, Commission and IMF, with Germany and France within the Eurogroup acting independently as key national governments placing pressure on a reluctant, resentful and defiant political establishment in Greece. The ESM acted merely as an agent in these talks.

Spain

Spain in contrast, like Ireland, fully accepted the terms of the ESM treaty and of the financial assistance provided to it via the ESM, with exception of noting that the aid was being provided for banks rather than the government. Given that interest rates had hit 7% on 14 June 2012 after two years of decline and an extended period of government denials that it would require assistance, the government had little choice but to approve the ESM and its terms.

The ESM first approved 100 billion of assistance with 39.5 billion disbursed on December 2012, and further 1.8 billion in February 2013 to the FROB (*Fondo de Restructuración Ordenada Bancaria*: the state agency restructuring and recapitalizing Spanish banks), while toxic assets were unloaded into the bad bank SAREB – Asset Management Company (AMC) for Assets Arising from Bank Restructuring. Conditionality included bank restructuring plans aimed to improve application of EU state aid rules, plus other reforms in governance, supervision and regulation of financial services. Spain met all of these demands without complaint and exited the ESM financial assistance on 31 December 2013. It will continue paying for the assistance until 2027, when the last of the financial instruments mature (ESM 2013b).

Ireland

Ireland asked the EU, and Germany in particular to approve an EU-funded recapitalization of Irish banks in June 2012 as part of its approval for the ESM Treaty, as the European Council was dealing with the request for a Spanish bailout, and again in February 2014, as the ECB and EBA conducted their Asset Quality Review (AQR) and stress tests (Chapter 5). That request meant not only compensating the Irish state retroactively for bailing out its own banking system at a cost of 28 billion euros, but covering any possible shortfalls in the Irish banking sector in the upcoming stress tests and AQR. Although the Irish government claimed that economic recovery had led to fewer non-performing loans, it was unsure how the ECB's methodology and the EBA's stress tests would value those mortgage-based assets. Irish Finance Minister Noonan underlined that German Chancellor Merkel had given a 'solemn promise' to provide such assistance in recognition that 'the Irish taxpayer protected the European banking system from any possible contagion' (Cage 2014).

Ireland passed the ESM Treaty in both houses of parliament in June 2012. The Irish government was under the impression that it would be able to secure funds from the ESM by September of that year to reduce taxpayer exposure to bank bailouts in exchange for voting yes on the basis of a unanimous agreement among the EU's finance ministers. Although ESM money would not erase the debt, it was hoped to increase debt sustainability through restructuring, and increase market confidence in the country's solvency (Beesley 2012). The Irish government was perceived as desperate, given a regular IMF review of the country's financial position in October 2012. Hence the target date of September, even though it was clear that ratification in other member states might not be complete or forthcoming by then.

Italy

Italy gave assent on 23 July 2012, while everyone waited on a legal challenge in Germany over the ESM to be decided by the constitutional court there. Finance Minister Vittorio Grilli showed confidence that if the ESM should be held up, that the EFSF would continue to be in place to provide support across national lines (Tortaro 2012). Before that point, Prime Minister Mario Monti argued unsuccessfully with Angela Merkel that the ESM should have increased borrowing and lending capacities ('a proper bank licence') in order to help out Southern Europe (Armitstead 2012).

Portugal

Portuguese ratification was on 13 April 2012, (after ratifying the TSCG on 2 March). Support and opposition for both Treaties was forthcoming from the same parties, with the conservative and socialist parties in favour (PPD/PSD and CDS/PP), and the far left and Greens against (PCP, BE and PEV). The government underlined the establishment of a permanent financial institution for states with weak own financial resources, and contributing to financial stability together with the TSCG (Casa Europa 2012). The government underlined the existence of a consensus across European member states that the terms of ESM and TSCG were necessary for completing EMU and making it work (Government of Portugal 2012). The Portuguese bailout lasted 11 quarters – the last instalment approved on

24 April 2014 (EFSF 2013). The ESM was pleased with Portuguese being forthcoming on the reforms which were demanded.

Cyprus

Cyprus provides a good case of process tracing to test the hypothesis that decisions and actions to ensure financial stability are taken outside of the EU (H1), that significant costs are pushed on states other than Germany (H2) and that imposition is used if necessary to ensure that national governments follow the rules that the great power has set out for them (H3.2). This is not simple hard bargaining under conflict but imposition. Cyprus first made a request for financial assistance for its collapsed banking sector in June 2012. The ESM opened negotiations with the demand that it would provide no assistance without Cyprus imposing haircuts on unsecured creditors and depositors (no bailout without a bail-in).

What happened afterward was a back and forth between the Eurogroup and the Cypriot government over the size of acceptable haircuts as a condition of financial assistance. The Cypriot government, concerned that a substantial haircut would initiate capital flight by wealthy Russian nationals with deposits in Cypriot banks which keep the banking sector there afloat, insisted that they would not concede to demands for haircuts that exceeded 10% of assets. In other words, a larger bailout from the ESM would be required. The ESM responded that it would not subsidize Russian oligarchs. The Finance Ministers of the Eurogroup insisted instead on an average haircut of 15.6%. Cyprus responded with an offer to keep the haircut on uninsured depositors and creditors at 10%, coupled with haircuts on covered deposits (that should have been legally guaranteed under EU rules) of 6.7%. In other words, Cypriot nationals rather than the ESM would be called on to subsidize Russian oligarchs.

The Eurogroup then made a deal with the Cypriot government in which they countered accepting haircuts on secured deposits at lower levels of 3%, increasing to a maximum of 12% to the largest unsecured deposits. The Cypriot government withdrew from the deal when the public learned of it and revolted on 22 March 2013. Under these conditions the Eurogroup withdrew its willingness to provide financial assistance in two stages over the next few days. The Eurogroup President announced the Dijsselbloem Principle on 24 March, saying that taxes on secured deposits remained acceptable and could serve as a model for managing resolution in the rest of the European Union (Salmon 2013). Schäuble countermanded this the next day, noting that stability and security of the European banking system had to be provided by leaving deposit guarantees intact. The Cypriot government went to Moscow seeking Russian financial assistance shortly thereafter but was unsuccessful.

Under these conditions, the Eurogroup adopted an IMF proposal on how to proceed with resolution of banks in Cyprus and providing enough financial assistance to prevent contagion. Laiki Bank would be closed, secured deposits transferred to the Bank of Cyprus, and large haircuts imposed on unsecured deposits, which were eventually set at roughly 40%. In this outcome, costs fell on Cyprus and

Russia rather than the ESM. Later, Dijsselbloem would underline that the method ensured that costs for resolution generally would be pushed back on the country from which the credit event originated.

In other words, the outcome ensured that national responsibility would remain the guiding principle with the ESM as a tool reserved for emergencies *for the Eurozone* (not countries in distress). The IMF underlined days later that it viewed the outcome as financially unsustainable for the government of Cyprus, which had to stand in to fund the consequences of the intervention under the terms of how and to whom the ESM provides financial assistance. The terms included Troika control of national budget policy and a memorandum of understanding that the Cypriot government would ensure that the banking sector in Cyprus would shrink, thereby undermining the strategic goals of the Cypriot state. The consequence was that it recommended debt relief for Cyprus, a pattern that would later repeat itself in the confrontation with Greece in 2015. But the imposition of terms on the Cypriot government, which included the minutiae of economic and social policy as part of national budgeting in return for the financial assistance that would be funnelled through the national government, went far beyond the coercion and hard bargaining before that point.

At what point in this picture should we see hard bargaining, coercion or imposition as confirmed? Eurogroup–Cyprus negotiations had gone on for the better part of a year before they were brought to a head in summer 2013. The imminent demise of one or two of Cyprus's largest banks in the absence of a deal raised pressure on the participants, but their behaviour is best classified as hard bargaining until Germany insisted that secured deposits remain protected in accordance with EU law. This was not a negotiating position but a demand, and made the condition for Germany approving partial financial assistance for the Cypriot banking system through the ESM. This is still not imposition outside of EU law and institutions, however. That came in the form of Eurogroup demands on the minutiae of Cypriot economic and social policy, including but not limited to the banking sector as a condition of receiving the assistance.

Cyprus proceeded quickly with ratification under these conditions, despite its disappointment with the outcome. The ESM made aid conditional on downsizing the financial sector, fiscal retrenchment, structural reforms and privatization. Nevertheless, given further differences between the Cypriot government and the Eurozone over the terms of resolution (covered in a chapter) there was a considerable gap between application for assistance (25 June 2012) and first disbursement (13 May 2013) (European Stability Mechanism 2013a). It negotiated a supplemental MoU to initial conditionality in 2014.

The ESM, the Eurogroup and imposition: the Greek Crisis of 2015

The Greek Crisis of 2015 shows the capacity for coercion and imposition even more strongly than the Cypriot case, as well as the German-led nature of the ESM/Eurogroup mechanism outside EU structures. The Greek Crisis revolved ostensibly around a conflict between the Greek government and a German-led coalition of states over whether the Greek government should be granted debt relief or financial assistance from the ESM or both, or whether it should exit the euro or even be forced out as a prelude to defaulting on its debt as an alternative.

Greek negotiations over the terms of a second bailout in 2015 take place alongside innovations to the SGP. As the election neared and a Syriza victory became more likely, the Juncker Commission proposed a relaxation of the SGP so that money invested in future growth (European Fund for Strategic Investments) would not be counted in the SGP (13 January, agreed in principle in the Council on 27 January). This did not prevent a Syriza victory, however. Greece's pre-Syriza history was one of accepting demands for reform, grudgingly but then with poor implementation that led to the next crisis. Syriza was different in that its opposition to Eurogroup demands was out in the open.

Syriza was elected 26 January 2015. Its attempts at garnering support from Italy, Spain and Portugal against Eurozone rules and Eurogroup demands failed (Hirst 2015). Spain's conservative government was attempting to contain the recession-induced rise of the political left. Portugal's conservative government was doing the same thing and attempting to pay back loan instalments to the ESM in April.

The Eurogroup responded to the election by demanding that Greece 'rebuild trust' with the rest of Europe, a combined accusation and demand that would define the relationship from that point onward, and fuel a series of escalating ultimatums through the rest of the year. This opening shot was followed by a hardening of positions on both sides: German conservatives demanding Greece be pushed out of the euro, and Greek demands for German reparations for WWII (Fahmi & Behrmann 2015). Meanwhile, Dijsselbloem used the 'broken trust' mantra throughout the negotiations to maximize his demands and leverage over Greece, a method that those who knew him well suggested was typical of his negotiation style (Brother & Oberdorff 2015). Eurogroup style also extended to the Council, where most national governments found themselves shut out of talks and consigned to the hallways throughout much of the fights that would ensue over the course of the year. Already in April, Irish Finance Minister Michael Noonan protested that the Eurogroup presidency and the Troika had shut out ECOFIN ministers during the process of making demands on Greece (Varoufakis 2015a). Chiming in, other smaller countries reported being upset at having been excluded from negotiations between France, Germany and Greece (Macdonald 2015a).

The unfolding of talks reveals how conditionality, coercion and imposition work in the Eurozone. By the 24 April Riga Summit – Dijsselbloem, as head of the Eurogroup, presented the government with its demands: a detailed list of reforms. On 10 May the Greek cabinet insists on no reforms to pensions. It hints at requesting help from Russia but is warned off by the US Treasury Secretary Lew. The IMF was reported to object to the treatment of Greece by the Eurogroup, meaning imposition of unreasonable demands (Evans-Pritchard 2015). A leaked IMF document from mid-May considered it impossible for Greece to meet Eurogroup demands before summer (Paul Mason News 2015).

Greek Prime Minister Tsipras railed publicly against the Eurogroup's stance toward Greece, accusing it of putting a great deal of effort into painting the Greek government as intransigent and unwilling to negotiate, and using that as an excuse to impose wide-ranging demands on the Greek government. He contended that in fact his government had tried to negotiate a path towards economic recovery through smart economic reforms that steered away from privatizations and pension protection for Greek citizens (Tsipras 2015).

At the beginning of June, with a Greek payment to the IMF due, France and Germany met with the Commission and ECB Presidents and the head of the IMF, to agree on the conditions under which Greece could access 7.2 billion euros worth of assistance in what the Economist depicted as 'an offer it can't refuse' (Economist 2015). Germany and France had not been able to agree at previous G7 talks on the subject. The result is that Germany's more restrictive demands, backed with an effective veto on disbursement, became the Eurogroup's standard operating procedure. Nor was there negotiation with Greece. The latter's attempt to trade acceptance of pension reforms for debt relief in June were turned down. The group's conditions were non-negotiable.

Negotiations in June reflected the Eurogroup's demand for unconditional surrender, while Greece attempted to shape the details of reforms or secure quid pro quos. In the aftermath of the early June breakdown, Greece missed its payment to the IMF on 5 June, announcing it would pay the money together with later payments of 1.2 billion due later that month. In a rift between the IMF and the Eurogroup, on 12 June the IMF left talks as Greece and EU stood off (Tuner 2015; Spiegel, Donnan & Hope 2015). It announced subsequently that Greece's debt would be unsustainable unless the Eurogroup forgave some of the debt (Gersemann 2015). Eurogroup and Commission pressure ensued on Greece to concede to demands unconditionally and sent the Greek delegation to Brussels back to Athens after it arrived with its own plan (15 June). Mutual recriminations resulted. Schäuble and Dijsselbloem underlined that they no longer trusted the Greek government, whatever it promised. Tsipras accuses European institutions of trying to humiliate Greece and engage in 'financial strangulation' (Gatopoulos 2015). As of 16 June, his attacks extended to the ECB and the IMF as well (Baker 2013).

The 18 June Eurogroup meeting took place in shadow of Merkel's agreement to extend Greece's payment deadlines to 30 June, provided Greece accepted the group's demands (Donahue & Delfs 2015). Greece was supposed to generate a fiscal surplus of 3.5% for 2015, introduce deep pension cuts and engage in widespread privatization and liberalization. The Greek government tabled plans that deviated from the Eurogroup's demands, seeking a path that would minimize the deflationary impact of the reforms. It planned to increase VAT on luxury items and introduce structural reforms agreed separately with the OECD before the summit. It also introduced privatization plans, though at lower levels than demanded and under conditions for the future owners that they would protect the socially weak. However, the plan foresaw leaving pensions untouched (Watt 2015). Varoufakis contended in public at the time of the meeting that Greece had reached its capacity to implement targets given 48% reductions in pensions and that wages, state employment and consumer spending and GDP had dropped by a third (Varoufakis 2015b). The plan to protect pensions from further cuts, however, alienated the IMF, which had advocated their reduction. The result was an impasse between the Eurogroup and the Greek government as the clock ticked on its repayments to the IMF, the EFSF and other creditors in June.

The 18 June meeting failed to generate an agreement, meaning that a new EUCO meeting on 25–26 June was scheduled before the next round of payments was due 1 July. The ECB responded to the impasse by buying time with Emergency Liquidity Assistance (ELA) for Greek banks, in which cash would be loaned against assets on Greek balance sheets (Georgiopoulos 2015). Steinberg and Vermeiren (2015) argued that Germany accepted unconventional measures by the ECB as the price of minimizing taxpayer-funded bailouts of Greece. June saw a series of Franco-German talks (Traynor & Hooper 2015) that produced no change in Eurogroup demands. On the contrary, the impact of German demands became stronger. In advance of EUCO meeting, the Five Presidents' Report (Commission, Council, Eurogroup, ECB and Parliament) advocated a position close to that of the Eurogroup, incorporating stronger fiscal controls and a European finance minister. The basis of economic policy would shift from voluntarism to legal obligations for EU member states (Juncker 2015).

The summit failed to produce agreement by the 26th deadline. In this context, pressure from the IMF and United States to reach a deal increased. On the 27th, the IMF released a Debt Sustainability Analysis report on Greece, saying that the country would need 50 billion euros of assistance to stay afloat, implying that if it were not part of the agreement, that Greece would collapse financially. According to Reuters, the EU tried to prevent the report's release, while the United States insisted on it (Taylor 2015). On Sunday, 28 June the White House released minutes of phone call between US President Obama and German Chancellor Merkel in which Obama urged Merkel to 'make every effort to return to a path that will allow Greece to resume reforms and growth within the Eurozone' (White House 2015; Doncel 2015). US Secretary of the Treasury Jack Lew, meanwhile, put similar pressure on Greece to accept the need for reforms in exchange for assistance, and to ensure financial stability (Ahmann 2015). Greece announced that it expected the Eurogroup to renew talks on Monday the 29th, but the Eurogroup remained silent. ESM head Regling indicated no knowledge of talks. Given the collapse of talks on the 28th, the ECB capped further growth in ELA facilities at 89 billion euros. This forced Greek banks to shut down for a week, effectively introducing capital controls as had been the case in Cyprus. ATMs were besieged, started running out of money, and limits on withdrawals introduced.

In the midst of this collapse, the Greek government announced that it would hold a referendum on Eurogroup demands on12 July. Meanwhile, Tsipras himself wrote a letter to the ESM and EG President Dijsselbloem on afternoon of Friday 30 June asking for financial assistance to meet interest payments on its existing debt and a new MoU, this time from the ESM, involving a restructuring of the Greek debt in ways that the IMF had proposed (Spiegel 2015). The government hoped that favourable terms would be forthcoming before the announced referendum, and that the ESM would effectively work as the public backstop for the country. The German government called the Greek government's bluff, however, by announcing that it would await the results of the referendum. In this it had support from both conservatives and from Social Democrats (Durden 2015).

On 1 July Greece went into arrears by failing to make all payments to the IMF. The subsequent Greek referendum voted no to Eurogroup demands by a wide margin of 60–40%. Conservative German politicians responded by demanding that Merkel start pushing Greece out of the euro. German FDP grandee Lambsdorff underlined that Greece's only hope of restoring economic competitiveness and solving its balance of payments problems would be to return to the drachma and devalue it. Any concessions would send a devastating signal to other states undertaking austerity reforms. CSU spokesperson for EU affairs Ferber concurred, asserting that the EU had to use the Greek case to demonstrate to other countries that EU rules would be enforced rather than negotiated, and that Greece's departure would strengthen the euro by strengthening respect for the rules (Becker 2015). Meanwhile, domestic CSU rhetoric from Bavaria reached new lows. Party General Secretary Andreas Scheuer insisted that 'leftist blackmailers and demagogues like Tsipras cannot be allowed to get away with their dirty schemes' (Bayrischer Rundfunk 2015). Dutch Prime Minister Rutte warned Greece that it would not get any concessions as a result, and former EU Commissioner Bolkenstein wrote an open letter to the government insisting that it show resolve in pushing Greece out of the Eurozone (Bolkenstein 2015).

German support for the Greek position, and for a relaxation of terms came only from the European Parliament wing of the German Green Party and from the German Linke (Left) Party, neither of which had any impact on domestic debate. The Social Democrats nationally remained unwilling to support this position, and indeed noted that Greece had 'burned its bridges to the Eurozone' (Traynor, Hooper & Smith 2015), while the European Parliament wing demanded that the heads of state and government take over from the finance ministers to hammer out a political compromise (Becker 2015).

Varoufakis stepped down on 6 July, claiming that the Eurogroup had treated him as *persona non grata* and that remaining would be counterproductive. French President Hollande met with German Chancellor Merkel the same day and tried to convince her to compromise on terms for Greece but failed. Merkel underlined in a statement that evening that Greece must be responsible for its own salvation. The IMF Managing Director Lagarde stated that the IMF would assist Greece if requested (presumably moving outside the Eurozone) (Associated Press 2015).

In light of this, a transnational coalition to reform EMU rallied again against the direction of Eurogroup demands, the methods of imposing it and on the effects. Five prominent economists including Thomas Picketty and Simon Wren-Lewis critiqued Merkel's decision to remain steadfast, by pointing out that the impact of the reforms had been so tough that they were unreasonable, unworkable and unhumanitarian (Picketty et al. 2015). Two days later, on the same day that the Greek government, with its new finance minister, approached the Eurogroup with a set of reform proposals, IMF Chief Economist Olivier Blanchard maintained that the need for the Eurogroup to compromise on debt sustainability was even greater than the IMF's pre-referendum report, against the preferences of the political masters of the Eurozone, while acknowledging Greek culpability in their own predicament (Blanchard 2015). Paul Krugman issued a similar assessment shortly thereafter (Krugman 2015). The Greek government's plan of 9 July followed Eurogroup demands in a number of key areas: it increased income and value added taxes, closed VAT exemptions for Greek islands, and cut the defence budget along Eurogroup demands. In other areas, it sought what it maintained was a sustainable compromise: it accepted rising primary surpluses for the public budget (though not as high as the Eurogroup had demanded – starting at 1% rather than 2.5%), and it sought longer transition periods for the poorest 20% of pensioners in the process of reforming the country's pension system (Merler 2015).

Within the Eurogroup, Schäuble issued a statement at that time to the other finance ministers insisting that the Greek government's plan was insufficient and therefore unacceptable in labour market, public sector, banking sector and structural reforms, as well as privatizations. His proposal was threefold: that Greece transfer 50 billion euros of its own assets to the ESM, which the ESM would then sell on Greece's behalf and use in place of Eurogroup assistance; that new laws be passed that would implement budget cuts automatically in the future rather than subjecting them to political debate and parliamentary voting and that Greek administration be de-politicized. If Greece refused these terms, it could enter debt relief negotiations, but only on the condition that it left the Eurozone.[1] These terms, but not the Grexit option, were taken over directly into the Euro Summit Statement of 12 July (Eurogroup 2015). This initiative was seen as useful to dissuade protest movements in Spanish and Portuguese elections to back off demands for EMU reform, starting with a dismantling of the enforcement pyramid.

The leak of the Schäuble plan ultimately weakened the German position somewhat by leading the German Social Democrats to break away from their support for the hard line. General Secretary Hubertus Heil underlined that such tactics were outside the bounds of respectable behaviour in the EU and said the SPD could not support it.[2]

In light of the Eurogroup's unflinching stance, the Tsipras government chose to accept the group's demands and seek whatever support it could muster in parliament. This meant abandoning a good number of Syriza members of parliament, and relying on the opposition as well. With the new political constellation in the Greek parliament, the Greek government reversed course over the next week on austerity policy, accepted Eurogroup demands in principle and came back with a plan to raise tax revenue to meet fiscal targets. Its hopes that Germany would approve debt relief as part of a compromise were again thwarted by the German Finance Ministry (Koutantou & Kambas 2015).

The Eurogroup met until 12 July and then again in the night between 13 and 14 July and concluded new demands for Greece, giving the country a 72-hour ultimatum to pass them in the Greek parliament. In this new context, hard liners in the Eurogroup wanted to block any emergency financing to bridge the time between the Greek parliament passing the reforms and the reforms having the desired financial results,[3] while Greece in particular saw this as impossible to achieve. Indeed, given that cuts to public spending would lower GDP and tax revenues, measures would have worsened public finances before they could recover.

The Eurogroup meeting of 12–13 July lasted 17 hours, going through the night, with heads of government present. The limits of Germany's capacity to get all of what it wanted became apparent, however. Schäuble had rebounded from the debacle of his Grexit proposal with a new one to suspend Greece temporarily while it repaired its finances (Karnitschnig, Turner & Palmeri 2015). The other demands remained in place, including the most explosive one for the transfer of 50 billion euros of Greek assets to Luxembourg. During the night, most of the attendees (other prime ministers and finance ministers, ECB President Draghi and the European Commission) had to endure repeated closed-door sessions between Council President Tusk, German Chancellor Merkel, French President Hollande and Greek Prime Minister Tsipras over what would happen. Hollande made it clear to Merkel that he would not accept a conclusion to the crisis which involved forcing Greece out of the Eurozone. A Greek time out from the Eurozone had remained a persistent German demand until 4 a.m., but differences on the collateral fund remained after that point. Council President Tusk determined at 5 a.m. that the next round of talks would either succeed, or he would declare a failure. The Greek government accepted the need for 50 billion euros of collateral being put in a special fund, but not in Luxembourg, while the German government insisted on Luxembourg until 7 a.m. before giving in. It eventually conceded the Greek demand to have the privatization agency located in Greece as long as it was politically independent. Although the Greek government then insisted that the IMF no longer be part of any Greek assistance arrangement, that demand was of lesser importance and it dropped the demand by 9 a.m. (ibid.). An IMF update on Greece underlining the unsustainability of Greek debt was announced on 14 July (IMF 2015).

Greek demands that the country required some sort of investment measures to re-start the economy were handled through the 50 billion euro investment fund (of which half was to support moribund banks), while demands that the Eurogroup make concessions for humanitarian reasons were handled through a side-payment of humanitarian assistance alongside the austerity measures rather than adjusting the austerity demands themselves. The latter compromise came at the suggestion of IMF Director Lagarde (Steinhauser 2015). The plan for that humanitarian assistance would amount to 35 billion euros gathered together from EU structural and investment funds (for regional development) and agricultural subsidy funds, and was presented two days later on 15 July (European Commission 2015). A bridge loan of 7 billion euros for three months was approved by the Council on 17 July to keep Greece afloat while the regular loans were being arranged. In doing so, the Council underlined that the use of the EFSM would be structured (through collateral and conditionality) in such a way as to prevent any non-Eurozone member states from incurring any risk of loss (European Council 2015).

The Greek government subsequently brought a Memorandum of Understanding between Greece and its creditors to Parliament on 16 July. The measures were passed with opposition support, but the divisions within the Syriza party remained. Tsipras: 'I acknowledge the fiscal measures are harsh, that they won't benefit the Greek economy, but I'm forced to accept them' (Maletzou & Koutantou 2015). The Greek government also temporarily ceased criminal proceedings against the head of the Greek statistical agency, Andreas Georgiou. The proceedings had been initiated on the charge that the head of statistics had been acting in a treasonous manner by reporting budget and economic statistics to the Troika and the Eurogroup in ways that put more pressure on the Greek government to make cuts than they had previously preferred (Pitas 2015). Later, however, the case re-opened leading to a conviction in 2017 (Brunsden & Hope 2017). This did not mean an end to further conditionality, however. Further measures demanded by the Eurogroup were due to be passed by 20 August 20 to ensure that the first tranche of assistance would be paid out.

Publicly at least, Dijsselbloem underlined more strongly than Schäuble had done previously that the Greek government had done what they must in acceding to Eurogroup demands, since the social cost of Grexit to Greeks would have been enormous. He therefore expressed surprise at the Greek government's decision to hold a referendum, and then to return to the Eurogroup with new, more relaxed proposals, emphasizing that any expectation that the Eurogroup would offer a better deal after a no vote were not realistic. That was particularly so since the banks had been closed for some time and the Greek situation continued to deteriorate. Given the lack of trust from the Eurogroup, the German government and the German Bundestag in particular, which would have to approve any assistance, being tough on Greece requiring additional assurances of future implementation in exchange for help was necessary (Steinhauser 2015).

Schäuble remained convinced that being strict on Greece and other countries to be self-sufficient was indispensable and the correct course of action. He denied that Germany had any power over Europe, illustrating (strangely) that unlike France and the UK, it had no military dominance in Europe. But again he underlined that it was essential for Greece to undertake structural reforms as a prerequisite for bringing back economic growth, and hence for the Eurogroup to extend aid. Special mention was given to Portugal, Spain, Ireland and the Baltic countries which had already undergone these reforms. German demands for reforms on all these countries, including Greece to gather together the financial resources to bootstrap themselves into economic recovery, had 'successfully stabilized the Eurozone'. Schäuble maintained that the German policy of resolve had therefore proven correct, and that he had always tried to help Greece, not harm it. Even more, he staved off critique that Germany should have been more lenient by saying that 'My grandmother used to say: Benevolence comes before dissoluteness. There is a kind of generosity that can rapidly produce the opposite of what is intended' (Brinkbäumer, Sauga & Reiermann 2015).

The Greek government negotiated with creditors up to and including 11 August. The MoU contained concessions of slightly revised fiscal surplus, but mostly strongly imposed conditionality, including 50 billion euros of asset sales. The

Greek parliament approved overnight on 13–14 August, with 40 Syriza MPs defecting and the opposition voting in favour (Henley 2015a).

As a result of these events, Greece received a third bailout with 86 billion euros of assistance from the ESM starting in fall 2015. It was required to deliver a primary government budgetary surplus in 2018, and engage in widespread deregulation, privatization of the public sector and liberalization of the private sector, meaning allowing the sale to non-Greek firms (Böcking & Christides 2015). The first tranche would comprise 25 billion euros, 10 of which would be reserved for the banking system (Guardian 2015a). The German Parliament approved the assistance (Financial Assistance Facility Agreement) to Greece on 19 August on the basis of the Memorandum of Understanding regarding Greek reforms to be taken in return. The other ESM national parliaments did as well. An immediate consequence was the sale of 14 publicly owned Greek airports to the Frankfurt airport group Fraport AG (Guardian 2015b).

In light of Greece's acceptance of Eurogroup demands, the Syriza-led coalition government lost a vote of no confidence, resigned and called a snap election on 21 August. It appeared to harbour the hope that (other) anti-austerity parties and party members will be sufficiently weakened that the conditions can be passed in the Greek parliament (Henley 2015b).

Reaction in the Eurogroup emphasized that it expected Greece to maintain the commitments made and hoped that 'the elections will lead to even more support in the new Greek parliament' for the bailout terms. Meanwhile, the spokesman for the President of the European Commission supported the election call in the hope that it would consolidate support for the legitimacy of the ESM-Eurogroup mechanism (Macdonald 2015b).

The Greek government devoted considerable attention to tackling tax evasion. However, there is some indication that the government failed to target large companies and the country's oligarchs, where great gains could be made (Christides 2015a). The Eurogroup imposed new conditions on 2 December 2015 for the release of 1 billion of the ESM programme, after the passage of reforms that had previously been agreed, including the establishment of an office to expedite privatizations, and widespread pension reforms.

More was at stake, however. The major issue for Greece was hope of debt relief. This had been discussed as a possible quid pro quo for reforms, but the Eurogroup insisted that there would be no discussion until Greece had fully implemented all demands. Given the Eurogroup's intransigence with Ireland, however, the potential cross-border transfers it implied that the Eurogroup wanted to avoid, it seems likely that responsible sovereignty will be successfully imposed without concessions. Eurogroup approval was required to secure 15 billion euros of assistance for the Greek banking sector, specifically four systemically important banks. It was also necessary for Greece to enter negotiations in 2016 over some measure of debt relief. Although the Eurogroup refused to discuss any reduction of Greek debt, Tsipras hoped that at least the debt could be restructured, interest rates reduced and the repayment schedule adjusted to current GDP growth (Christides 2015b).

The Greek government eventually delivered on these demands in parliament on 18 December 2015.

Conclusions

The politics of bailouts and firewalls in the Eurozone demonstrate the primacy of national governments over European institutions in three ways: by the fact that national governments remain responsible for dealing with the cost of sorting out insolvent banks in the event of a financial crisis, by the fact that European financial assistance for national sovereigns and their banks was designed to underline the responsibility of national government for the monies handed out and the conditions under which they would be lent, and by the fact that German power appears to have been the only power that mattered in determining the contours of the EFSF and the ESM and the subsequent behaviour of those institutions. This is a significant reshaping of EMU architecture and a bridge to shaping Banking Union in the way that Germany wanted in the pursuit of managing financial interdependence with a view to distributional gains.

The result is that the architecture of public backstops is characterized by the continued primacy of national government and the weakness of European institutions and funds in providing for financial stability. The ESM was created to be used sparingly, as a failsafe for disaster that can be opened under the discretion of the contributing countries. Its voting rules, which require a 75% weighted majority to approve funding and 85% in an emergency, further entrench a German veto on providing aid, given that Germany has nearly 27% of the weighted votes. This architectural arrangement therefore replicates the design features of the IMF that gave the United States control over IMF policy and governance to the present day.

The second facet of the Eurozone's bailout architecture, in which national responsibility is reinforced, was a political choice imposed on debtor countries by creditor countries. It was not a voluntary choice by those confronted with a treaty they did not like, but an existential question of survival for Ireland and Southern Europe in an environment of unsustainable financial market pressure. The money provided to stave off disaster (for the creditor countries as well) consisted of loans, not transfers, and ensured that national government would be held accountable to the consortium of lenders acting collectively in a new body outside the EU. This is not the establishment of further EU institutions as neofunctionalism or neoliberal institutionalism would expect, but the establishment of new institutions outside the realm of the EU that have both discretion and can only decide under the shadow of German veto power.

A neofunctionalist outcome would have seen the development of a federal Europe that kept EMU intact but damaged Germany's conception of its national interest. Liberal intergovernmentalism, given the large distance between the parties and the need to agree on moving forward, would likely have generated inertia and lack of agreement. Classic realism would have been consistent with a breakup of the Eurozone. New intergovernmentalism would have expected elite management with voluntarism.

The conditionality that the ESM places on recipients at the behest of its most important suppliers of capital reinforces the responsibility of national government, both legally and factually, for ensuring that ESM funds are only employed in the rarest of circumstances, after national bank supervisors and resolution authorities (where applicable) have imposed the highest possible cost of adjustment on private sector creditors and depositors. This may impose a cost on the banks of those creditor countries that national governments may take into consideration and make them more reluctant to insist on such stringent conditionality, but as national regulators in all EU member states continue to force banks to reduce their exposure to banks in other countries, the sensitivity of banks and governments in northern European creditor countries to the risk of default in the Eurozone's southern periphery weakens over time. To the extent that this renationalization or decoupling continues over time, the vulnerability of northern banks to a southern default that led Germany to keep Greece within the Eurozone and to agree to more lenient terms for Spain and Italy in June 2012 than for other programme countries, will eventually melt away. This leads to the conclusion that pressures on Germany and other countries that provide money for national bailouts to do so, and most importantly, to increase the amounts available, will decline by design. In that context, the bargaining power of Germany, the Netherlands and Finland through the ESM increase, meaning that conditionality will also remain strong in the future. In that case, the incentive for national governments to adopt ex ante national responsibility for ensuring a sound banking system without European assistance increases. Moreover, it increases that incentive for countries that might have previously been thought too big to fail, as Spain was in 2012.

To the extent that this is true, further austerity and deflation (Matthijs & Blyth 2011) are pre-programmed as a result of Germany ensuring no sizeable common backstop to Eurozone banks. In this situation, the ECB's Outright Monetary Transactions (OMT) is the only backup to national lending capacity, which in turn is restricted by the terms of the TSCG. The only policy room that remains for national governments is internal deflation, in which wages and other labour costs, including payroll taxes, are pushed downward to increase export-led competitiveness. That drives further spending cuts elsewhere in public sector budgets (Münchau 2014). Under the right conditions, it can lead to large reductions in current account deficits as domestic consumption shrinks (Stiglitz 2015).

The consequence is that neofunctionalist expectations of ever-increasing supranationalism do not appear to be supported. The bailout mechanism for banks in the EU, and for the national governments that provide their public backstop, provides help only where it is deemed necessary to avert an existential threat to the Eurozone and above all its core economies, and focusses strongly on reinforcing national responsibility, not collective responsibility for the health of the banking sector.

In contrast, these cases show that realist institutionalist expectations are fulfilled, and some detail added. Europe, specifically Germany, avoided the pressure of path dependence, securing institutions outside the EU. Increasing forcefulness of method, meaning escalation into coercion and imposition was employed to secure adherence to Germany's rules of the game. A centralization of oversight results but remains based on the organizing principle of responsible sovereignty.

There is nothing revolutionary about this outcome, internationally speaking. It replicates the principles of financial assistance as practiced by the IMF outlined in Chapter 1. It is only in the context of expectations held by some analysts and proponents of European integration that there should naturally be more supranationalism in European bank bailouts that this outcome is puzzling. The assumption that turns out to be incorrect amongst the functionalists in bailout policy is that national governments, when faced with a financial crisis, will attempt to secure transnational economic activity and all of the welfare gains that it provides. The European response to bailouts, which reinforces national funds and responsibility, disproves this expectation, however.

Internationally, and for the contributing states to the ESM, there are reasons to believe that the strategy will not cost money, but actually earn it over time, which in turn can be used to build up the ESM's own capital buffers. That will shield its largest contributors, particularly Germany and France, from having to put forward real money in a bailout situation. The ESM was already making money on interest payments made to programme countries in 2013 (Business Week 2013). And the Bank for International Settlements classified ESM and EFSF bonds in March 2014 as 0% risk weighted by the Basel Committee. This means that they are attractive for banks holding them to fulfil their capital adequacy requirements under the Basel Accords as Level 1 High Quality Liquid Assets on their balance sheets (Bank for International Settlements 2014). This further ensures that the ESM, in addition to being limited in size, and under control of Germany, provides little chance of being a reliable bailout mechanism.

Notes

1 The document was leaked by Sven Giegold, German Green MEP. Via Mathieu van Rohr (2015).
2 Tweet from @hubertus_heil, 11 July.
3 Finnish Finance Minister Stubb declares opposition, declaring the euro group has no mandate to discuss it. Emergency assistance for banks will have to come from privatization of assets transferred by Greece to the ESM. See tweets from @alexstubb on 13 July.

References

Ahmann, T. (2015) U.S. Treasury's law urges steps toward resolving Greek debt crisis. *Reuters*, 28 June.

Alderman, L. (2015) France offers support, but not debt relief to Greece. *New York Times*, 1 February.

Alesina, A., Baldwin, R., Boeri, T., Buiter, W., Giavazzi, F., Gros, D., Micossi, S., Tabellini, G., Wyplosz, C., & Zimmermann, K. (2008) Open letter to European leaders on Europe's banking crisis: A call to action. *Vox*, 1 October.

Armitstead, L. (2012) Debt crisis: Finland threat to plans to unleash ESM. *Telegraph*, 2 July.

Associated Press. (2015) Spanish PM: Greece must follow Europe's rules, 6 July.

Baker, L. (2013) After Cyprus, Eurozone faces tough bank regime – Eurogroup head. *Reuters*, 25 March.
Bank for International Settlements. (2014) *Risk weight for European stability mechanisms and European financial stability facility*. Basel: March.
Bayrischer Rundfunk. (2015) CSU nennt Tsipras 'Erpresser und Volksbelüger', 5 July.
Becker, M. (2015) Reaktionen auf Referendum: "Merkel muss jetzt den Grexit organisieren". *Spiegel Online*, 5 July.
Beesley, A. (2012) EU bailout fund may take stake in Irish banks as part of debt deal. *Irish Times*, 11 July.
Blackden, R. (2012) Timothy Giethner: Europe must put in place 'stronger and more credible firewall. *Telegraph*, 25 February.
Blanchard, O. (2015) Greece: Past critiques and the path forward. *iMFdirect*, 9 July.
Böcking, D., & Christides, G. (2015) Griechenland und die Geldgeber: Bibbern im Oktober. *Spiegel Online*, 21 September.
Bolkenstein, F. (2015) Beste mark, dring aan op vertrek Griekenland. *Volkskrant*, 6 July.
Brinkbäumer, K., Sauga, M., & Reiermann, C. (2015) 'There is no German dominance', Interview with Wolfgang Schäuble. *Spiegel Online International*, 17 July.
Brother, T., & Oberdorff, M. (2015) De method Dijsselbloem. *Vrij Nederland*, 18 May.
Brunsden, J., & Hope, K. (2017) Greece warned over trial of former statistics chief. *Financial Times*, 15 September.
Bundesministerium der Finanzen. (2014) *Minister Schäuble's keynote speech: Bundesbank symposium on financial stability*. 28 February.
Bundesverfassungsgericht. (2012a) *Press release no. 67/2012*, 12 September 2012.
Bundesverfassungsgericht. (2012b) *Press release no. 42/2012, regarding 2 BvE 4/11*, 19 June 2012.
Business Week (2013) EU funds make a profit on Irish bailout', 4 December.
Cage, S. (2014) Ireland confident banks don't need more capital. *Reuters*, 12 February.
Casa Europa. (2012) Aprovação pela Assembleia da República do Tratado que cria o Mecanismo Europeu de Estabilidade, 13 April.
Cermak, C. (2013a) Schaeuble will have negotiating mandate. *The Main Wire*, 14 November.
Cermak, C. (2013b) Asmussen: SSM, Res Mech Cld be operational by Summer 2014. *The Main Wire*, 28 May.
Cermak, C. (2013c) ECB's Asmussen: ESM bank backstop needs only ESM treaty change. *The Main Wire*, 25 September.
Christides, G. (2015a) Kampf gegen Steuerhinterzieher: Griechenland verhaftet Maronenverkäufer statt Millionäre. *Spiegel Online*, 17 December.
Christides, G. (2015b) Tsipras' Reformagenda: Zu viel, zu schnell. *Spiegel Online*, 8 October.
De Witte, B., & Beukers, T. (2013) Court of justice approves the creation of the European stability mechanism outside the EU legal order: Pringle. *Common Market Law Review* 50: 805–48.
Deen, M., & Sterns, O. (2012) OECD Urges Europe to strengthen firewall as growth trails U.S. *Bloomberg*, 29 March.
Dettmer, M., Elger, K., Hawranek, D., Hesse, M., & Huelsen, I. (2012) Fear and uncertainty: The Euro endangers German economy. *Spiegel Online International*, 3 July.
Deutscher Bundestag. (2012) Abstimmung über Fiskalpakt und Euro-Rettungsschirm, 29 June.
Donahue, P., & Delfs, A. (2015) *Merkel says Greece accord possible only if Tsipras moves*. Bloomberg, 18 June.
Doncel, L. (2015) EE UU espió a varios miembros del Gobierno alemán y del BCE. *El País*, 2 July.

Durden, T. (2015) Greece asks for 2-year Bailout from ESM, Merkel shoots it down. *Zero Hedge*, 30 June.

Dyson, K. (2016). Germany, the Euro crisis, and risk management: Europe's reluctant and vulnerable hegemonic power. In D'Ottavio, G. & Saalfeld, T. eds., *Germany after the 2013 elections: Breaking the mould of post-unification politics?* Abingdon: Routledge: 49–66.

The Economist. (2015) An offer it cannot refuse, 2 June.

Elliott, L. & Smith, H. (2012) France and Italy add to pressure on Germany to prop up the euro.] *Guardian*, 31 July.

Elliott, L., Smith, H., & Kollewe, J. (2012) World Bank warns that euro collapse could spark global crisis. *Observer*, 16 June.

Emmott, R. (2012) Euro crisis needs "mother of all firewalls": OECD. *Reuters*, 27 March.

Epstein, R. A. (2014) Assets or liabilities? The politics of bank ownership. *Review of International Political Economy* 21, 4: 765–89.

Epstein, R. A. (2017) *Banking on markets: The transformation of bank-state ties in Europe and beyond*. Oxford: Oxford University Press.

Escritt, T. (2014) Dutch PM threatened in 2012 to quit Eurozone over reform contracts. *Reuters*, 30 April.

Eurogroup. (2015) *Euro summit statement SN 4070/15*. Brussels, 12 July.

European Commission. (2011) *Green paper on stability bonds*, 23 November.

European Commission. (2015) *A new start for jobs and growth in Greece: Commission mobilises more than €35 billion from the EU budget*. (Press Release IP/15/5373). Brussels, 15 July.

European Council. (2015) *EFSM: Council approves €7bn bridge loan to Greece*. Brussels, 17 July.

European Financial Stability Facility. (2011) *Master agreement with Portugal*, 11 May.

European Financial Stability Facility. (2013) EFSF board of directors approves final disbursement to Portugal.

European Financial Stability Facility. (2014) EFSF issues €5 billion 7-year bond. Luxembourg: 8 April.

European Parliament. (2013) *Article 136 TFEU, ESM, fiscal stability treaty: Ratification requirements and present situation in the Member States*. DG Internal Policies (Constitutional Affairs), 12 December.

European Parliament Research Service. (2014) *German constitutional court decisions on EU anti-crisis measures*. Strasbourg, July.

European Stability Mechanism. (2013a) FAQ: ESM financial assistance for Cyprus, 18 September.

European Stability Mechanism. (2013b) *Spain successfully Exits ESM financial assistance programme*. Luxembourg, 31 December.

European Stability Mechanism. (2014) *Klaus Regeling welcomes German constitutional court's ruling*. Luxembourg, 18 March.

Evans-Pritchard, A. (2012) Europe's debt crisis credibility hangs on thin Irish thread. *Telegraph*, 16 October.

Evans-Pritchard, A. (2014) Tim Geithner reveals in the raw how Europe's leaders tried to commit financial suicide. *Telegraph*, 12 November.

Evans-Pritchard, A. (2015) Greece's 'war cabinet' prepares to battle EU creditors as anger mounts. *Telegraph*, 10 May.

Fahmi, D., & Behrmann, E. (2015) Germans tired of Greek demands want country to exit Euro. *Politico*, 16 March.

Gatopoulos, D. (2015) Greece Prime Minister Tsipras: We are facing 'financial strangulation' *Business Insider*, 18 May.

Georgiopoulos, G. (2015) ECB boosts emergency funding as Greek banks bleed, Tsipras calm. *Reuters*, 19 June.

Gersemann, O. (2015) Der Währungsfonds bringt Merkel in die Bredouille. *Die Welt*, 16 June.

Gore, G., & Roy, S. (2012) Spanish bailout saves German pain. *International Financing Review*, 29 June.

Government of Portugal. (2012) *Intervenção do Primeiro-Ministro no debate parlamentar sobre ratificação dos Tratados que cria o Mecanismo Europeu de Estabilidade e sobre Estabilidade, Coordenação e Governação na União Económica e Monetária*. Lisbon, 12 April.

Grabel, I. (2015). The rebranding of capital controls in an era of productive incoherence. *Review of International Political Economy* 22, 1: 7–43.

Guardian. (2012) 'Friend of Greece' Francois Hollande gives bailout ultimatum, 14 June.

Guardian. (2015a) Greece to receive first bailout cash after German MPs and ESM approve deal, 19 August.

Guardian. (2015b) Germans to run Greek regional airports in first wave of bailout privatisations, 19 August.

Henley, J. (2015a) Alexis Tsipras hit by Syriza rebellion as Greece approves bailout deal. *Guardian*, 14 August.

Henley, J. (2015b) Greek bailout: Alexis Tsipras steps down to trigger new elections. *Guardian*, 20 August.

Hirst, N. (2015) Greece finds no solidarity in Club Med. *Politico*, 16 February.

International Monetary Fund. (2015) *Greece: An update of the IMF staff's preliminary public debt sustainability analysis*. IMF Country Report 15/186.

Jenkins, Patrick. (2014) Greece's plight offers clue to future of EU banking system. *Financial Times*, 26 February.

Juncker, J.C. (2015) *Completing Europe's Economic and Monetary Union*. Brussels: European Commission.

Kanter, J., & Eddy, M. (2012) Europe urged to increase firewall to a trillion Euros. *New York Times*, 29 March.

Karnitschnig, M. (2017) Merkel quashes hopes of ambitious Eurozone reform. *Politico*, 29 August.

Karnitschnig, M., Turner, Z., & Palmeri, T. (2015) The all-nighter that kept Greece in the Eurozone. *Politico*, 15 July.

Kingston, S. (2013) Pringle judgement breaks new ground. *Irish Times*, 4 February.

Koutantou, A., & Kambas, M. (2015) Greek PM Tsipras seeks party backing after abrupt concessions. *Reuters*, 10 July.

Krugman, P. (2015) Austerity and the Greek depression. *New York Times*, 10 July.

Lynch, S. (2012) Van Rompuy says decisions on ESM cannot be blocked. *Irish Times*, 4 July.

Macdonald, A. (2015a) Benelux states grumble at Greek-German-French talks at EU. *Reuters*, 19 March.

Macdonald, A. (2015b) EU calls on Greece to stick with reforms, stresses positives. *Reuters*, 20 August.

Maletzou, R., & Koutantou, A. (2015) Greek parliament approves bailout measures as Syriza fragments. *Reuters*, 16 July.

Market News International. (2014) Germany schäuble: Will not change ESM treaty, 28 February.

Martin, M., & O'Dell, J. (2013) Reluctant Germany casts cloud over Europe's bank revamp. *Reuters*, 15 November.
Matthijs, M., & Blyth, M. (2011) Why only Germany can fix the euro. *Foreign Affairs 17:* 117–35.
Merler, S. (2015) *The Greek last-chance proposal: stepping backwards to move forward?* Bruegel, 10 July.
Milano Finanza (2012). The market stabilization program: Legal issues, 27 June.
Münchau, W. (2014) What eurocrisis watchers should look for in 2014. *Financial Times*, 6 January.
Neuger, J. G., Bodoni, S., & Stearns, J. (2012) Greece wins easier debt terms as EU hails rescue formula. *Bloomberg*, 27 November.
Paul Mason News. (2015) Leaked IMF memo on #Greece saying "no possibility" of Greece meeting debt obligations this summer (via Twitter) 16 May.
Picketty, T., Sachs, J., Flassbeck, H., & Wren-Lewis, S. (2015) Austerity has failed: An open letter from Thomas Piketty to Angela Merkel. *The Nation*, 7 July.
Pitas, C. (2015) Greek judges drop felony charge against stats chief. *Reuters*, 19 July.
Salmon, F. (2012) How Europe can force Greece out of the euro. *Reuters*, 14 May.
Salmon, F. (2013) The Dijsselbloem Principle. *Reuters*. 26 March.
Sarcinelli, M. (2012) Euro crisis or public debt crisis? With a remedy for the latter case. *PSL Quarterly Review* 65, 262: 215–36.
Scally, D. (2012) German finance minister denies pushing ESM deal. *Irish Times*, 12 July.
Schmidt, S. K. (2013) A sense of Deja Vu: The FCC's preliminary European stability mechanism verdict. *German Law Journal* 14: 1–20.
Spence, P., & Fraser, I. (2015) Greek PM: IMF has 'criminal' responsibility for situation. *Telegraph*, 16 June.
Spiegel Online. (2015) Schäuble's push for Grexit, 17 July.
Spiegel, P. (2014b) Inside Europe's plan Z. *Financial Times*, 14 May.
Spiegel, P. (2015) Leaked: Tsipras letter requesting a 3rd bailout. *Financial Times*, 30 June.
Spiegel, P., Donnan, S., & Hope, K. (2015) IMF quits Greece talks amid 'air of unreality' as deal unravels. *Financial Times*, 11 June.
Steinberg, F., & Vermeiren, M. (2015) *The limits to German power in the Eurozone*. Real Instituto El Cano ARI 25/2015, 11 May.
Steinhauser, G. (2015) WSJ's Interview with Jeroen Dijsselbloem: The full transcript. *Wall Street Journal*, 16 July.
Stiglitz, J. E. (2015) Reconstructing macroeconomic theory to manage economic policy. In Laurent, E. & Le Cacheux, J. eds., *Fruitful economics*. Basingstoke: Palgrave Macmillan: 20–56.
Taylor, P. (2015) Europeans tried to block IMF debt report on Greece: Sources. *Reuters*, 3 July.
Telegraph. (2013) Ireland may not need financing backstop to exit bailout, 12 October.
Totaro, L. (2012) Italian parliament gives final approval to bill ratifying ESM. *Bloomberg*, 19 July.
Traynor, I. (2012) IMF urges Europe to build bigger firewall around Italy and Spain. *Guardian*, 23 January.
Traynor, I., & Hooper, J. (2015) Creditors offer Greece six-month bailout reprieve as Tsipras weighs response. *Guardian*, 21 June.
Traynor, I., Hooper, J., & Smith, H. (2015) Greek referendum no vote signals huge challenge to Eurozone leaders. *Guardian*, 5 July.
Tsipras, A. (2015) Alexis tsipras: Non à une zone euro à deux vitesses. *Le Monde*, 13 May.

Tuner, Z. (2015) Frustrated IMF pulls out of Greek talks. *Politico*, 9 June.
Van Malleghem, Pieter-Augustijn. (2013) Pringle: A paradigm shift in the European Union's monetary constitution. *German Law Journal* 14: 141–68.
Van Rohr, M. (2015) Here's the Schäuble Grexit plan everybody is talking about – via @ sven_giegold. (via Twitter), 10 July.
Varoufakis, Y. (2015a) *Greece's proposals to end the crisis: My intervention at today's Eurogroup*. Yangisvaroufakis.eu, 18 June.
Varoufakis, Y. (2015b) Yanis Varoufakis: A pressing question for Ireland before Monday's meeting on Greece. *Irish Times*, 20 June.
Watt, A. (2015) Reach a deal! The Greek offer is a basis for a compromise. *Social Europe*, 16 June.
White House. (2015) *Readout of the President's call with chancellor Angela Merkel of Germany*. Office of the Press Secretary, 28 June.

5 The SSM

Supervising Europe's biggest banks

This chapter is about the establishment of the Single Supervisory Mechanism, or SSM. If anything has become supranational in the context of Banking Union, this is it. The vision of a single bank supervisor with direct responsibility for all EU banks, coupled with powers to wind them down in an orderly fashion was never achieved, but more supranationalism was achieved in this area than in any other. Accordingly, proponents of neofunctionalism point to its establishment as proof that institutions followed functional necessity, allowing for the necessary political negotiations to reach the deal about how (Epstein & Rhodes 2016; Schimmelfennig 2016). They further maintain that the European Central Bank created facts that were very difficult for national governments, including Germany, to resist, with the consequence that the SSM has more direct power than the member states intended to provide in the first place. This shows that national preferences ultimately lost out to the functional need for a central bank for the euro area.

However, the establishment of the SSM, and the terms on which it was done, are also consistent with an intergovernmentalist interpretation of events. The SSM was established within the EU using intergovernmental negotiation. However, the ESM hinged on finalizing agreement on the SSM – no money without control – so that Shadow EU institutions and realist institutionalism remain vital to understanding the prioritization of supervision within BU, both in terms of institutional strength and the speed of its introduction. This is particularly remarkable after the establishment of the EBA in 2011, which coordinated but could not control like a de novo institution (Bickerton et al. 2015). The institutional architecture within the EU is changed to fit a new architecture outside it new architecture outside it (H1) and impose real control using coercive means to impose commitments (H3.2). This is accomplished in ways that de novo bodies like the EBA could not have done (against the expectations of new intergovernmentalism). Indeed the domestic politics of Banking Union in Germany reveal that the country's support for the ECB as bank supervisor was so strong that it continued to push for it when few others would. The SSM, like the TSCG, was a project pushed by Germany, and its importance was so great in making German assistance to other countries politically feasible that withdrawing support for the ECB's expanded role was not possible. Changing attitudes within the country about whether state-owned Landesbanken should be supervised, and how local savings and loans banks (Sparkassen) could

DOI: 10.4324/9780203702130-5

be protected squared domestic needs with international demands (Howarth & Quaglia 2016; Lombardi & Moschella 2016; Deeg & Donnelly 2016).

This chapter seeks to answer two questions. To what extent does the timing and form of the SSM's establishment reflect realist institutionalist politics, in particular the backing of Germany and its allies? What are the consequences of granting supervisory power to the ECB in its current form, and how are we to understand the ECB's own initiatives in building out supervision and related activities aimed at keeping the Eurozone together? It suggests that liberal intergovernmentalism, within the confines of EU rule-making explains the more modest development of the EBA as a supervisor, but that realist institutionalism best explains the establishment of the SSM as a core feature of Banking Union that primarily only Germany wanted. The result is a hybrid supervisory system with the EBA coordinating national supervisors for most banks and the ECB acting directly at a relatively small list of large, systemically important institutions. Future tensions in supervision are therefore pre-programmed.

The SSM in short: supervision, stress testing and financial stability

The European Central Bank commenced its role as the EU's leading bank supervisor on 4 November 2014, following a political agreement by the member states in December 2013 to grant that status, and subsequent regulatory details that had been agreed by April 2014. The ECB directly supervises 128 European SIBs covering more than 80% of assets on bank balance sheets. The remaining 6000-plus banks in the EU are supervised by national authorities. Those authorities are required to take ECB directives on best supervisory practice into account, through a so-called Single Rulebook, they have a legal duty to provide timely and complete information to the ECB as it requests it (in the search for potential threats to financial stability), and they must yield to the ECB if it decides to take over supervision of a bank directly. Although the balance of central direction and national discretion remains to be tested, the relationship between the ECB and national competent authorities is structured in a way that closely resembles the vertical network relationship between the ECJ and national courts, or the European Commission's DG Comp and national competition authorities.

Germany made the SSM a prerequisite for making ESM assistance available to banks, which led other states to agree, even those whose priority was clearly for financial assistance first. The scope of the ECB's authority, however, was largely determined by the ECB itself, with the permission of the EU's member states. The list of 128 banks that the ECB supervises is the result of an algorithm that the ECB developed itself to replace what it saw as an arbitrary and ineffective German proposal to task the bank with supervising no more than 25 banks. Instead, the ECB algorithm chose to supervise banks having assets in excess of 30 billion euros, amounting to more than 20% of national GDP, or belonging to the top two banks in any EU member state. The Single Rulebook is also a tool that the ECB influences as much as it can. The Asset Quality Review, which the ECB announced and conducted prior to assuming its duties as supervisor in 2014, also provides the bank with its own view of balance sheets in the Eurozone, rather than relying on the assessments of national supervisors. Finally, although a function of the ECB's role as guarantor of financial stability rather than as supervisor, the ECB's provision of Emergency Liquidity Assistance to banks in distressed situations influences the likelihood that supervision has adverse, neutral or positive effects on banks in the short term.

The rest of this chapter examines how the ECB got to this situation. It starts with the record of the ECB's predecessor in this regard, the European Banking Authority, and then pays attention to the timing and context of the decision to support the ECB as banking supervisor over the EBA, as well as the extent to which the ECB displaces the Authority through the SSM. Although the ECB's initiatives strengthen its hand in all four relationships (to member states, national authorities, the EBA and banks themselves), coverage is not complete.

The European Banking Authority

The idea of establishing a single bank supervisor for the European Union, or at least for the Eurozone, went back to the early days of the financial crisis in 2009, when the De Larosiere Committee, a group of experts given the responsibility of pointing the lessons from the crisis for the EU, recommended the establishment of the European Banking Authority. The EBA would pool together national regulators and task them with sharing information and best practice on the state of banking in their jurisdictions, recommending new regulations and legislation to the Commission, including recommendations on the adoption of international banking regulation standards known as Basel III, and collectively supervising the quality of oversight in individual member states. In those cases where banks operated in more than one member state, the EBA would also host supervisory colleges – groups of two or more bank supervisors working together on the oversight of a bank's cross-border operations. The EBA was therefore less than a single supervisor, but as much as the group of experts could manage to recommend, and as it turned out, as much as the member states in the Council were willing to accept during the legislative process. In this sense, this underlines that the onset of the financial crisis was insufficient to prod European decision-makers to consider a single bank supervisor for the EU or for the Eurozone. The EBA came into being on 1 January 2011, after legislation passed in late 2010.

In keeping with the thrust of the De Larosiere report, the EBA's primary mission was to raise the general level of supervision in the EU, both within the banking sector and in the larger context of financial stability within the European Systemic Risk Board, in conjunction with its fellow supervisors in the pensions and securities sectors (EIOPA and ESMA). It was also tasked with carrying out stress tests of EU banks, albeit indirectly, supporting and overseeing the quality of work undertaken by national supervisors. The EBA in theory had the power to overrule a national supervisor by qualified majority vote, but never attempted to do so, and could have run into legal obstacles under the Meroni doctrine had it tried (Moloney 2014; Véron 2013). As a consequence, the EBA in practice operated much in the same way that other so-called open methods of coordination in the EU and the OECD operate – on the basis of country reporting, peer review, but ultimately voluntarism on the part of the individual member states. This means that if they chose to withhold information, not conduct their supervisory duties with due diligence or resist suggestions for improvement or calls for cooperation, there was little the other member states or European bodies could do about it (Véron & Wolff 2013). Similarly, if the other member states have an equal interest in not rocking the boat and encouraging collective investigations into the behaviour of one of their own, action is unlikely. Unlike the case of the SGP, which places the Council of Ministers under a legal obligation to decide whether a national government is in violation of its commitments and obligations, the Commission cannot challenge the EBA's failure to act against one of its own by taking the body to the ECJ.

In theory, the EBA's mission was designed not only to take bank supervision to the next level, and ensure that everyone was adopting the state of the art together, but also to instil investor confidence in the European economy by exposing weaknesses that banks would have to correct. There would be a moment of pain followed by a fresh start. In the context of the ever-deepening Eurozone crisis, this meant identifying and exposing non-performing loans and other assets (including derivatives) that would have to be written down, and loans in danger of slipping into non-performing territory as the economy continued to stagnate and decline. It also meant conducting rigorous stress tests, or ensuring that they were carried out by national supervisors, in which regulators would test the capacity of banks to withstand one or more economic setbacks, ranging from a significant downturn in the economy, the collapse of a major European bank, or even the bankruptcy of one of the EU's member states. All of these events would reduce the value of assets associated with the setback that banks held on their balance sheets, requiring them to undertake potentially costly adjustments. Recessions would lead to declines in the value of stocks and bonds, in the income that they generate, while the threat of a sovereign bankruptcy would undermine the value of treasury bills held on balance sheets as part of a bank's reserve capital. To ensure the resilience of banks in the face of periodic setbacks, supervisors need to ensure that banks have sufficient stockpiles of cash to serve as insurance. In order to do that, they would have to either retain earnings in a tough economic environment or sell new shares to raise money. In the parlance of bank regulation, the EBA needed to ensure that banks complied with benchmarks for capital adequacy (Howarth & Quaglia 2013) by raising equity. The stress tests would say how far this effort would have to go.

In the European context, stress testing and bank adjustment were also deemed necessary to break the so-called doom loop between insolvent banks and insolvent national governments. Banks had been hit first during the financial crisis of 2008, finding themselves short of capital with which to fund their operations. National governments, preferring not to close the banks or sell them off to foreign owners, stepped in with cash injections and asset guarantees that turned the banks from general economic assets into direct economic liabilities. Combined with the general deterioration of public finances during any economic downturn, financial markets began to question the capacity of some governments to repay and started raising interest rates in Southern Europe by a factor of two to three times between 2011 and 2012, to the point where the interest burden became unpayable and bankruptcy appeared imminent. Under these circumstances, the value of treasury bills from Southern European countries on the balance sheets of banks declined, leading to a renewed need to raise capital that markets refused to supply. This again required the banks to turn to their national governments, which were now up against the wall. That moment was reached earliest in Greece, in 2010, and threatened to crack the capacity of Italy to borrow in November 2011 (but did not), and finally affected most of Southern Europe simultaneously in May–June 2012. The intent was that if stress tests were to lead banks to face up to the weaknesses on their balance sheets and to take corrective measures, that they would be able to secure their own funding on private capital markets once again and return to being assets to the economy rather than a liability for both economy and government.

It is in that context that EBA failed its own test of public confidence toward the end of 2011. Tasked with conducting stress tests for European banks, or rather agreeing on a set of criteria that national supervisors would apply to their own national banks, the EBA had to agree on what trends and credit events it would simulate in testing bank resilience. At a time when the European Council was openly deliberating with the IMF and the ECB on a common position toward Greece and its request for further financial assistance, the EBA failed to consider the possibility of a partial or total Greek default on its public debt, or of imposed haircuts on bondholders (reductions in the value of the bonds' worth) that would have imposed similar losses on banks holding those bonds. This put into stark profile the complaint from observers on the inside of the EBA that national representatives were undermining its work by dragging their feet on agreeing to common positions, demanding exemptions and otherwise shielding their national champions.

This type of behaviour more strongly reflected the modus operandi of the EBA's predecessor, the Committee of European Banking Authorities (CEBS), in which no attempt was made to encroach on the prerogatives of national competent authorities, rather than the mission and powers on paper that the EBA had been granted. The EBA's powerlessness in the face of national opposition, and particularly toward powerful countries was underlined when the German supervisory authority allowed two German Landesbanken (regional, public sector banks) to withdraw from the stress testing and then attacked the Authority's algorithm for assessing capital adequacy (Wilson 2011). The EBA's humiliation was complete. By 2017, the Authority's reputation had still not fully recovered (Binham 2017).

A great deal was at stake in the decision to defy the EBA. Had the stress tests gone forward without the blockages, they would have created problems for banks in Germany and France in particular. According to Blundell-Wignall and Slovik (2010), non-Greek EU bank exposures to Greek government debt alone exceeded 50 billion euros (with Greek banks themselves exposed to 56 billion), while non-Spanish bank exposures to Spanish debt was at around 51 billion (Spanish banks being exposed to 203 billion). The value of government debt would have declined significantly in value as a result of either an orderly default, which the Council was deliberating, or been entirely at risk in the event of an uncontrolled one.

This meant that under the period of supervision coordination by the EBA, national governments continued to determine for themselves how they would muddle through the crisis and eventually exit it, if they ever did, without regard for the integrity of the supervision process. This means that there was no full enforcement pyramid (H3) which Germany later sought to rectify. National governments acting collectively within the European Council and in conjunction with voting and rule-making were not terribly important in determining whether there would be a major credit event. As the previous chapter on bailouts showed, Germany, France, the United States and the IMF were the only governments effectively involved. National governments within the EBA could decide collectively to turn a blind eye to major credit events when it suited them, and individual member states could simply defect if they believed they could get away with it. It made a mockery of the commitment to establish the EBA in the first place. The sections below outline in more detail specific aspects of the supervision process, coupled with how the EBA handled them.

Capital requirements

One of the key features of any stress test is to ascertain whether banks hold the quantity and quality of capital required to weather a significant downturn or credit event. Here as well, the EBA had no independent authority. Instead, capital requirements were negotiated by the European Commission, the member states and the European Parliament in the adoption of most, but not all international Basel capital adequacy standards in the Capital Requirements Directive IV (CRD IV), and by the Commission and the member states in the Capital Requirements Regulation (CRR), which provides for further details (Howarth & Quaglia 2013). In the context of the CRR, the EBA provides advice to the Commission for the adjustment of capital requirements over time. In the case of Basel III standards, the EBA recommended against the full adoption of international standards, preferring to set the bar lower for EU banks, much to the dismay of the UK government, which had wanted to apply higher limits.

In the context of capital requirements, *deleveraging* became a key issue for banks everywhere, but European banks in particular, which started the crisis with higher leverage ratios than their American counterparts (Reidhill 2013). An issue discussed broadly across bank supervisors internationally therefore was the power of bank supervisors to order banks to lower their leverage ratios. This means relying more for their operating capital by raising it on stock markets and less on bond markets. The rationale was threefold. First, banks would be less vulnerable to fluctuations in interest rates and even the availability of new loans to cover bonds coming due. In September 2008, the drying up of the interbank market affected not only overnight loans, but this element as well. Second, in the event of a crisis leading to the downfall of a bank, money raised by equity would not lead to complicated debt contracts that had to be sorted out by a resolution authority. Third, shares give holders the right to vote on company policy, to review financial statements and even vote on the selection of the company's leadership, placing management under increased supervision from the company's shareholders.

Deleveraging can be accomplished by raising new capital on the stock market (which can backfire by driving down share price), retaining earnings (which also tend to drive down share price by keeping dividends low), converting debt to equity (use of hybrid instruments) and redemption below par in the case of callable bonds. Only 10% of the effort to meet EBA capital-to-risk-weighted-asset (RWA) ratios of 9% was met by shedding assets. Another 9% was made by negotiating recalculation of RWA with national regulators, essentially negotiating a more optimistic assessment of default risk. The other 77% was met by various capital measures, spread across increased equity and debt conversion (Bank for International Settlements 2012: 6–7). Redemption below par means that the bank pays back the bondholder before the bond is repayable and pays a penalty for doing so. This is only attractive to the bank if the current market rate is significantly lower than the normal price. At the time of sale, a callable bond must pay a higher interest rate in order to attract buyers. Deleveraging took place partly as well by Western European banks reducing their loan portfolios (Jones 2014). Credit to the real economy shrank considerably, even as interest rates stayed persistently in negative territory in 2016.

However, the capacity to deleverage in this context is less than these figures indicate. The Bank for International Settlements reports that Eurozone banks made extensive use of the ECB's Long-Term Refinancing Operation (LTRO) program to raise capital outside of these options, accounting for 80% of the funding required to pay down debts coming due (debt redemption). Greece, Portugal and Ireland had made the most extensive use early on and then tapered off, after which Spanish and Italian banks stepped up their use massively, followed by Belgium and France, while other northern European banks made far less extensive use. In contrast, Germany, Luxembourg and Finland massively increased their deposits with the ECB. Southern European countries benefited from the LTRO through lower yields (interest payments) on their borrowing (Bank for International Settlements 2012: 3).

Banks in Europe remain almost everywhere far more highly leveraged than anywhere else in the world, however (OECD 2017), meaning that it was difficult, if not impossible for European governments, or anyone else for that matter to consider giving the SSM the power to decide on leverage ratios, despite the urgent prodding of the US government. This also means that the move toward new regulations on leverage ratios, as in the United States, are difficult to contemplate for much of the Eurozone, with the possible exception of France. The leverage ratio is a measure of the Core Tier 1 capital that a bank holds divided by its outstanding exposure (assets), whereby the higher the leverage ratio, the greater the security. The United States chose in the wake of the financial crisis to demand high leverage ratios in relation to all assets, which it considered to be more transparent and less vulnerable to manipulation than the Basel-based system of measuring core capital against risk-weighted assets. The UK followed this approach, setting it apart from other regulators in the European Banking Authority (Bank of England 2013: 69). The ECB's designated chief of supervision was reported in early 2014 to favour such a focus on leverage ratios (Fleming, Ross & Jones 2014).

Although some banks in the Eurozone had reduced leverage in anticipation of the ECB's new role as supervisor for the Eurozone's largest systemically important institutions, only some of that deleveraging could be accomplished by reducing the creation of loans. An increasingly common method of deleveraging was to do it contingently – by raising capital through hybrid mechanisms, particularly contingent convertible bonds that would revert to shares in the event of a bank's insolvency (Avdjiev, Kartasheva & Bogdanova 2013).

National involvement and friction

Italy

Italy's supervisor, the Bank of Italy, had a relatively lenient approach to supervision and converted very late to prefer innovative methods of bank resolution and recapitalization. Once the SSM was in effect, the results were visible in that half of all banks failing to fulfil capital adequacy standards in 2014 were Italian. Italy was the only major economy of the Eurozone that did not institute a bad bank system to help clean toxic waste out of its banking system. As a result, it proved to perform particularly badly in 2014 and onward in deleveraging and raising capital. In the context of the 2014 asset review the Bank of Italy tabled plans for a bad bank for Italy's banks, but government denied the need, stating that its banking sector was in good shape (Za 2014). Meanwhile, the Italian Banking Association reported that its members had 156 billion euros on non-performing loans in 2013 that they were concerned about, and the Bank of Italy was concerned that three Italian banks were not forthcoming with data in preparation for stress tests (Klimes 2014). In the absence of such a public bad bank plan, which the government opposed because it feared a downgrade of its sovereign credit ratings, the Bank of Italy pressured banks to do the work themselves. This meant making provisions for non-performing loans (a combination of writing off the value of those loans and raising capital, or setting up an internal bad bank), or selling those loans to funds like KKR which specialized in problem assets (Sanderson & Dinmore 2014).

According to Reuters, the Italian government and Bank of Italy, as the bank regulators, were also recorded as saying that they would 'exempt banks that had mandatory European Commission-approved restructuring plans . . . from the harshest of stress tests in 2014'(Reuters 2014a). This took advantage of concessions made in the European Banking Authority to assess all banks undergoing mandatory restructuring on the basis of projected improvements in the balance sheet and on the profit and loss statement over 2014 to 2016, rather than an assessment of actual worth in 2014. Italian authorities were particularly concerned about Monte dei Paschi bank (Bernabei 2014). Monte dei Paschi at the time faced great difficulties in raising capital to bolster its balance sheets due to legal infighting with a shareholder group that promised to drag on (Bernabei 2014a). Other Italian banks, UniCredit and Intesa to be exact, were able to work on private solutions instead, which involved securitizing loans and selling them to hedge funds to deleverage (Bernabei & Semeraro 2014).

Spain: recapitalizing with convertible debt

In Spain, the central bank acted differently than in Italy. After a period of deregulation prior to the GFC, the Bank of Spain and the Spanish government reversed course to re-regulate Spanish banks, supervise them more stringently and force resolution of insolvent institutions (Epstein 2017; Quaglia & Royo 2015). Banks responded in part to impending stress tests by selling off debt from the asset side of the balance sheet. A significant portion of that debt was in Spanish treasury bonds, which the banks bought as foreign investors sold it at the start of the Eurozone crisis. Spanish banks as a consequence have to rely more strongly on traditional banking business for income, which ties their profitability to the general state of the Spanish economy. This can be positive or negative, depending on the state of the economy. If banks lend more to the real economy and it generates growth, it is positive. If the growth fails to materialize, it is negative. The Spanish state has to rely more strongly on foreign investors to buy its bonds (moving from 35 to 41% of holdings in February 2014) (Penty 2014).

Spanish banks, as well as Portuguese and Irish banks, also prepared for stress tests by issuing new debt in 2013 and 2014. In the early stages this debt was covered, meaning that the bonds were secured by collateral, which provides creditors with heightened security that their investments are secure. Not only does the normal collateral serve as a hedge against default, but covered bonds were explicitly protected in European rules on bail-ins (next chapter). Toward the end of 2013, sufficient creditor optimism was present for the banks to issue normal, unsecured debt that exposes creditors to a normal risk of default and bail-in. One financial analyst suggested that the fresh investment in bank bonds reflected both an impression that the economy was improving (witnessed by an expansion of corporate debt) and more importantly, that creditors saw banks improving their internal finances and putting problems behind them. To what extent creditors based this assessment on facts or supposition is unclear, but banks were able to increase capital through bonds by over 50%, thereby easing the pressure on them to sell further assets (Thompson 2014). In the case of Spain, the government pressured banks to increase capital in this way or face nationalization (Toyer & Ruano 2014).

Another observer underlined that confidence was not the only story, but that these new debt instruments were contingent convertible bonds (known as cocos) that transformed into shares if the price dropped below a pre-selected threshold, or if the supervisor intervened to stop the bank paying interest on the bonds. This means that creditors would have the opportunity, as newly minted shareholders, to replace the bank's management before a bailout or bail-in became necessary or imminent. Banks would be relieved of paying interest in an existential crisis with bondholders taking the financial loss. Issuing cocos would allow banks to pay a lower rate of interest, increasing their profitability and viability. Spanish bank BBVA could pay 7% interest rather than 9% in early 2014, for example, and the method became widespread thereafter (Jeffery 2017). Although supervisors had some serious worries that this interest rate discount was too great, by irrationally failing to consider conversion or supervisory intervention as a real possibility (Thompson & Arnold 2014), some advantage to the various parties remains, even as creditors reconsider the risk of default and charge more for the instrument.

The short-term effect of using cocos was the capacity of Southern European banks, along with northern European banks, to access capital needed for the stress test, and to do so without resorting to covered debt, which causes problems for supervisors in the event of a bank's collapse. In such a circumstance, there would be little left for resolution authorities to bail in, making a taxpayer bailout and/or collapse more likely. Since the supervisor reviews the nature of such debt instruments as well as of assets, this is a welcome trend that enhances financial stability. It likely would have happened in the absence of ECB supervision (as evidenced that the trend to convertible bond is as strong outside the Eurozone as inside it), but the nudging function of the EBA stress tests and ECB AQRs are likely to have been significant in pressuring banks to secure the capital. The strongest move toward convertible bonds has been in the higher tier of banks that fall under ECB supervision (Thompson & Arnold 2014).

It must be noted, however, that in the medium to long term, the ability of banks to use cocos to meet regulatory requirements for increased capital depends on market behaviour that can shift overnight from accommodating to impossible. If the price of bonds drops below the threshold, or if interest rates rise significantly in anticipation of declining profitability or the risk of default, then the advantage of issuing such instruments declines. Indeed the Bank of England demonstrated concern that markets were creating instability by lending too much to banks at too low an interest rate, and that when interest rates eventually rose, and CoCo bonds dropped in price as markets woke up to their mistake, that a pre-programmed crisis for the banks would result (Carney 2013; Bank of England 2013).

And in the private sector, the resort to cocos is still considered to be second best to retaining earnings (if available) and selling off assets (if they can be sold without a loss), due to the fact that the interest rates remain high for strong banks and up to 50% higher for smaller and weaker banks (Vaughan 2011). For governments providing bailouts, however, it is more attractive to resort to a combination of receiving interest on their loans to banks, and not scaring away investors from the stock market, who would be diluted if the banks were to raise capital by issuing more shares. One result is that the extremely high leverage ratio that typifies European banks, which constitutes a significant vulnerability when interest rates rise, and therefore poses a significant risk to financial stability during times of stress, is not addressed by the practice (Vaughan 2011). This is despite the fact that both American and British regulators, as well as the OECD, have underlined that deleveraging is essential to long-term financial stability (Bank of England 2013: 65–6; Reidhill 2013; Wehinger 2012).

The EBA authorized the use of CoCos in December 2011 for banks trying to raise capital to meet their capital requirements. It estimated then that banks required 153 billion euros of new capital to meet them. The supervisor is interested in CoCo conversion when a bank's tier 1 core capital ratio drops below a fixed percentage. But the threshold chosen (7%) was considered too weak by some (Vaughan 2011), reflecting European unwillingness to fully implement Basel III agreements (Howarth & Quaglia 2013).

Greece

Supervision in Greece proved further from generally accepted practice than Italy. Greek banks and government found themselves in February 2014, before the stress tests had taken place, in conflict with the Troika and other outside investors regarding the degree of capital needed to restore Greek banks back to health. Greek bank and government representatives insisted that 6 billion euros was required to recapitalize the banking sector, and had shopped around private analyst firms seeking confirmation of that outcome, while Troika analysis, particularly by the IMF, saw a figure of 20 billion as necessary. This review was taken in light of Troika–Greece talks over whether Greece would require a third bailout in 2013/2014 (Spiegel & Hope 2014).

Part of the sought reduction was found by lowering the standard to which Greek banks would be held. The Troika had originally applied Basel standards on capital ratios (9% core tier 1 capital), but reduced it to the 8% used for the rest of the EU after lobbying by the Greek government (Georgiopoulos 2014). The Greek government (not the central bank) had already commissioned and received the results of its stress testing at that point but was not able to meet the target without the reduction, leading it to argue with the Troika for easier terms (Reuters 2014).

Meanwhile, the Bank of Greece, which had been keen to issue loans to the economy but had wanted to see the results first, was kept out of the loop and eventually increased the supply of credit to banks without looking at the results. In its view, the large percentage of non-performing loans that it believed were on the balance sheets of Greek banks (one-third of all loans) made it all the more necessary to increase central bank loans without delay (Noonan 2014). For the Greek government and central bank, therefore, the stress tests were not intended to examine the health of banks critically and recommend needed improvements, but to prop up foreign investor confidence in Greece (Georgiopoulos 2014a) regardless of the findings. In particular, the Greek authorities and banks needed to find outside investors for Greek banks which would then be expected to pay increased capital (rather than deleveraging by getting rid of non-performing loans, as the stress test would otherwise require them to do). Although that stress-test-induced deleveraging would help the Greek banks to return to eventual health, it would indicate that the work had not already been done, which the banks and government wanted to avoid.

This squares with the behaviour of regulators in Italy and Ireland as well, pushing to soften the probe of the stress tests. This gives further credence to Andrea Enria's claim, as EBA Chair, that national protectionism continued to run rampant in the European body.

The single supervisory mechanism

The main point of contention was not about capital requirements, but about the establishment of an EU bank supervisor, however. Two visions of supervision for the EU contrast functional design for the Eurozone (not even the EU), with a more highly politicized design led by creditor countries. The two versions have different scope and powers and key functions in the regulatory process. A functional design would stress central oversight and strong powers, coupled with external financial resources at the EU level to restructure banks found wanting, whereas the politicized design stresses national responsibility for support mechanisms, buttressed by European oversight of banks likely to trigger a request on EU assistance by the national competent authorities and its constituent banks. A more politically sensitive model, reflecting expectations of new intergovernmentalism, which was chosen for the EBA, would allow for continued national ownership of policy implementation and enforcement in the context of collective benchmarks on the broad parameters that national regulators should employ.

Despite the mission to break the negative mutual reinforcement of banks and sovereigns in Europe, the EBA's first wave of stress tests was followed by the unexpected bankruptcy of the French-Belgian-Luxembourgish bank Dexia, among others that had been given a clean bill of health. This undermined confidence in the broader European economy and in the seriousness with which supervision was being undertaken in this context. For this reason, the expectation grew that Europe's banks would transition to zombie banks, neither shedding their toxic assets, nor improving their ability to secure private finance, nor facing any hope of general economic recovery as loans to the economy ceased to flow, nor making an exit of public support for banks possible. The short form for this series of expectations was the Japanization of the European economy, which makes reference to Japanese economic stagnation since 1991 as a result of banks and supervisors colluding to allow banks to operate with high levels of non-performing loans. The EBA's failure on stress tests fuelled suspicions that it was powerless to push national supervisors to act vigorously against their own banks, leaving national champions weak and exposed or in a state of existential threat while the banks of other countries continued to benefit from lax oversight – suspicions that had not been dispelled entirely by 2017 (Gandrud & Hallerberg 2017), despite some cautiously optimistic assessments (Schoenmaker & Véron 2016). This in turn raised expectations of continuing pressure on public finances as banks required support. Even as late as 2016, the EBA continued to be the object of critique on stress tests (Bloomberg 2016).

It is partly, though not solely in this context that the need for an alternative form of supervision became apparent to the policy community. Europe could have muddled through without imposing change on its banks and for the intent of the latter to reduce future financial exposures if it had not been for the incapacity of some governments to borrow on capital markets, and for the knock-on effect that that had on northern European countries. Small countries in trouble were also easier to ignore than larger ones. As that incapacity forced Greece, Portugal and then Spain to follow Ireland in requesting financial assistance from the EU and from the IMF, the interest of northern European countries in providing some type of financial assistance rose. This was a straightforward interest in quelling the contagion of financial instability from Southern Europe into Northern Europe. As the previous chapter demonstrated, this meant visiting the question of how generous government-to-government bailouts should be.

The moment of demand for a single bank supervisor with more power than the EBA came in the context of Spain asking for financial assistance for its banking sector in June 2012. Bankia was in line as the first bank to fail without a bailout, and the possibility was real that more banks would need assistance given the steep decline in the economy since 2008. Given the size of the Spanish economy, the potential contagion effects were much higher than they had been for Greece or Portugal, making the payoff for Germany and other states more obvious. In return for allowing the ESM, as yet unratified, to be used to bail out banks rather than sovereigns, however, Germany demanded the establishment of a supervisor who would ensure that the money would very rarely be required, and that if lent, that it stood a reasonable chance of being repaid. This meant rigorously exposing the assets and liabilities on bank balance sheets on a regular basis, to reduce the likelihood over time of a bank getting into serious trouble, and opening up the accounts of banks that required direct and immediate assistance to survive, to ensure that an informed decision could be made that the bank could be saved if given the assistance. If not, the bank would be left to collapse or be wound down, which leads to the issue of bank resolution, discussed in the following chapter. Either way, a European supervisor would be required that could expose the accounts of the banks so that further decisions could be taken about the level of assistance to be extended and the terms attached.

By June 2012, the EBA's shortcomings coupled with the Spanish financial crisis provided an opportunity for the ECB to nominate itself as the likely candidate to take on the responsibility. The remainder of the negotiations between the EU member states, the Commission and the ECB demonstrate a number of points. First, the German negotiating position within the Council wanted supervision in principle, but wanted it limited to the EU's 25 largest banks, known as SIFIs – systemically important financial institutions. In December 2012, it secured this concession from its fellow member states, pushing back arguments by both the European Commission and the ECB that supervision should extend to all EU banks. Second, the ECB was successful as a political entrepreneur at claiming the role of single supervisor, and in expanding the scope of its remit from 25 banks to 128, and rights to take over supervision of any other bank that it considered a threat to financial stability (De Rynck 2016). The Bank's announcement of an Asset Quality Review, and its involvement in developing the Single Rulebook for national authorities further increased its influence over the EBA. The ECB therefore succeeded at replicating the network model of cooperation between European and national authorities that had already been developed and used effectively by both the European Court of Justice and by the European Commission in its role as competition authority. These extensions were achieved on the basis of arguments of both technical expertise and policy credibility that Germany and the other member states eventually accepted in April 2013. Third, the member states nevertheless succeeded at ensuring that their own supervisors would dominate decision-making within the SSM through the EBA over the larger questions and execution of supervision itself. This potentially limits the capacity of the SSM to work in a fully independent manner. Finally, the Commission may have set the stage and facilitated negotiations, but the agreements that came to place and the initiatives taken reflect other actors in the process, particularly the member states and the ECB.

Overall, the outcome of the decision to create a single supervisor demonstrates that a supranational institution like the ECB does indeed have the capacity to shape events in ways that constrain the options available to national governments. However, it would be going too far to say that supranational institutions got what they wanted, when they wanted it and how they wanted it. The Commission's and the ECB's plans right up until the December 2012 Council meeting were firmly in favour of an independent supervisor with wide-ranging powers extending into bank resolution, as in the United States, and covering the EU's 6000 plus banks. Both argued that supervision would not succeed without those powers. That they did not secure those powers is testimony to the limiting power of intergovernmental agreement. The SSM is therefore simultaneously both the Banking Union's greatest achievement and the strongest support that can be found in favour of neofunctionalism/neoliberal institutionalism. Even so, the intrusion of national authority into the SSM decision-making process and the persistence of national capacity to shield banks remain real. This is not just a question about the limits of supranationalism, but given the history of the EBA, and the fact that it will continue to play a significant role in the supervision of EU banks, that nationalist undermining of attempts to establish European power will remain a relevant factor. The recent history of bank supervision in the EBA underlines above all that one cannot assume that national actors within the SSM will act in as technocratic a fashion as have national judges working with the ECJ or national competition authorities working with DG Competition, the Directorate General of the Commission that acts as Europe's competition authority.

Moral hazard and forbearance

The demand for emergency assistance for banks generates demands for robust, common supervision as well. Moral hazard is reckless and dangerous behaviour enabled by actors who believe they will not be held responsible for the consequences of their actions, but that others will have to pay instead. The quality and robustness of bank supervision determines in large part whether banks are able to act recklessly in ways that make a collapse more likely, and through that, a demand for deposit guarantees and resolution to be deployed. Within the resolution mechanism itself, this fear of moral hazard is the incentive to establish an independent resolution authority that is unlikely, due to a legislated mandate and mission, to exercise the least practicable amount of forbearance with regard to restructuring and winding down banks.

Forbearance, which refers to delaying the recognition of losses within a bank in order to give the appearance of liquidity or solvency, is common in the banking industry by virtue of national authorities seeking to give home banks more time to sort out their problems, and can be countered by a common authority that is unlikely to take such decisions on the basis of national preference (ESRB 2012: 5). Since forbearance is one of the key parameters in allowing zombie banks to continue doing business while burdened with toxic assets, a more aggressive resolution approach is also considered vital to restoring lending to the real economy by healthy banks in the wake of a financial crisis. The need to look soberly at bank balance sheets and do the required surgery becomes particularly important at the point when quantitative easing is tapered to the extent that banks can no longer hide the extent of impaired assets (BIS 2011: 42), and in which national governments (some more than others: programme countries in Southern Europe being the weakest) are incapable of providing capital injections to recapitalize banks in a crisis (BIS 2011: 57, 72–83), which is widespread in the weaker regions of the Eurozone.

The Academic Advisory Committee of the ESRB underlined the necessity of applying supervision with a minimum of forbearance. Whereas supervisors may be inclined to give banks breathing space until they can rectify their financial positions, and to avoid systemic fallout, the Committee concluded that such leeway most frequently merely postponed the moment of crisis to the disadvantage of the general public. The preferred mode of supervision, it argued, should focus on setting out ex ante rules of engagement on forbearance, ex ante roles for the various supervisors involved, and make it a priority to make systemic stability rather than the fate of one institution the measuring stick against which forbearance is evaluated. That insistence puts at a premium well-established rules and guidelines regarding the resolution of problem institutions to prevent contagion to the broader financial sector, including clear rules regarding the protection of depositors in that process (ESRB 2012: 1).

The Committee's expectation that the EU banking sector would eventually evolve into a market populated by several banks doing business across the single market (rather than the current system of limited cross-border exchanges) informed its opinion that a strong European Resolution Authority was required to make swift, authoritative decisions in the event of a banking collapse (ESRB 2012: 2). This requirement for swiftness reflects ongoing experience of the relationship between the time taken to resolve banks and sort out the impact on depositors and creditors, and the aggregate impact of a bank failure on the entire financial system (Feteke-Györ 2013). Whereas the Committee cautioned against excessive forbearance for credit events involving single banks, it recognized that there may be good reasons to do so when stringency would place the entire financial system under pressure, under very limited circumstances. Reasons for forbearance are reflected in the American approach to debt default in Latin America in the early 1980s, when banks were not forced to write down losses lest they become insolvent themselves.

Reasons against forbearance are that it gives banks the room to engage in risky speculation to make up their losses (US Savings and Loans in the 1980s), or allowing them to hide their losses indefinitely and persist as zombie banks (Japan since the 1990s). On the whole, the Committee underlined that forbearance normally backfires, delaying a crisis but making it worse (ESRB 2012: 8–9). It was all the more urgent in Europe due to 'rampant' forbearance by national supervisors in the EU. The Centre for European Policy Studies recommended the model employed by the Federal Deposit Insurance Corporation (FDIC) in the United States, which incorporates a combination of mandatory capital adequacy and quality thresholds past which supervisors are obligated to intervene to start resolution proceedings, and mandatory release of relevant information by banks to the public that aid the supervisor to see when that threshold is reached (Carmassi, Di Noia & Micossi 2012: 7).

Micossi, Bruzzone and Carmassi (2013) also mention an additional issue that allows one to see the seriousness or laxness with which European legislators set up supervision. They indicate a preference for focussing on overall leverage levels within the bank, which the FDIC employs as a measure that is objective, transparent and linked to the overall risk attached to individual banks, rather than the risk-weighted averages typically employed in Europe and in the Basel Accords. The FDIC itself underlines that such risk weights are prone to creative interpretation by banks and credit rating agencies that undermines the usefulness of such information in assessing when a bank is at severe risk of failure or actually insolvent, requiring resolution to start (Reidhill 2013). If the ECB and national legislators were to introduce such standards, they would have to contend with the fact that leverage levels in European banks remain five to six times higher than in the United States on average. American regulators forced down bank leverage levels after 2008, whereas their European counterparts did not, as they issued more debt to keep them afloat, particularly in the Eurozone.

The ESRB Committee noted in this regard that intervention in the internal affairs of banks (corporate governance) by national governments was far lower once the crisis erupted than required to correct behaviour. As a result, the tendency toward moral hazard by banks had not diminished. Cash injections and loans were provided through hybrid instruments, which are bonds that can be converted to (voting) shares in the company, with the result that governments never directly had votes or representatives on the boards of directors of the banks they were supporting. The result is that banks had not started cleaning up the assets on their balance sheets until the ECB was instituted as the supervisor. This approach had been further enabled by the use of accounting tricks associated with bad banks, that take assets off the balance sheets without the public sector truly taking responsibility for them (ESRB 2012: 10). The alternative favoured by the ESRB Committee is a hands-on approach in which the public sector authorities 'step in, take control, sort out the business and then restructure, recapitalise and reprivatize the good parts of the businesses' (ESRB 2012: 11), as Swedish authorities did in the early 1990s.

The formula offered for combining supervision with other measures to combat moral hazard is a combination of corporate governance, private oversight, public oversight, resolution regime and deposit guarantee system that provides incentives for pre-crisis private diligence (Reidhill 2013). A political difficulty in making this happen lies partly in the realm of improving company law and more importantly, partly in the unwillingness of public authorities to prosecute and otherwise hurt business interests. The unwillingness to prosecute is reflected in the Holden Doctrine (Too big to jail) (Taibbi 2013). The management of deposit guarantees also requires more reliable, standardized deposit information (which is often lacking: Fekete-Györ 2013) which would, if a European authority were established, collide with bank secrecy laws, in Austria and Luxembourg in particular.

All of these points emphasize the need to establish supervisory authority to the greatest extent possible at the European level, as well as establishing other European banking authorities and funds in related areas, in all three areas. There are clear expressions of intent by EC and global actors (ECB, ESRB, IMF, IADI) in favour of centralized institutions. In the run-up to the ECB officially taking over its role as supervisor in November 2014, it was possible to observe the degree of relative degree of influence that the ECB and the EBA would have in future supervision. While the EBA was given responsibility once again for stress testing, and for establishing a common rule book for bank supervision (Regulation 575/2013 and Directive 2013/36) (thereby removing an important tool for mission expansion from the ECB that it had used to increase its remit from 25 to 128 banks), the ECB elected to conduct its own Asset Quality Review to assert its authority and involvement, and to put the EBA under additional pressure to conduct a fair and objective stress test. The interplay between those two parallel processes sheds light on the relative power of national authorities and European ones in the supervision process. They are investigated below.

Stress testing and the Asset Quality Review

This section looks at the ECB's role in establishing an enforcement pyramid as distinct from what preceded it in the EBA. The first plan of action for restoring the European banking system to health, and restoring the confidence of financial markets in it, was to conduct stress tests, as the US had done with its own banking system.

Andrea Enria, the Chair of the European Banking Authority, for his part, acknowledged in 2013 that the EBA was not fit for purpose, either in stress testing or in mediation during a bank resolution or another supervisory intervention. He cited intergovernmental politics within the EBA as the reason why this was so. The need for committees to take decisions made decision-making slow, cumbersome and 'impossible'. 'They give us responsibilities but they put so many national safeguards on every task we need to do that sometimes I am concerned we will not be able to perform [them]' (Jenkins & Fleming 2013).

Enria underlined further that the purpose of the stress testing was not only to provide for financial stability, but to take a first step toward re-establishing the single market in capital, given its renationalization in the wake of the Eurozone crisis. Faced with the prospect of financial contagion across national borders, he noted that national supervisors had pressured banks with operations and connections in more than one member state to scale these back so that they could be regulated entirely as national entities without the interference of other regulators. Not only would colleges of national supervisors not become necessary, the reach of European regulation through the EBA would be minimized. The result was a triangle of national banks, national governments that were ultimately responsible for losses in the banking sector, and national regulators that not only forced on the banks to renationalize, but allowed banks that should have been closed for insolvency to remain in business. The same view was expressed the same day by Benoit Coeuré at the ECB, who feared that the EU's incapacity to conduct meaningful stress tests would lead its default to be to allow zombie banks to persist, leading to a Japanese-style zombie economy with artificially propped-up banks rather than doing the surgery required to restore banks to proper health (Klimes 2013).

A key issue flagged by Enria at the EBA was the valuation of sovereign bonds held by banks. Whereas banks had traditionally been able to value assets at purchase value, the Eurozone crisis had shown that national treasury bills could lose their value during a crisis of economic confidence. Rather than rely on historical values, Enria considered it vital to take the current market value of national treasury bills, and to incorporate the risk of default into the assignment of risk weights for such bonds in the process of undertaking a stress test (Klimes 2013). The result of such a valuation is to make the sovereign debt of countries with weaker credit ratings less valuable to banks as a type of asset in which to invest. In the absence of new sources of capital that could be set aside to provide for potential losses in a crisis scenario (in accordance with Basel III rules), banks would have to dump at least some of their treasury bills from Southern European countries, creating further pressure on those governments to tighten government finances. Indeed, by early 2014, the first signs that Southern European banks were doing precisely that were visible in Spain.

The Economist quotes an unnamed French banker suggesting that Germany had Landesbanken shielded from the review to ensure that they would not be ordered to increase their capital buffers. It also pointed out that in the event of a dispute between the ECB and a national supervisor, there would be little the ECB could to do to force the situation other than to cut the bank off from ECB liquidity facilities, which would cause the bank to collapse (Economist 2012).

In this context, German demands for a functioning bank supervisor in exchange for making ESM money available for bank recapitalization required another actor to take on the job. The ECB put itself forward as early as 2012 as a likely candidate, competing with the European Commission, which also coveted the job, on the basis of expertise and political independence. Relevant in the debates that ensued was that no other institution could credibly claim the capacity to function properly, and to remain above the fray of governments protecting their own national champions.

However, the ECB was not given the power in the legislation establishing the SSM to conduct stress tests. Instead, this power and responsibility was handed back to the EBA, which had been unable to and unwilling to conduct the tests with due diligence in the first place. In response, the ECB announced that in addition to the EBA conducting stress tests on selected European banks, it would conduct its own Asset Quality Review (AQR) in 2014 with the assistance of outside rating agencies to help maximize the independence of the review. One of those firms raised questions about the integrity of the process, however. The company Oliver Wyman, which gave Anglo Irish Bank a clean bill of health before it failed in 2008 (Waterfield 2013a), and conducted a stress test of the Spanish banking system in 2012 using questionable methodologies, was chosen to assist the ECB (Durden 2012).

The ECB's role as supervisor started on 4 November 2014. In preparation, and to enhance confidence in the integrity of the process, the ECB announced draft framework regulations for AQR and for supervision after that moment on 7 February 2014. That document lays out that supervision of the biggest 128 EU banks is a joint responsibility of the ECB and national regulators. Other banks are the responsibility of national regulators, unless the ECB finds that regulating other entities from the EU level is required to fulfil its mandate. The text outlines that these powers are designed to ensure that bank entities it doesn't supervise, but are connected to banks it does, do not lead to banks evading effective supervision (Black & Blundsen 2014).

The AQR was designed to find non-performing loans, and measure them against loss absorption capacity (sources of money that can compensate for the losses), so that the need for recapitalization can be quantified. Loss absorption capacity is comprised of bank provisions (banks themselves setting aside money), asset protection schemes (government compensation schemes for non-performing loans), future profits and the excess capital buffer. The capital buffer is money acquired by selling debt worth multiple times the bank's shortfall. The questionable aspect of the Oliver Wyman stress test is that it assumed that Spanish banks could sell hundreds of billions of euros in debts as they deleverage in the midst of a severe economic downturn. Most importantly, that debt was already used as collateral for loans from the ECB under the LTRO program.

The AQR was also designed to ensure that assets on the balance sheet are properly valued. The stress test then models what would happen to that in a crisis (Dixon 2014). The AQR takes place in three stages. The first phase is planning, in which the ECB and national regulators request information from banks regarding loans and trading assets. In the second phase, the ECB and its agents examine loan portfolios, inspect the quality of collateral and the soundness of level three assets, which are significant but hard to value as they are not bought and sold very frequently (Noonan 2014).[1] The AQRs and stress tests also need to factor in that national regulators are keeping capital pooled within national borders of international banks, and there is nothing the ECB can do about this (Economist 2012).

The plan of attack by the ECB and the EBA on AQR and Stress Tests provided a gap of three months between the completion of the exercises (risk assessment done in February 2014, AQR following, and stress tests completed by June/July 2014) and the publication of the results in October 2014. On the one hand, it provided banks with the opportunity to correct problems before the markets and the public are certain they exist. On the other hand, however, it provided time and opportunity for political actors to push for a friendly review and interpretation of the facts, for banks to dispute the results rather than comply, as happened with Bank of Ireland in February 2014, for national regulators and banks to drag their feet on full compliance with reporting requirements, and can therefore undermine market confidence in the integrity of the reviews.[2]

At the same time, the ECB and the EBA chose to apply a less stringent review of bank solvency than the IMF. Whereas the IMF chose to model potential losses to loans over a 30-year period, reflecting the nature of some treasury bills, corporate bonds and mortgages, the ECB and EBA reviews had a decidedly shorter time horizon of three years, enough to seek out impending disasters and dealing with them, but not potentially larger problems down the road (Jenkins 2014). Given that debt restructuring in program countries like Greece partly involved the partial delay of payment past the three-year horizon, this means that potential risks were knowingly factored out of the review.

Banks prepared for stress testing and implementation of Basel III standards by reducing their holdings of risk-weighted assets, including sovereign bonds in 2013 and 2014. It relieved pressure on banks to raise more capital at a time when it is more difficult and costly to acquire and fulfils regulatory requirements for higher capital ratios. However, it also dampened economic growth. A review undertaken by the Financial Times in 2011 revealed that the principal vulnerability of large Spanish banks was in Spanish treasury bills. German and French banks, particularly Deutsche, had significant exposures still to peripheral European debt (Economist 2013).

Supervision in 2014 primarily raised the prospect of banks having to raise more capital in order to become more resilient to contagion. This led to political battles over what rules would apply. The ECB's starting point was that Basel III rules should be largely adopted. One key consequence of such an adoption would have forced banks to list derivatives as assets on their balance sheets instead of holding them off-balance sheet in a shadow bank subsidiary. Doing so would require banks to raise capital through increased equity holdings (cash and other convertible instruments), to counterbalance the risk of assets declining in value or defaulting completely. Although increased deposits and loans from other institutional investors could also be used to counter the risk of default in principle, European banks were already considered to be far more heavily indebted than banks in North America, and therefore more sensitive and vulnerable to waves of deleveraging (loans being called in rather than issued or extended), which initiates a downward spiral for banks).

National exceptions

National exceptions to ECB supervision came primarily from Germany. While the Landesbanken had been successfully withdrawn from EBA stress testing prior to 2014 so that they would not have to increase their capital buffers (Economist 2012), a change in domestic political opinion, by banks and government in particular, generated a permissive consensus on allowing them to be supervised from Frankfurt afterward. The savings and loans banks, the Sparkassen, however, were spared supervision (Deeg & Donnelly 2016). Similarly, the public banking institution KfW, with the backing of the German government, pushed successfully in 2014 to ensure that the ECB did not supervise its public sector export bank, IPEX as it had planned to do. The bank is Germany's third largest measured by the size of its balance sheet, but argued that it should remain under the sole jurisdiction of the German regulator (Huebner 2014).

Supervision-resolution matrix and credibility

Those involved in the planning of the SSM expressed fear that stress testing would not be effective as long as funding was not available to cover shortfalls. The ECB could not credibly make banks and regulators believe that it would expose shortfalls, at least to their full extent:

> 'It is madness to expose capital shortfalls if you don't know where new capital is going to come from,' says one bank supervisor.
>
> (Economist 2013)

OECD senior economist Wehinger weighed in separately to note that stress testing without financial resources to plug capital shortfalls is a source of financial instability (Wehinger 2012: 6). This is a problem for the stability of the European banking system and for the supervisory mechanism as a whole, since stress tests were scheduled to take place in autumn 2014, before any envisaged European Resolution Mechanism would go online that could intervene to prevent a credit event. The ECB warned about this repeatedly to little avail. The consequence is that national banks, national supervisors and national governments and taxpayers are responsible for their own shortfalls before Banking Union is completed. This has the benefit for countries with easier access to capital markets, if the stress tests and asset quality review are thorough and successful, of ensuring that legacy assets are out in the open and not the subject of cross-border transfers. It has the drawback, however, of putting pressure on the European Central Bank, as the single supervisor, to consider closely whether to be extra cautious in formulating its conclusions regarding the amount of capital required by banks in order to meet their capital requirements. It also puts pressure on the ECB, as the head of the single resolution board, to also exercise leniency. In early 2014, the ECB's designated head of supervision, Danièle Nouy, sent a clear message that the ECB was prepared to expose and shut down banks that did not meet the regulatory criteria (Fleming, Ross & Jones 2014). However, she did not entertain questions of whether the ECB as supervisor would weigh the considerations of financial stability against those of rigour in supervision. While it might be conceivable for a small bank to fail as a sign to the system as a whole, sufficient public backstops were not in place to ensure the orderly closure of a larger bank. The ECB underlined that banks that performed poorly in the AQR and stress tests might have to be bailed out by their national governments. They would not be let off the hook (Taylor & Suoninen 2014). This would enhance the credibility of the SSM at the same time that it potentially pushes problems within banks back to the national governments dealing with the conditions of an ESM loan, potentially unleashing a new round of the Eurozone Crisis in the process. Indeed, financial markets appear to be concerned about precisely this (Münchau 2013), which would mean continued expectations of EU banking being dominated by zombies for the foreseeable future. If so, it will hinder European banks in raising equity to the extent they would like and put the European banking market at a competitive disadvantage to other jurisdictions, without increasing financial stability.

Conclusions

The SSM demonstrates the successful development of supranational power within the EU, but under specific conditions. It is the only element of reform where Germany supported increased powers to establish an enforcement pyramid (H3) linked to distributional issues (H2) and linked to Germany's willingness to proceed with ESM as a lender of last resort (linked to H1 and H3.2). Still intergovernmental negotiations within the EU mean that compromises were still made that fall short of a full enforcement pyramid. These continued risks of institutional incompleteness are important for European supervision in that they underline the importance of differences of opinion between national regulators when setting up a single rule book for stress tests and supervision. Those national regulators continue to have considerable control of the process, even in areas where the ECB is ostensibly in charge. Although the ECB initiated the AQR and pins its hopes for establishing its credibility versus banks, and the credibility of stress tests versus markets, the AQR only looks at one half of the balance sheet, and lacks the capacity to tackle the question of bank leverage directly. The EBA's stress tests necessarily look at both sides of the balance sheet, and therefore consider issues like convertible bonds that an AQR will not necessarily consider. Moreover, the high reliance of European banks on bonds to finance their operations rather than selling shares on the stock market, securitizing and selling off their assets on derivative exchanges or inviting equity investment from hedge funds and money market funds (as in the United States and UK)[3] mean that there are few alternatives to the CoCo practice spreading throughout the EU's banks in countries with weaker public backstops. It is therefore difficult to imagine, given the alternative that banking systems in Southern Europe would otherwise undergo massive contraction, that the EBA could muster a majority of member states to push through lower leverage ratios. This means that significant challenges remain in increasing the financial stability of the European banking sector, despite the limited success of the ECB in expanding its original mandate.

That mandate, in turn, needs to be considered in light of what made it possible. The EU, without German insistence on a single supervisor capable of looking into large EU banks, was only prepared to let the EBA be the supervisor. That the ECB came into question at all was entirely a result of Germany pushing for investigation powers focussed on rooting out bad loans, which were most prevalent, and the greatest source of financial instability in the southern periphery of the Eurozone, and Ireland, rather than countries like Germany that had weathered the crisis fairly well. Although the ECB did manage to convince others it should be responsible for more than 25 banks, it remains responsible directly for less than 1% of all banks in the EU, has little to say about stress testing, has little power to look at the liability side of balance sheet, or rather do something about it, is dominated in its decision-making role as supervisor by national authorities that have demonstrated national, not transnational allegiance (in contrast to national central banks within the single currency) and must live with the constraint that if it does act to expose a bank, that it could unleash a chain reaction of financial contagion, because the mechanisms of resolution are underfinanced, complicated, fragmented on national lines and continue to reinforce the doom loop of mutually reinforcing weaknesses between banks and sovereigns (discussed in the next chapter). If the SSM is to work, it will have to be on the basis of medium-to-long term trends in which banks retain earnings, and raise capital through equity markets to slowly improve their positions. This is still a significant effect and could be seen in the run-up to the launch of the SSM in 2014.

Notes

1 For the treatment of level three assets under International Accounting Standards, which are used in the EU, see Deloitte (2014).
2 Black and Brennan (2014) report that the Bank of Italy claimed special consideration on financial accounting standards. This is despite the fact that companies are required to comply with International accounting Standards in the EU.
3 See Bank of England (2013); Reidhill (2013) and Wehinger (2012) for suggestions that European banks deleverage more.

References

Avdjiev, S., Kartasheva, A., & Bogdanova, B. (2013). CoCos: a primer. *BIS Quarterly Review*, September 2013, 43–56.

Bank for International Settlements. (2011) *82nd annual report*. Basel, 24 June.

Bank for International Settlements. (2012) European bank funding and deleveraging. *BIS Quarterly Review*, March.

Bank of England. (2013) *Financial stability report*. November 2013, Issue 34.

Bernabei, S. (2014) European regulators to exempt some banks from harshest stress tests. *Reuters*, 10 February.

Bernabei, S. (2014a) Watchdog asks Monte Paschi if it will challenge cash call delay. *Reuters*, 8 January.

Bernabei, S., & Semeraro, G. (2014) RPT-unicredit, intesa in talks to pool 1 bln euros of restructured loans. *Reuters*, 13 February.

Bickerton, C. J., Hodson, D. & Puetter, U. (2015) The new intergovernmentalism: European integration in the post-Maastricht era. *Journal of Common Market Studies* 53, 4: 703–22.

Binham, C. (2017) Banco popular and Monte dei Paschi dropped from EBA stress tests. *Financial Times*, 7 June.

Black, J., & Blundsen, J. (2014) Big Euro-area banks to face joint probes by ECB, national teams. *Business Week*, 7 February.

Bloomberg. (2016) Europe's stress tests fail again, 1 August.

Blundell-Wignall, A., & Slovik, P. (2010) EU banks and sovereign debt exposures. *VOX: CEPR's Policy Portal*, 14 September.

Carmassi, J., Di Noia, C., & Micossi, S. (2012) *Banking union: A federal model for the European Union with prompt corrective action.* CEPS Policy Brief No. 282, 18 September.

Carney, M. (2013) *Opening remarks by the governor, financial stability review press conference*. London: Bank of England, 28 November.

De Rynck, S. (2016) Banking on a union: The politics of changing eurozone banking supervision. *Journal of European Public Policy* 23, 1: 119–35.

Deeg, R., & Donnelly, S. (2016) Banking union and the future of alternative banks: Revival, stagnation or decline? *West European Politics* 39, 3: 585–604.

Deloitte. (2014) *IFRS 13 – Fair value measurement.* www.iasplus.com/en/standards/ifrs/ifrs13

Dixon, H. (2014) ECB faces severest stress test. *Reuters*, 24 February.

Durden, T. (2012) How Oliver Wyman manipulated the Spanish bank bailout analysis. *ZeroHedge*, 28 September.

The Economist. (2012) Made in Brussels: The Eurozone needs a banking union, but this isn't it, 17 November.

The Economist (2013) Til default do us part: A half-hearted Banking Union raises more risks than it resolves, 8 June.

Epstein, R. A. (2017) *Banking on markets: The transformation of bank-state ties in Europe and beyond.* Oxford: Oxford University Press.

European Systemic Risk Board. (2012) *Forbearance, resolution and deposit insurance*. Reports of the Advisory Scientific Committee, 1 July.

Fekete-Gyor. (2013) *Evolution of the deposit insurance framework: Design features and resolution regimes*. Presentation to the Research Conference of the International Association of Deposit Insurers, Basel, 9–10 April.

Fleming, S., Ross, A., & Jones, C. (2014) Eurozone's new super-regulator prepared to be unpopular. *Financial Times*, 9 February.

Gandrud, C., & Hallerberg, M. (2017) *How not to create zombie banks: Lessons for Italy from Japan*, Bruegel Policy Contribution 6/17.

Georgiopoulos, G. (2014) Greece's lenders accept lower capital ratio for bank health test. *Reuters*, 27 February.

Georgiopoulos, G. (2014a) Greek rescue fund worried stress test delays may deter investors. *Reuters*, 6 February.

Howarth, D., & Quaglia, L. (2013) Banking on stability: The political economy of new capital requirements in the European Union. *Journal of European Integration* 35, 3: 333–46.

Howarth, D., & Quaglia, L. (2016) Internationalised banking, alternative banks and the Single Supervisory Mechanism. *West European Politics* 39, 3: 438–61.

Huebner, A. (2014) Germany's KfW wants its export bank removed from ECB oversight. *Reuters*, 12 February.

Jeffery, E. (2017) AT1 capital/CoCo bonds: What you should know. *Euromoney*, 20 July.

Jenkins, P. (2014) Greece's plight offers clue to future of EU banking system. *Financial Times*, 26 February.

Jenkins, P., & Fleming, S. (2013) EU bank watchdog in govenance plea. *Financial Times*, 18 November.

Jones, Marc. (2014) Taper tensions, ECB tests to keep banks deleveraging in emerging Europe. *Reuters*, 14 February.

Klimes, M. (2013) EBA's Andrea Enria: too many banks survived the Eurozone crisis. *International Business Times*, 18 November.

Klimes, M. (2014) Italy's troubled banks crammed with E156bn in bad loans. *International Business Times*, 18 February.

Lombardi, D., & Moschella, M. (2016) Domestic preferences and European banking supervision: Germany, Italy and the Single Supervisory Mechanism. *West European Politics* 39, 3: 462–82.

Micossi, S., Bruzzone, G., & Carmassi, J. (2013) *The new European framework for managing bank crises*. Brussels: Centre for European Policy Studies. (No. 8620).

Moloney, N. (2014) European Banking Union: Assessing its risks and resilience. *Common Market Law Review* 51, 6: 1609–70.

Münchau, W. (2013) An exercise in prolonging a banking credit crunch. *Financial Times*, 23 December.

Noonan, L. (2014) Eurozone regulators gather for detail on bank review plans. *Reuters*, 17 February.

OECD. (2017) *Banking sector leverage (indicator)*.

Penty, C. (2014) Spain: Banks ditch debt in pre stress test makeover: Euro Credit. *Bloomberg*, 7 February.

Quaglia, L., & Royo, S. (2015) Banks and the political economy of the sovereign debt crisis in Italy and Spain. *Review of International Political Economy* 22, 3: 485–507.

Reuters. (2014) Greek central bank chief says will announce stress tests results next week, 27 February.

Reuters. (2014a) Fitch: EU bank stress test raises hurdle, but lacks key details. *Reuters*, 5 February.

Riedhill, J. (2013) *Guidance papers on deposit insurance coverage and moral hazard*. Presentation at IADI Research Conference, Basel, 9–10 April.

Sanderson, R., & Dinmore, G. (2014) Italy rejects 'bad bank' over credit rating fears. *Financial Times*, 10 February.

Schoenmaker, D., & Véron, N. (2016) European banking supervision: The first eighteen months. *Bruegel Blueprint Series* 25: 1–6.

Spiegel, P., & Hope, K. (2014) Greece in dispute with troika over banks. *Financial Times*, 25 February.

Taibbi, Matt. (2013) Gangster bankers: Too big to jail. *Rolling Stone*, 14 February.

Taylor, E., & Suoninen, S. (2014) Lautenschläger: ECB will not let banks failing tests off the hook. *Reuters*, 28 February.

Thompson, C. (2014) Periphery bank debt issuance hits post-crisis peak. *Financial Times*, 26 February.

Thompson, C., & Arnold, M. (2014) 'Red hot' coco bonds win broader acceptance. *Financial Times*, 21 February.

Toyer, J., & Ruano, C. (2014) Bank confidence, structural reforms needed for European jobs, says Spain's de Guindos. *Reuters*, 13 February.

Vaughan, L. (2011) Investors may shun banks' contingent convertibles as regulator adds limits. *Bloomberg*, 13 December.

Véron, N. (2013) *A realistic bridge towards European banking union*. Brussels: Bruegel Policy Contribution (No. 2013/09).

Véron, N., & Wolff, G. B. (2013) *From supervision to resolution: Next steps on the road to European banking union*. Brussels: Bruegel Policy Contribution (No. 2013/04).

Waterfield, Bruno. (2013a) ECB hires controversial Wyman for bank stress tests. *Telegraph*, 25 September.

Wehinger, G. (2012) Bank deleveraging, the move from bank to market-based financing, and SME financing. *OECD Journal: Financial Market Trends* 2012/1.

Wilson, J. (2011) German regulator attacks EBA stress tests. *Financial Times*, 7 June.

Za, V. (2014) Bank of Italy mulls public guarantee on banks' bad loans – paper. *Reuters*, 24 February.

6 The SRM

Resolving banks without deposit guarantees

Although initially overshadowed by the headline issue of bank supervision in Europe, experts considered bank resolution (bankruptcy management, restructuring and closure) to be key for Banking Union to work successfully, alongside a European Deposit Insurance System (EDIS) (Donnelly 2016). Resolution and deposit insurance contribute to financial stability by preventing further contagion throughout the financial system when a bank becomes insolvent. They therefore complement the SSM and constitute core components of a Banking Union (Véron & Wolff 2013; Baglioni 2016). They also complement each other, since both manage the affairs of insolvent banks.

Establishing the SRM started out as a case of intergovernmental negotiation without realist elements until distributional issues became unresolvable. Germany's concerns about the possibility of resolution funds growing beyond its control and even eclipsing the ESM led it to insist that a Single Resolution Fund (SRF) at 55 billion euros, roughly 1/20th the size of the ESM's financial capacity, would remain outside the EU as well, and only accessible once resolution actions had been taken by national authorities under the supervision of a European agency (establishing an enforcement pyramid based on conditionality). EU state aid law then adjusted to this realist demand – resolution costs would borne by banks and investors, then member states would have to funnel their own money into shutting down banks in an orderly fashion.

Instead of an EU resolution authority with significant powers and financial resources – an option favoured by most actors, national, European and international – Europe established an EU agency, the Single Resolution Board (SRB), to oversee and coordinate national authorities regarding the resolution of ECB-supervised banks, plus the SRF placed outside of EU jurisdiction, where it could not be used or expanded without German consent.

Resolution involves the appointment of a manager for the bank who winds up the institution by prioritizing who gets whatever money is left in the bank, forthcoming from deposit insurance and otherwise claimable from other counterparties. Counterparties are other institutions with whom the bank transacts, who may have outstanding claims on or debts to the bank under administration. This process of resolution means not only sorting out the position of retail depositors, who are covered at least in part by deposit insurance, but also commercial ones who

DOI: 10.4324/9780203702130-6

are not, including other banks who may owe the defunct bank money. Optimally, a resolution authority can restructure the bank proactively before a collapse actually occurs, leaving behind a smaller, but healthier and viable institution. Resolution mechanisms therefore overlap with day-to-day supervision, which is responsible for ensuring that banks avoid behaviour leading to failure, or issuing an early warning of trouble in a bank if it gets into trouble, whether for bad behaviour or outside events like a national bankruptcy that then bankrupts the bank. A specific overlap may be a demand for banks to increase their capital buffers to better withstand the collapse of other banks. The latter has happened in Cyprus and in Greece. Resolution has two key functions during a bank crisis: to ensure the continuity of financial services for normal bank clients, even when that must happen at a new bank, and to minimize the impact of the bank's closure on other banks.

The most important mechanism for fulfilling these functions is restructuring bank assets. The way in which this is done affects the cost to the bank and its creditors, to the resolution fund in place to cover additional claims, and to the public backstop that provides additional capital in winding up the bank so that it does not threaten other banks. Restructuring is done through three mechanisms: separation of assets, transfer of business and bail-ins. Separation of assets involves removing toxic assets (non-performing loans or other financial instruments that have a negligible market value) from the bank. On the bank's financial records, this replaces a fictional display of healthy income and wealth with a realistic assessment, which may approach zero. Transfer of business involves selling what is left of the bank to another bank, normally after asset separation. It sometimes involves the establishment of a public entity known as a bridge bank that holds on to what is left until a buyer can be found. Bail-ins form a counterpart to the separation of assets, in which the resolution authority terminates or alters the contracts that the bank has with its creditors (bondholders). These creditors are typically other institutional investors such as pension funds, hedge funds, mutual funds, money market funds and other banks. In the process of resolution, the authority will attempt to ensure that the bail-in compensates as much as possible for the writing down of toxic assets. What remains of the bank is a much smaller institution stripped of most of its assets and liabilities that can be transferred to another bank as it is closed as an independent business.

Resolution funds are deployed at the point where a bail-in large enough to fully compensate for the write-down of toxic assets would exceed the capacity of the further financial system to absorb. This would endanger financial stability for the system as a whole. The resolution fund can be used to ensure that the severity of the bail-in is contained, so that what remains of the bank (which will mostly be the deposits of insured depositors and remaining safe assets) can be transferred to a new owner and that the solvency of the bank's creditors is not threatened. Understandably, the bank taking control would want the resolution fund and bail-ins to work beforehand to ensure that the new acquisition is not a liability.

Although bail-ins were uncommon and bailouts widespread at the beginning of the financial crisis, and could not be viewed as an alternative to pubic backstops (Goodhart & Avgouleas 2014; Avgouleas & Goodhart 2016; Jones 2016), they gained traction in European, American and global circles as necessary to reduce the public cost of dealing with bank failure, but also to incentivize stronger creditor oversight of banks (Coffee 2010). Institutional investors would have greater incentives to sit on boards of directors, insist on more transparent reporting and regular controls in ways that retail depositors cannot and do not do (Mayes 2013). Bail-ins also reduce to some extent the possibility that bailing out an insolvent bank could bankrupt the state providing the bailout. The alternative to bail-ins by private creditors, or a supplement thereof through the resolution fund, is a bailout with public funds.

As with deposit insurance, there are clear functional reasons for setting up independent resolution authorities and funds before a crisis erupts. Uninsured depositors and creditors need to be aware that the resolution authority can and will impose losses on them in the event of insolvency. This increases the incentive on them to monitor the bank diligently, in cooperation with supervisory authorities (Reidhill 2013).

In the European context. Gros and Schoenmaker (2012) argued for the establishment of a European Deposit Insurer and Resolution Authority (EDIRA) that can carry out these functions. The ECB's Coeuré did as well, coupled with deposit insurance, if it were to effectively break the negative feedback loop between bank debts and public sector debts in Europe. The Resolution Authority would require the power to close a bank swiftly (in the interest of preventing contagion that could damage financial stability) and impartially (to ensure that investors from the member states are not discriminated against in such a proceeding). It would have to have access to a single resolution fund, and the authority would have to be able to call on additional public funding at the European level to supplement the fund in extraordinary circumstances, meaning situations in which not one bank is being closed down, but several at the same time in the course of a system-wide crisis. Coeuré underlined that a coordination of national resolution authorities would not provide financial stability (Coeuré 2013).

Coeuré also laid out the necessity of working out the details of a European Deposit Insurance System and incorporating it into the resolution mechanism. For the resolution authority to do its job properly, legal certainty about the status of guaranteed deposits had to be established, alongside the pecking order of claims to protection in the event that a bank is subject to resolution and decision is taken to bail-in creditors and uninsured depositors. Further comments advised on the sequencing of steps that determine how bank resolutions should be funded. The resolution fund requires deposit insurance funds to contribute to the costs of winding down a bank and ensuring the continuity of critical functions for the broader economy. To minimize the likelihood of public funds being used in resolution to pay outstanding claims on the bank, private actors should be expected to contribute first (unsecured creditors and uninsured deposits), followed by a resolution fund that is paid for by banks themselves, coupled with contributions from DGSs, and only then via a public sector backstop that would extend loans to the resolution fund. Those loans would be repaid by the fund at a later date after the resolution, and the fund would collect the balance from banks insured by the system (Coeuré 2013). This formula echoed recommendations by the Scientific Advisory Committee of the European Systemic Risk Board. The ESRB placed additional emphasis on ex ante funded funds, as asking banks for capital during a crisis would be countercyclical for the general economy, and impractical when banks lack the capital to pay (ESRB 2012: 14).

The Scientific Advisory Committee also urged the establishment of a Single Resolution Authority and fund as necessary to overcome the mismatch between home country control as a principle of assigning competence, and the impact on various subsidiaries in the firm, especially those operating in different countries, to deal with cross-border shifts in deposits during a crisis, and to deal with the impact of a weak state being inundated by claims against a national resolution fund and/or deposit guarantee system (ESRB 2012: 20–1). The Committee for these reasons saw a combination of supervision, resolution and deposit guarantee as necessary at the European level, coupled with access to the ESM as a public backstop and expressed concern that the Council had made no mention of such (ESRB 2012: 22–5). In this context, the ESRB noted that only the UK has set up a bank resolution system, but even that is underdeveloped regarding cross-border resolutions (ESRB 2012: 12).

In the absence of common deposit guarantee and resolution systems, the next best option is to coordinate national systems. In the European case, the proposal for a European Deposit Insurance System (EDIS) has a number of components to ensure standardization and cross-border transfer of data and home/host mutual assistance (Kuczynski 2013). Coordination protocols are also needed for cross-border payment, communication and public awareness. The latter includes issues of deposit coverage (scope and limits), payment methods and timing, in order to manage public expectations and avoid panic (Fekete-Györ 2013).

Supply of European resolution

Resolution came late on to the European legislative agenda. The draft Bank Restructuring and Resolution Directive (BRRD) was tabled on 6 June 2012 (COM 2012 280/3), three months before the proposal for the SSM. Like the draft Deposit Guarantee Systems Directive (DGSD), the draft BRRD attempted to coordinate national systems rather than establish a European authority and fund.

One of the key issues removed from discussion at the beginning of intergovernmental negotiations was the prospect of a resolution fund large enough to help wind down insolvent banks. The same was true for a European deposit guarantee scheme. The Economist quoted one national representative saying:

> 'The numbers are simply too big,' says one person involved in the talks. 'If it were pushed it would blow up the whole discussion [about Banking Union] because it would scare the creditor countries'.
>
> (Economist 2012)

It added that the Swedish banking crisis of the 1990s cost taxpayers and banks 3.6% of GDP for resolution and other related costs, which would imply a fund of nearly 350 billion euros for the Eurozone (Economist 2012). This contrasts to the decision of the Eurogroup to build up a fund of 55 billion euros gradually between 2015 and 2026.

Council let the SRM issue rest on the back burner while it sorted out the details of the SSM. It then scheduled debate on a Council response to the Commission's BRRD proposal at the June 2013 summit. Before the Council could meet on 27 and 28 June, France and Germany issued a policy document on 30 May 30 and met on 10 June to prepare their own positions (Bundesregierung 2013). Both opposed the Commission or any other European body having authority over bank resolutions. Instead they supported the establishment of a 'single resolution board involving national resolution authorities', and insisted that private sector money be tapped before public money in the event of resolution and related restructuring (Duffy 2013).

France agreed to Germany's desire to ensure that ESM funds would remain unavailable for resolution until the European Parliament had accepted both the SRM and a national-based European deposit insurance system. In return, it got assurances that Germany would support greater 'economic governance' within the Eurozone, but not pursue changes to EU treaties in the process that would grant important new powers to EU institutions (Duffy 2013). This seems not much of a concession from Germany, which only held out the prospect of discussing EU treaty changes in 2018 but not Fund commitments. Meanwhile, the ECB's Asmussen underlined the urgent need for a decision on resolution, noting that failure to do so would render the ECB's role as single supervisor a 'paper tiger, since there would be no plan for how to resolve banks if the ECB found them insolvent in the AQR' (Cermak 2013a).

As Gros and Schoenmaker suggested, Germany, the Netherlands and Finland also adopted the position, and later the Eurogroup, that national governments would have to take responsibility for legacy debts of national banks made before any European resolution mechanism would enter into force, thereby blocking recapitalization of Southern European and Irish banks by their northern European neighbours, as the potential recipients had requested (Walsh 2013). Financial assistance through the ESM would only be possible in resolution and restructuring cases, discussed below. That the Gros/Schoenmaker plan factored transaction costs and legacy debts out of the negotiation equation, and nevertheless failed to clear the way for supranational institutions and funds underlines the centrality of national regulatory and financial control to the outcome. Given the dominance of the German coalition within the ESM, funding would therefore only be negotiable for future crises, and only when the recipients would be required to accept Eurogroup demands on when and how a bank is to be closed, as in the Cyprus case (Hadjipapas 2013; Spiegel 2013).

Calls by the ECB, Portugal and Ireland for a single, credible fund that would allow resolution authorities to take decisive action thereby went unheeded. Commissioner Barnier acknowledged that Germany's political opposition to taking on more financial responsibility for public backstops limited how much could be done, even if he thought that those fears were overblown, and even if he recognized that a central resolution fund was essential to secure financial stability (Christie 2013; Christie, Buergin & Stagno Navarra 2014). This shortcoming led to concerns by other countries that delayed ratification into late 2015 and threatened the Fund's launch in 2016 (Stagno Navarra, Verlaine & Christie 2015).

A further strengthening of national authority was agreed in the case of cross-border resolutions. While national authorities would have a free hand to engage in national resolutions, the EBA would undertake mediation in cross-border resolutions. It would have to make recommendations within 24 hours. Whether that would be possible given the EBAs track record of paralysis at the hand of entrenched national interests is questionable, however (Jenkins & Fleming 2013).

This contrasts with the European Commission's proposals regarding the SRM. They supported ECB demands that the Board be able to finalize a resolution within hours, suggested that the Board be able to finalize a resolution over the weekend, to minimize negative contagion in financial markets, in accordance with standard practice.

However, Germany demanded in February 2014 that the Board have no less than four business days (exclusive of Saturday and Sunday) in which to work. Germany also insisted on taking away final decision-making on resolutions from the Board and vesting them in national governments and regulators. The Board would have to flag recommendations to the Council when 5 billion euros or more were required from the European Resolution Fund in any given year (effectively all use of the fund), or when intervention would cost more than 20% of the fund in total (on a multi-year basis, or 10 billion euros). It would further require a double majority, involving two-thirds of the countries represented on the board and representing more than half of the paid up capital. These difficult thresholds made independent EU control of resolution highly unlikely, and generated opposition not only from the Commission, Parliament and EU member states likely to need resolution assistance, but notably the Netherlands as well, which supported most other German initiatives (Brunsden 2014).

These demands built on previous Council agreements that were dedicated to setting minimum standards for national resolution laws, authorities and funds. Other deliberations focussed on technicalities of coordination between national authorities to establish a coordinating regime (Donnelly 2010; Bickerton et al. 2015). The Council's position of 28 June 2013 on the draft directive stipulated that member states should appoint independent resolution authorities, ensure involvement of finance ministers of the affected member states in the event of resolving a multinational bank, and of the authorities in accordance with guidelines agreed in the EBA (Council 2013: 7–8) in resolving the bank without extraordinary public support, including finance from the general budget (Council 2013: 11,15, 23, 33). While left up to the member states to decide how stringently to apply such a principle, this recommendation reverberates with a Council agreement, separate from the BRRD, that any loans made to a country for resolution purposes through the ESM must honour the principle of minimizing the size of the public backstop.

For instances in which a country might request assistance from other EU member states through the ESM, the recommendation becomes a demand.

The key to resolving banks with a minimum of public support (bailout) lay in maximizing the cost paid by private actors (bail-in). This was a central component of the BRRD at the insistence of the Netherlands and Germany at the head of the Eurogroup, and opposed by governments in Southern Europe, France and Ireland, although they signed in the end in order to secure access to ESM funds in the event of an emergency. Bail-ins nevertheless raised national differences in how to choose which private investors should suffer first and most (creditor seniority). Although the ECB urged member states to decide on one algorithm for determining haircuts, the Council could not come to an agreement on a single standard (Council 2013a: 12). It also deferred the requirement for countries to put bail-ins before bailouts until 2019. Although the Eurogroup could coerce such a choice for Cyprus at the moment of insolvency, it was not able to do so for countries that could act without ESM assistance. Indeed, as will be shown later, the Eurogroup's predominant instinct in the Cypriot Crisis was to give the national government as much room as possible to determine its own priorities in resolution until it became clear that the government could not survive its own proposals. This is an important nuance in economizing on compulsion that reflects Proposition 4 in Chapter 2: coercion was used if necessary, but otherwise national coordination in line with expectations of new intergovernmentalism was used rather than supranational agency expected by liberal intergovernmentalism.

The Council's negotiations on the BRRD included setting out to some extent the seniority of claims on bank assets in the event of closure by protecting a wide range of creditors. It first confirmed the protection of guaranteed deposits up to 100 000 euros in the event of a bank closure, followed by payments due to employees, payments owed to other banks on a short-term basis (up to one week), payments owed to small and medium-sized enterprises and covered or collateralized debt, in which banks had secured loans in exchange for a guaranteed collateral. Only then would losses be imposed on unsecured creditors (Council 2013a: 2). These exemptions confirm the manner in which Cyprus resolutions were handled (Salmon 2013). Under the draft, national authorities could make further exceptions to classes of creditors during a bail-in on a case by case basis where imposing a haircut would prevent the provision of 'critical functions' or unleash further contagion. In other words, national differences in insolvency and resolution proceeding could continue. A condition was that bank doesn't fall under ECB supervision and the SRB allows it.

The ECB critiqued the Council's preference to wait until 2019 for the bail-in provisions of the draft directive to take effect. Resolution authorities would lack one of the most important tools in being able to do their jobs, which would undermine the intent of the BRRD. It also criticized the Council for refusing to spell out the reasons for which national resolution authorities could protect certain assets or exercise general forbearance toward a bank, which leads to legal uncertainty for investors and supervisors (Asmussen 2013). The same was true for the Council failing to set out rules regarding the pecking order of creditors who would be called on to contribute to a bail-in. This would create an incentive for political manoeuvring at the national level, making bail-ins work differently from country to country, and more slowly. It also engineered room for national governments to defect from common rules in order to protect banks for nationalist purposes, where nationalist means on the grounds that the bank is valued as a national resource. The Cypriot Crisis, discussed below, showed that this was a real possibility. Later, in the SRM Regulation of June, progress was made in moving up the time frame for the SRF to 2016 and fully capitalizing it within 8 years. But the size remained capped at 55 billion euros.

The issue of which national resolution authority or authorities would have the power to direct such matters was also an issue when multinational banks were involved. As with deposit insurance, resolution authority was awarded to the country in which a bank was headquartered, (Council 2013a: 12). Although there were provisions under discussion to form resolution colleges of multiple national authorities, the Council's position was that the lead authority would have the power to act even over the objections of other authorities (Council 2013a: 30). This strengthened the power of national authorities supervising the EU's largest multinational banks at the expense of countries served by those banks (Epstein 2008; Epstein 2013). This outcome has long-term market advantages for banks headquartered in countries where the sovereigns are able to provide lender of last resort services in the form of cash injections or debt guarantees – in Germany and a few selected countries allied with it. Subsidiaries are also managed this way rather than handled by different national authorities.

Tonveronachi notes that the EU legislative proposal of 2013 included the possibility for member states to intervene in a cross-border resolution process when their national interests were significantly at stake (Tonveronachi 2013: 377–8). This would apply to situations in which the state insisting on intervening would protect its perceived rights regarding the resolution of a subsidiary that is owned by a bank situated in another member state and otherwise subject to that national resolution authority, or perhaps even the SRB.

The Council's BRRD draft also specified the establishment of national resolution funds rather than a European fund, despite the fact that resolution of a multinational bank could require pooled resources, unless one country has a vast surplus of funds to contribute. The handing of resolution authority to one country therefore mismatches decision-making power and funds. Cross-border resolution fund contributions remained voluntary in the Council's 2013 position, making national autonomy and responsibility the default organizing principle (Council 2013a: 12). Nor was the Commission successful in proposing that an EDIRA be established that would only have powers and funds to deal with cross-border banks. Thus, national control of regulatory power and budget resources made a deal impossible (Brunsden & Christie 2013).

Progress was made in bringing the member states to agree on the establishment of ex ante resolution funds at the national level *as an option* (Council 2013a: 32) with assets of 0.8% of covered deposits 10 years after the directive enters into effect (rather than the international norm of 1.5% immediately). Banks would be required to pay for the fund, based on liabilities and risk. The Council's version of the draft BRRD allowed for countries to make the resolution fund part of deposit insurance or bank insurance, allowing for a minimum of adjustment in national systems, provided the assets available for resolution are in fact in addition to deposit insurance, paid on an ongoing basis and made available during a resolution. Lending between national systems would be voluntary only. The resolution fund could be used for direct recapitalization, but only after creditors had been forced to take a haircut of no less than 8% of the bank's liabilities, reflecting the wishes of the German-led coalition (Council 2013a: 3–4). This points to restrictions on the use of resolution funds to recapitalize across countries. It also sets the parameters of a 'level playing field' across EU member states in how strongly they can protect their banking sectors.

The BRRD in its final version became a means of capacity building for national governments in the form of institutions and resolution plans and common procedural standards. The main focus of the directive is to set out the powers and responsibilities of national resolution authorities. National governments must establish resolution authorities, resolution plans and ensure that systemically important banks draft resolution plans that plan out how the bank can be wound down in an orderly fashion in the event of insolvency. The BRRD specifies specific tools that national authorities must possess, including asset transfer, bridge banks and bail-ins. The SRB then becomes responsible for reviewing those plans for banks supervised by the ECB. It is also empowered to demand improvement of those plans.

Single resolution mechanism as authority and fund

The draft BRRD acknowledged the stakes of establishing a resolution authority. It accepted that an EDIRA would have powers to affect the rights of creditors, shareholders and owners by transferring businesses (to another company or bridge institution) and selling assets within the group without the approval of shareholders if necessary (Council 2013a: 19, 25). However, the preamble noted that the principles of European company law would have to be respected (Council 2013a: 37). Those principles stipulate special rights of shareholders and stakeholders that cannot be set aside in the event of a corporate takeover or merger, and allow national tax authorities to block the migration of a company away from its home jurisdiction, that could impede for resolution to transfer parts of a bank or an entire bank from one EU member state to another (Donnelly 2010).

A key issue of debate that took place during negotiations over resolution was whether they should take place within the context of EU treaties or outside them, and whether envisaged EU treaty changes would reinforce supranational or national powers for Banking Union. France opposed any treaty changes for fear of negative voter backlash against the EU in a referendum and a negative impact on its economy (Duffy 2013). Meanwhile, Germany, backed by Austria, preferred changes to the EU treaties that would ensure member state control of resolution regardless of any claims to EU powers of economic governance (Business World

2013). This meant changing the nature of the EU itself, in which the Commission or other EU bodies are delegated authority to act on the member states' behalf. In this context a compromise was reached close to the substance of German demands being established, but not a fundamental remake of the EU toward a more intergovernmental body in its core treaties as it had sought. Nevertheless, the substantive changes underpin an ad hoc shift to greater intergovernmental politics as the modus operandi of EU regulation.

This left the question of an EDIRA open. Internal Market Commissioner Barnier suggested in July 2013 that the ESM act as a resolution authority under the Commission's oversight, expanding on the role it had played in the Cypriot banking crisis at the time. The ESM would become an EU institution rather than an intergovernmental body outside the European Union (Buergin & Christie 2013). This suggestion did not meet with approval by the German government, however, which stood to lose control over an institution it had set up to meet its wishes, which it controlled as a creature of international, not EU law.

In October 2013, Barnier made a follow-up proposal to that ESM be made an EU institution – an EDIRA – rather than an international organization outside the EU. He was willing to promote treaty changes that would make that possible. However, he also insisted that as a resolution authority, it would have to be responsible for all EU banks. Germany countered that the ESM could only come into question as a resolution authority for banks under ECB supervision. This would ensure that national responsibility for resolution would be ensured for all but the largest systemically important banks in the Eurozone (Hudson 2013), that special dispensations for its own cooperative banks remain intact (Howarth & Quaglia 2016; Deeg & Donnelly 2016) and that the liabilities of the ESM would remain contained. In this point, ECB executive board member Yves Mersch supported a German-friendly compromise by arguing that an EDIRA could be established without treaty changes, at least for banks already falling under the ECB's supervision. However, this prospect was easier said than done, at least if the ESM was to become involved. Klaus Regling, head of the ESM responded that it would not be able to act as a resolution fund or provide money for a resolution fund without a change to the international ESM treaty that created it (Buell 2013). As ECB Vice President Jörg Asmussen remarked 'This is not at all related to European treaties' (Cermak 2013b). Germany and all states would have a veto on changing terms. The government of Luxembourg, otherwise an ally of the German cause, lent support to Barnier (Buergin & Christie 2013), but without any impact. Germany's opposition led Barnier to solicit EU-level alternatives that would work for smaller banks as well like Bankia (Hamilton & Brunsden 2013).

Germany's further stance on the relationship between the ESM and the SRM was that the ESM could be used to recapitalize banks in the event of a resolution for ECB-supervised institutions, but only after other sources had been drawn on in accordance with Council demands, with a clear hierarchy of claims and protection, and only as a last resort. Before the ESM could be called on, junior and then senior creditors would be expected to take losses, followed by institutional investors, depositors, trading partner banks, other EU banks and finally national governments. Germany also rejected Irish calls to make ESM funds available retroactively to relieve the burden of Irish taxpayers in propping up the Irish banking system (Scally 2012).

The German demand to establish the main responsibility of the private sector and member states for resolution generated pushback from a variety of actors. In the private sector the Economist noted that a resolution authority would likely be undermined by national bankruptcy laws and the absence of a legal court in which complaints could be adjudicated (Economist 2013). But the main objection was over money. Wolfgang Münchau of the Financial Times underlined that a resolution authority with neither a common public backstop, nor a capacity to borrow would be 'pointless', and undermine the ECB's credibility as supervisor (Münchau 2013). It would face greater negative consequences of forcing a bank into resolution. As we shall see later, Münchau's warnings proved insightful in the trepidation of both the Commission and SRB to wind down banks, though the ECB itself exercised its duty to announce that banks were indeed insolvent, triggering resolution. A market analysis of the December 2013 deal concluded that the small size of the fund would reinforce pressure on banks and national authorities as the primary providers of a public backstop. It would prevent the SRB from resolving banks in an orderly fashion, pressuring governments with fragile finances to provide more state aid for restructuring and resolution that they could not provide. It would furthermore do this at the moment when stress testing of European banks was being launched, requiring banks to access additional capital (Thompson & Barker 2014).

More central to political negotiations, however, both Commission and Parliament warned that without a significant authority and funding on which to draw, the renationalization of banking systems, which had proceeded apace since 2008, would continue and consolidate, reversing the integration of the single capital market. The European Parliament wanted the fund to be able to issue debt and to be managed by a powerful resolution authority. US Treasury Secretary Lew echoed these concerns, assessing the fund to be too little too late. Parliament additionally viewed the establishment of a resolution fund outside the EU's legal and institutional framework as illegal because it bypassed the ordinary legislative procedure (Carnegy 2014; Fontanella-Khan 2014). The EP did not secure these goals, but eventually (in April 2014) succeeded in having the member states shorten the time in which the SRF would be capitalized and mutualized to 8 years.

In November 2013, Schäuble was busy holding talks with his own party and the opposition Social Democrats (SPD) to establish a united front on the resolution mechanism. Social Democrats had critiqued the government for agreeing to any use of ESM funds for recapitalization, regardless of the terms and conditions (Goldbach & Zuckerman 2015). This even more hawkish stance underlines the pervasive and central place that Germany's distributional concerns vis a vis Europe held with the electorate. Above all, Schäuble wanted to ensure agreement on two things: that the Council, and not the Commission, would take final decisions on bank resolutions, and that mutualized debt in the form of Eurobonds would be ruled out. Given the SPD's critical stance and national bent on Banking Union, which opposed using the ESM for market intervention or bank recapitalization, as the EU had agreed for Spain in June 2012, this was not difficult. To ensure its own control, Germany rejected the Commission's proposal to base the SRM legislation on Article 114 of the treaties, which would have allowed the Commission to take decisions involving financial consequences for the member states. Germany insisted instead on Article 352, which would prevent the Commission from intruding on the prerogatives of the member states (Scally & Lynch 2013).

Agreement on the SRM

In a political agreement struck in April 2014 between the Commission, Council and Parliament, the EP succeeded in reducing the role of the Council in resolution processes, and in increasing the role of the ECB. The ECB as supervisor would effectively trigger resolution proceedings by indicating insolvency to the SRB, which would recommend to the Commission that this happen and on what terms. Those terms would involve a recommendation of the funding required from the SRF. The Council would retain the right to decide the ultimate level of disbursement and determine the weight of the public interest in intervening (European Parliament 2017).

The German position, and the fact that both preferences were incorporated into the legislative text, demonstrates Germany's capacity to get what it wanted in demanding institutions and their (lack of) coverage under EU law over the objections of the European Commission, Parliament and ECB. As with the SSM, not all of the details within EU law could be controlled, however. This reflected a mix of intergovernmental politics whenever strategy focussed on giving powers to EU institutions or establishing coordinating regimes, and realist institutionalism involving Shadow Europe on distributional issues.

In the SRM Regulation, the SRB became an agency with legal personality and responsibility for banks in the Eurozone. It comprises an Executive Director and Vice-Chair and four others (voting), a representative of the Commission (no vote), and the ECB in its role as bank supervisor (without a vote) as the daily executive board, and representatives of the national competent authorities (voting) (107–8). The Board is appointed by the Council on recommendation of the Commission, after hearing the opinion of Parliament. The Board in the first instance oversees resolution plans by banks, and resolution interventions by national authorities, including separating and selling assets, mandating bail-ins and debt-equity conversion for creditors, calling on deposit insurance and resolution fund contribution. The Board, together with the Commission, has the competence to manage the relationship with national competent authorities on these matters through Memoranda of Understanding, at least for standard procedures.

The SRM Regulation also foresees significant reservations for national authorities, but seeks to clarify potential conflicts. One national resolution authority would be designated lead in the case of a transnational bank involving more than one regulator (27), though the Board consults with all. If a member state rejects the Board's decision, national insolvency law is the default (Art 6 (4)). The Board consults on resolvability with the ECB and any national competent authorities where the bank has significant business (40).

Also important was the threshold for SRM involvement. A credit event would have to involve

> significant adverse consequences for the financial system or negative impact on financial stability. . . . [This refers to] a situation where the financial system is actually or potentially exposed to a disruption that may give rise to widespread financial distress liable to jeopardise the orderly functioning, efficiency and integrity of the internal market or the general economy of one or more Member States.

The Regulation also provided for a resolution fund to be built up over 8 years starting in 2016, to be used for resolution purposes. Member states would not be held liable for shortfalls. The Board would own the fund, and the Commission would decide on its future level. These proposals elicited UK demands for protection against any need to pay into the single resolution mechanism (Waterfield 2013b) and eventual intergovernmental agreements that the size of the fund would be fixed at 55 billion euros and paid for with intergovernmentally-negotiated quotas rather than adjusted by a supranational body. But it also elicited resistance from Germany, which wanted to keep the fund beyond the reach of supranational institutions, including the Commission and the ECJ. For this reason, the Fund would be established outside EU law to prevent attempts at control or judicial review.

For its part, the Parliament had objected to being bypassed in the establishment of the SRM and declared the intergovernmental agreement on the Fund reached by the Council illegal. Leaders of all political parties signed a letter declaring their 'firm disagreement' to the use of an intergovernmental treaty outside the EU to accede to German objections to an EU treaty, on supposed legal grounds. The EP would still have to approve of parts of the package that are to be passed through the normal legislative procedure. It favoured a strong central authority, which the Council did not envisage. It also wanted mutualization by 2018 (Fontanelle-Khan 2014). In the absence of such powers, the status quo would continue, in which the EP viewed political interference by the member states as an impediment to credibility, meaning the SRM has to find a way to do away with it. Its press release the day before Council negotiations insisted that the Fund be available from the start, and that it not be fragmented into national compartments during the build-up phase, as it would create an un-level playing field (European Parliament 2014b). Nevertheless, when the Council insisted later that week that the Parliament could take the intergovernmental agreement or leave it, but that it could accept minor amendments, the European Parliament passed the SRM (European Parliament 2014a).

The Council proved to have a number of key open points due to incomplete agreement between the member states over details after the 18 February 2014 meeting, before the deal was finalized. Most of the details regarded money, and in particular, whether other states would gain relative to the main paymasters. As Eurogroup Chair Dijsselbloem noted, the key open issues were the financing of resolution costs (who pays and in what order, or whether there is flexibility), lending between national compartments (who decides and how), rules applying to new members of the SRM later on, the bail-in conditions on using the SRF, and on burden-sharing in multinational resolutions (Eurogroup 2014).

The German concern about limiting overall exposure to fund liabilities was underlined by a rare disagreement between Germany and the Netherlands regarding the slow build-up of the fund, which the Parliament had criticized. Dijsselbloem suggested that the wait be shortened by allowing the Fund to issue debt. He nevertheless argued this was not a public backstop (not wanting to back such a proposal). Such assurances were not enough for Germany, however. Schäuble rejected the idea since taxpayers would ultimately be responsible, and in joint responsibility. As long as the EU agreed to apply bail-ins rigorously, the SRF would be sufficient at 55 billion (Wagstyl & Vasagar 2014).

The BRRD was passed 15 May 2014, followed by a SRM Regulation in July for the Board, and went into force on 1 January 2016. Over the course of the legislative process, the proposals for the Board and the Commission's role in resolution became stronger vis a vis the Council and the member states than originally envisaged. At the beginning of the process, the draft text for the SRM Regulation outlined that 'The resolution college should not be a decision-making body, but a platform facilitating decision-making by national authorities' (Recital 98). In this sense it built on the formula used for the BRRD, which provides for national resolution authorities supervised by national finance ministries, national resolution funds and bank resolution plans. The SRM reviews and points out needs for improvement.

Changes also weakened the automatism of Council approval for resolution decisions. Before a resolution is imminent, the SRB works with national authorities to ensure that resolution plans are workable. The actual moment of starting a resolution decision lies with the European Central Bank in its capacity as Supervisor, however. It decides whether a bank has insufficient capital to continue operating. This increases the likelihood of a decision that is not influenced by national authorities. In the event of an insolvency the Board then decides whether the bank can be resolved using national legislation only or whether a resolution needs to be initiated at the European level. Even in these cases the Board merely recommends to the Commission that resolution proceedings be started. The Commission then has 24 hours to decide whether to proceed. In the original version, the Council had to approve the decision and could take up to four days to decide. The result would have been that the SRM could take a long time to. This contrasts heavily with the need to resolve banks quickly to avoid financial contagion, often over a weekend or overnight. The final version of the Regulation allowed the Commission to choose whether to submit the decision for approval to the Council, thereby shortening the process. As was seen in the Italian and Portuguese cases outlined below, however, the Council's weaker role at the end of the decision-making process has been substituted with more pro-active involvement before the Board makes a recommendation. A key component of that recommendation is whether the bank can and should be resolved under European or national rules. The latter provides more leeway for national authorities to manage resolutions without rigorous bail-ins, and national governments have asked successfully to do this, keeping control largely national. This implies the country having no access to the SRF, but that is a price they appear willing to pay. The adjustments therefore strengthen the decision-making process, but do not appear to have affected the strong role that national authorities play in managing resolutions within their jurisdictions. In essence the construction of the SRM still puts the initiative back into the hands of national authorities and governments. This has the additional effect of ensuring that national authorities remain responsible for the financial costs of ensuring that a bank resolution does not negatively impact financial stability beyond the bank in question.

Since the passage of the BRRD and the SRM Regulation, the willingness of the Commission and the Board to take resolution into their own hands has been tested a number of times. Both institutions have chosen to provide considerable leeway to national authorities and finance ministries to resolve banks on their own terms. The main questions for the Commission are twofold. First, how stringently should be out in rule be applied? Second, what is the reasoning behind allowing national authorities to take the lead?

Regarding the first question, the Commission takes the view that there are two reasons to be less stringent about the bail in rule. The first is that there might be good reasons for sparing smaller banks the pain of a bail-in. The SRB demonstrated willingness to accept lower demands on smaller banks in 2016. Smaller banks are thought by some to be lesser risk of failure even if this is not objectively true, and more importantly forcing smaller banks to raise the type of capital that could be subjected to bail-ins in would raise their operating costs. In 2015 France, Germany and the UK acted together in proposing a relaxation of the rules for small banks which the Commission accepted. The second component of the Commission's reasoning is that financial stability is a local issue (Donnelly 2017). This means that the disruption of financial services in any EU country or even any region within the country is sufficiently bad that EU intervention should be smaller and the opportunity for state aid should be greater and faster.

Regarding the second issue of allowing national authorities to take the lead the answer seems to be that national authorities defend their rights very strongly – that they alone possess the financial resources to provide local financial stability. Furthermore the SRF is too small and too cumbersome to be used overnight in resolution. There are therefore built-in incentives for actors to rely on national resources and decision-making procedures to the greatest extent possible. The Board and Commission therefore push back responsibility and latitude to decide on national authorities.

The impact of these decisions is visible in the case of small banks and medium-sized banks that are still systemically important, which leads the Commission to view state intervention favourably, even if the BRRD's terms are not met. This can be seen in the Italian cases of Banco Monte dei Paschi di Siena (BMPS) and

Banco Veneto and Banco Popolar di Vicenza (V&V). Of these three banks BMPS is larger, operating beyond its immediate regional headquarters. In the context of Italy's economic decline during the GFC, it purchased a large insolvent bank that ultimately overwhelmed it and I forced it into insolvency. But as the world's oldest bank the political consequences of allowing to fail were large enough to incite the government into multiple initiatives to save the bank from being closed when it otherwise would have been.

While the BRRD forbids state aid without a bail-in resolution, it allows national governments to negotiate precautionary recapitalizations – capital injections to keep a bank afloat before a stress test officially finds a bank short of capital. A key condition of this financial aid is that it must be provided on market terms. This means that the state must charge an interest rate that other investors would normally charge the bank if they could be found. A precautionary recapitalization is distinguished by the fact that a bank's financial shortfalls have not yet officially been recognized by the supervisor. This provides a window of opportunity in which the supervisor indicates a potential need for the bank to raise the capital on the basis of an upcoming stress test to allow the Ministry of Finance to extend a loan to the bank until it can recover the capital itself by normal means on private capital markets. In the BMPS case this loophole was used to provide the bank with a precautionary recapitalization, in return for internal structural reforms. Competition Commissioner Vestager expressed hope that BMPS would return to lending money to the economy once its NPL problems were cleaned up (Barker & Sanderson 2017), while Bundesbank doubts about the temporary nature of the bank's problems were swept aside (New Europe 2016). The state effectively became a provider of patient capital to its own banking sector (Donnelly 2018).

This was not the case in the other two banks (V&V), however. In both cases the banks were small regional entities suffering from a dwindling client base and a rising rate of non-performing loans (NPLs) which in turn reflects a stagnating Italian economy. This renders them unable to turn to private investors to increase their capital. As a result of the straitjacket these banks, like many of their small regional contemporaries, resorted to selling bonds to keep themselves afloat. This was a measure of desperation. Retail depositors were paid a higher rate of interest than ordinary savings accounts. What the customers did not expect, however, was that under the new BRRD rules an insolvent bank could only receive state aid if a significant portion of those bonds were wiped out first. This meant that Italian households would have their savings wiped out in the event of an insolvency because the bonds were not deposits and so they would not be covered by deposit insurance. In 2015 the Italian government found itself confronted with a political nightmare in which the deposit insurance would effectively not work for the purposes it was designed. This led the government to reimburse bondholders regardless of the BRRD's restrictions. After a long period of lobbying by the Italian government,the Commission eventually agreed to permit the reimbursement and not classify it as state aid because banks had allegedly mis-sold the bonds to customers. However, selling bonds to retail customers is a long-standing practice especially amongst small banks. A 1999 report from the deposit insurance foundation FITD (*Fondo Interbancaria Tutela dei Depositi*) showed that regional banks had resorted to funding themselves since the 1960s (Pistelli 1999).

While these cases of reimbursing bondholders were made legal through a loophole and with the Commission's complicity, the further takeover of the V&V banks by Banco Intesa San Paolo (hereafter Intesa) was not. The Italian government had organized the establishment of two private funds in 2015 to support ailing banks without their being sold to foreign investors. The Atlas fund and the Atlante fund were set up to solicit private donations from Italian banks that would be used to help save banks that had gotten in trouble. Into 2015 half of the money had already been used for helping BMPS. This was partly due to the fund being so small (4.8 billion euros); there was not enough money to help them out without closing them.

In this context the government pressured Intesa to buy the banks. It refused. Eventually Intesa agreed to take over V&V but under strict conditions that disregarded the BRRD. First, it would only buy the good assets of the banks. Second, the state would give it €5 billion to do this. Third, acquiring the new banks would not lead to it having to acquire more core capital. In other words, Intesa was receiving state aid to purchase the assets without having to incur any costs or risks. These conditions were clearly beyond the intent and the letter of the directive. By fall 2017 they had not been challenged which means that both the Board and the Commission are limited even further by the reality on the ground in Italy. Furthermore, both institutions allowed Italian authorities to proceed on the basis that V&V were critical for local financial stability, not European (European Commission 2017). The ECB's Vitor Constancio publicly backed the position by arguing that the interest of financial stability would trump considerations of state aid legality (Binnie & Za 2017). Nor have there been any response to two Spanish complaints that the Commission allowed Italy to do what it wants, while Spain played by both the letter and spirit of the law.

Spain contrasts strongly with the Italian case in that it resolved banks quickly and thoroughly after the onset of the Eurozone crisis. Many of the problems in the Spanish-speaking sector where to be found at the local or regional level where credit unions and cooperative banks had engaged in risky behaviour during the decade preceding, lending reasonably large amounts to households that could not repay and which found themselves in financial distress. The Spanish government reacted in 2009 by establishing a national resolution authority, a national resolution fund (FROB) and selling the small insolvent banks to their larger, healthier commercial counterparts and retightening the regulation of those banks to ensure that they got rid of their problems (Deeg 2012; Quaglia & Royo 2015).

In 2017 the resolve of the Spanish authorities was demonstrated once again when Banco Popular was sold to Santander for the price of €1. The ECB had declared the bank insolvent after repeated failures to raise sufficient capital (Brunsden 2017), which set the SRB, the Spanish government, the Commission and Santander in motion. In contrast to Intesa, Santander acquired both the assets and the liabilities so that state aid was avoided, but also a bail-in as well in a way that preserved local financial stability, preventing disruption to depositors (SRB 2017).

But here the similarities with the Italian case end, and the centrality of local financial stability to European institutions is underlined. French Socialist MEP Pervenche Berès asked what would have happened had there been no buyer for Popular. The V&V/Intesa case demonstrates that EU authorities would have found another way to avoid closure. While Spain focussed on taking initiatives in the context of EU law, the Italian government put more effort into bending the rules on state aid, eventually with the constructive permission of the Commission. While resolution had taken place in Cyprus in 2013 in ways the national government did not fully support, the circumstances were special – the country was receiving financial assistance from the ESM, and therefore subject to Troika demands. This was not the case for Spain and Italy in 2017.

This means that within the context of EU resolution, the directive has fulfilled its purpose in Spain precisely because the Spanish government was willing to implement it faithfully, while in Italy that was not the case (Donnelly 2017a). German objections were not headed. A great deal of the difference in respecting the rules of directive appear to be whether the national government was willing to intervene early and forcefully in banking resolution the earlier they intervened the easier the problems were to stop without resorting to stay it. In both cases as well, handling resolution in this way avoided the sticky details of trying to access the SRF and the conditions Germany would surely demand.

A further consequence of these developments is that the Commission remains responsible for making decisions and negotiating with national authorities over issues that it no longer intended to deal with after the directive entered into force. DG Competition noted that after the Great Financial Crisis erupted into 2008 that it spent an enormous amount of time negotiating the terms of state aid with national authorities and then pushing them to look for an exit strategy. They also expected that these negotiations would become a thing of the past. While the directive did not forbid state aid it ensured that state aid should be the last resort. It stood to reason therefore that the Commission would only really be called upon to make a decision about sticky situations in which financial stability would be threatened in unforeseen ways.

What does this tell us about the outcome of the SRM? It tells us that decision-making authority and resolution proceedings still remain profoundly national. What happened later under the Juncker Commission was the expansion of financial stability concerns from large banks to small ones. Confronted with the lack of alternatives, the Commission and the SRB have elected to provide the widest scope passable to national authorities in normal times and to not challenge national authorities even when the rules of the directive are broken. This re-legitimizes national stabilization through government, which continues to be allowed as a last resort. This in turn reinforces responsible sovereignty in principle, at least with the consequence of limiting transfers. The responsible component is less than the original design intended, showing limits to the enforcement pyramid strategy within the EU legal framework.

Deposit insurance

As with resolution, there were two predominant visions of how deposit insurance systems should be structured in Europe – one with significant powers and financial resources at the EU level, and another based on a coordination of national systems without financial transfers. Financial transfers were the key issue, but also divergent risk behaviour of different banking institutions, and related demands that any European DGS have differentiated premia, to avoid establishing a system in which safe banks would not only subsidize banks engaging in riskier behaviour, but encourage that behaviour through cheap insurance. The result is that Commission efforts to get Germany in particular to accept a common DGS were unsuccessful, given that it would likely be a net payer for liabilities elsewhere.

The lessons of the global financial crisis underlined that deposit insurance had to be significantly reformed and upgraded to ensure a positive contribution to financial stability, but also to prevent enhanced insurance from leading to enhanced risk-taking. The key features designed to keep such effects to a minimum are: limits on insurance coverage, higher deposit insurance premiums charged for institutions with higher-risk portfolios, and excluding certain kinds of depositors from insurance (Reidhill 2013).

They therefore complement the single supervision mechanism and constitute core components of a Banking Union in Europe. They also complement each other, since both are involved in managing the affairs of insolvent banks. In 2008, and again in 2010, the European Commission proposed a European Deposit Guarantee System (DGS) as part of a broader package of legislative initiatives to improve financial stability in the EU. The 2010 legislation led to raising minimum standards of coverage, and including a duty of the member states to inform the others of major impending changes to their coverage. Attempts to transfer or lend money between systems failed.

Deposit guarantee systems require a number of attributes if they are to contribute to financial stability. *Broad protection of depositors* is required to ensure that bank clients do not panic when a bank collapse is feared or underway and shift their deposits elsewhere. International guidelines on deposit insurance schemes recommend covering 90–95% of depositors (not deposits) and all banks, including systemically important and public banks in order to ensure that the incentive to contribute to a bank run is low for most clients. The costs of covering so many depositors can be compensated by limiting the amount of insurance that each depositor enjoys (Reidhill 2013). This has a dual beneficial effect of preventing mass panic and giving rich, above all professional, depositors the incentive to monitor the bank's behaviour closely. The expectation is that such creditors will exercise market discipline by moving their deposits to another bank when they see that the bank is acting too risky for their comfort. The same principle applies to unsecured creditors in resolution situations. *Information* and a system that is not too complex are also required to make the coverage effective. Public awareness of coverage and reimbursement methods and times are also important to prevent runs (IADI 2013: 4–6). Finally, *timely intervention*, including the infrastructure and capacity to reimburse depositors within a week must be in place before a crisis ensues to forestall depositor runs before they occur (Reidhill 2013). Otherwise, delays can occur that fuel panic (Mayes 2013).

Beyond coverage, information and timely intervention, two funding elements are also considered essential to a deposit insurance system being able to perform its job properly. The first is that deposit insurance requires independent, dedicated funds that are funded by banks in advance of a crisis and replenished after the crisis has passed. *Ex ante funding* ensures that banks are not called on to contribute to a fund at the moment when they are least able to do so, leaving the public purse to pay the bill. The use of the reserve during an economic downturn affecting one or many banks also has a beneficial macroeconomic impact, of acting in a countercyclical fashion that softens the blow of economic downturn and makes a faster, more robust recovery possible. Replenishment, which is also ex ante funding for the next crisis, ensures that banks, rather than taxpayers, continue to be the primary paymasters of deposit insurance (the *polluter pays principle*). The intent is not simply to save public money, but to *combat moral hazard* by giving banks and their stakeholders (shareholders, creditors and employees) an incentive to monitor their own risk of collapse and restrain reckless behaviour (Datwati 2013). Deposit guarantees can be applied to more than cash deposits depending on how balances are kept. Money market funds experienced a run after the collapse of Lehman, for example, as most deposits were kept in that form (ESRB 2012: 17–18). This would cover issues such as junior bondholders in Italy if so designed.

While it is conceivable that national deposit insurance premiums could be calibrated to cope with national bank collapses, an integrated European banking market in which depositors and banks are often from different countries would be unstable unless the funding were aggregated and deployed at the European level. In Europe, attaining this would mean raising the level of protection in some countries, establishing depositor preference in the case of a bank's collapse (so that they would be paid before other creditors) in other countries, and more broadly, ensuring harmonized rules in Europe that depositors with accounts in more than one country would understand easily.

Beyond ex ante funding by banks, deposit insurance also requires a *public backstop* to deal with the collapse of multiple banks simultaneously that would otherwise bankrupt the deposit insurance fund, a position supported by the European Systemic Risk Board (ESRB 2012: 18). Since the cost of a systemic crisis is large and unpredictable, the Financial Stability Board underlines that guarantees need to be open-ended rather than capped (FSB 2012). In Europe, the mismatch between pan-European bank activity and the capacity of national DGSs to cope with collapses is aggravated by the unequal capacity of EU member states to provide financial guarantees that reinforce national deposit guarantee systems. For this reason, the dedication of pooled resources at the EU level to support banks once deposit insurance has reached its capacity is considered essential. In the absence of a fiscal union that some analysts consider essential to providing this public backstop, an independent fund backed by the member states like the ESM with sufficient funds, and the capacity to leverage its assets through the issue of euro bonds is considered the next best option (Wolff 2013).

Supply of European deposit insurance

Beyond the 2010 directive, demand was still high for an EDIS capable of transferring funds across borders and having the attributes outlined above. Despite the functional necessities of establishing EDIS and resolution systems at the European level to handle the financial risk of banks operating across European borders, there are a number of distributional issues that drive conflict. These issues primarily revolve around who should pay for financing the public backstop. They also involve the question of whether banks should all pay equally into the system, regardless of how high the risk of bankruptcy is. Here, financial institutions providing for deposit insurance and bank investment profiles set out divergent preferences. While large commercial banks favoured EDIS, cooperatives and public savings banks (Sparkassen) in Germany and Austria did not. Their low risk and built-in supervision as part of insurance meant that they were likely to pay in but never benefit, and shift to a system without the risk-averse supervisory influence (Bernet & Walter 2009). These concerns led Germany and Austria to view EDIS sceptically, to resist proposals to allow national funds to borrow from one another in an emergency, and to resist pressure to allow states to call on the ESM as an alternative to an EDIS fund. This undersupply of European deposit insurance was chosen despite the fact that all key decision-makers were interested in ensuring that deposit insurance and resolution mechanisms are provided throughout the European market, to minimize financial stability emanating from other countries.

Distributionally, there are choices to be made regarding the mix of public and private funding in such systems. For those countries that are most likely to be net contributors to the systems, there is an incentive to minimize costs by ensuring that private actors pay as much as possible, and that the collective funds are kept smaller rather than larger. They are also likely to be concerned that the fund can provide asymmetric benefits to countries with the weakest banking sectors, thereby damaging the competitiveness of their own banks, and providing countries with weaker banking sectors with incentives for reckless behaviour that the funds will bail out (IADI 2013: 5–7). For countries more likely to require outside assistance for national banks, the reverse is true.

Where disagreement existed was on the extent to which common European funds would be established, and on the threshold at which public guarantees would take over from privately funded deposit guarantees and resolution funds. The third is to what extent banks should have to pay risk-weighted premiums into deposit guarantee systems and resolution funds. Countries with a large share of banks and similar financial institutions (credit unions, building societies, cooperatives and public sector savings banks) with low risk profiles have an interest in paying a lower rate than their riskier, often larger counterparts.

An additional issue for national deposit insurance systems in Europe is the coordination of national practices in the absence of EU institutions. This extends not only to the technicalities of sorting out who pays and how in the event of bankruptcy affecting depositors in more than one country, but the issue of beggar-thy-neighbour policies that force other states to spend more on deposit insurance. The Irish introduction of unlimited deposit insurance in 2008, without consulting other EU member states, was viewed in other European capitals and in Brussels as such an act, as it threatened capital flight out of other countries into Ireland until other countries followed suit and provided greater deposit guarantees.

The initial response of the European Commission regarding deposit guarantee systems came in 2008, and was limited to modest technical measures to enhance efficiency in national systems. The draft directive proposed to shorten the pay-out times for depositors (to three days from three to nine months) to increase the amount covered (from 20 000 euros to 100 000) and to mandate cooperation between national systems in an unspecified manner.

The experience of bank failures during the Eurozone crisis led to a reformulation of the draft directive in 2010, as the previous draft had not been agreed upon. The Council counterproposal to that document in 2011 emphasizes that it intended to set minimum standards for national systems and provide for coordination between them, rather than introducing European deposit guarantees. Key issues were eligibility of deposits for reimbursement, liability for payment in closure involving two or more member states, and whether insurance premiums would reflect risk of failure or not. Measures were included to disallow coverage for deposits shifted across borders after the point of failure (in memory of such activity when Ireland offered unlimited coverage in 2008) (European Council 2011: 6). While not forbidding countries like Ireland from raising their deposit guarantees to unlimited levels, no European guarantee would exist to bolster the national capacity to act. Pressure by countries seeking to prevent such behaviour would have to be exerted outside the framework of European law – in a self-help fashion. Financial payments of national DGSs to depositors of multinational banks with branches in other EU member states were to be made by the host country in the first instance, but reimbursed by the DGS of the home country that supervises the bank (European Council 2011: 21). National governments would then be responsible individually for shortfalls in the system as the public backstop. These last details are important in confirming that the member states used this method of coordination to strengthen, not weaken the link between national governments and banks headquartered in their jurisdictions (Kapstein 1994). Commission plans to require risk-weighted premiums were rejected in favour of member states deciding how to charge banks (Council 2011: 10).

The European Parliament's main goal in the legislation in 2012 was to move the member states to agree to making 100 000 euros of deposit guarantee a permanent, rather than temporary measure. Other goals were to ensure guarantee funds equal to 1.5% of assets, reflecting international consensus on appropriate funding levels rather than the 0.8% that the Council would eventually agree on, to ensure subsistence money of 5000 euros within a week, and for riskier banks to pay higher insurance premiums than other banks, up to 2.5 times the low risk premium (European Parliament 2012). These demands, contrasted with the Council's position, underline how weak the latter's provision of European deposit guarantees was.

The Commission tabled a new DGSD proposal in September 2012, as consensus in financial circles had advanced on how deposit guarantees could be involved in bank resolution, but still no agreement on DGSD had been reached. The proposed right to borrow across national DGSs was expressed again as an option (Council 2011: 31), and then withdrawn entirely in a later Commission proposal, following German objections (Berschens, Kröner & Hildebrand 2017). The draft also provided for national DGSs to be used in recapitalization, rescue and restructuring efforts prior to failure in an attempt to ward it off. The logic that the DGSs would pay out less if helping to prevent a failure than in reimbursing depositors for an actual collapse reflected the state of the art in maximizing the contribution of deposit guarantee funds to financial stability.

The revised proposal was considered insufficient by a number of outside specialists. Rather than national coordination, the IMF made it clear that a truly European DGS which could insure depositors throughout the EU was essential for financial stability (IMF 2013: 11). Gros and Schoenmaker also argued for an EDIRA whose powers and funds would be phased in to take over from national authorities and funds over a 20-year period, minimizing the potential resistance of national governments to a European solution on the basis of transaction costs. The European authority and funds they proposed would initially exist alongside national schemes, acting where national schemes do not (so as to avoid a duplication of costs for banks), and then gradually assume responsibility for losses over a 20-year period. The fund would be based on ex ante contributions. Countries with such systems would transfer assets gradually to the European system, while countries with ex post systems, like the Netherlands, would be required to build up their contributions over time (Gros & Schoenmaker 2012).

Gros and Schoenmaker also tried to minimize the concern of Germany and others likely to have to be net payers into the system that they would be burdened with paying for the toxic assets of foreign banks. For this reason, they argued that only well-capitalized banks should enter the system, so that the fund's establishment does not make large transfers to cover past losses (legacy problems). Those debts will need to remain the problem of the member states in question, and have to be dealt with prior to the launch of the EDIRA. They point out that this would allow Banking Union to make a proper start (without distributional issues dividing the states). Countries would have to sort out whether the ESM could be used to help transfer toxic assets from the balance sheets of the banks to the public sector.

The Gros/Schoenmaker plan attempted to bring the member states closer toward a common system in part so that zombie banks, which had grown in number with the duration of the Eurozone crisis, could be brought back to health or shut down without jeopardizing the financial system. The alternative would have been to let them continue doing business, which merely delays the day of reckoning (in hope of staving off disaster, or at least waiting for economic recovery to turn the non-performing loans around), which was the status quo at the time of writing. This concern of zombie banks backed by public authorities that cannot afford to do so represents a fear by the countries that would have to pay that there are hidden liabilities in the banking sector. This is a principle reason why Germany insisted that any European DGS would only be allowed after the establishment of the ECB as the single supervisor for the European banking system (Economist 2012). As Gros and Schoenmaker underline, however, supervision and resolution would have to go hand in hand to make this happen, with the assistance of a deposit guarantee system.

Nevertheless, the Council remained firm on its plan for a coordinated national approach coupled with minimal cross-border transfers at the discretion of member states. It reached agreement on the outline for a European DGS in June 2013. Those principles included the coordination of national DGS, plus exemptions for certain categories of banks, such as credit unions, public sector savings banks and banking cooperatives, which the German government had defended heavily (Bundesregierung 2016). Funds from national deposit guarantee systems could be used in resolution systems, but subject to national discretion. Likewise, national systems would be able to request assistance from other national systems, but no legal right to aid was established.

The Cyprus Crisis of 2013 tested the implications of this nationally based regime of deposit insurance for weak links in the European financial system when two banks – Laiki and Bank of Cyprus – went bankrupt. Despite the fact that the European Commission still took an accommodating view to state aid for failing banks, the Cypriot government was not able to raise the cash required to provide a public backstop on capital markets. It then turned to the Eurogroup and requested assistance from the EFSF/ESM, triggering a defensive reaction from the Netherlands, Germany and Finland, who insisted that the ESM not be used. In the protracted negotiations that followed, the Eurogroup insisted that ESM funds would only be used under strict conditions, and as a last resort. The country requesting assistance would have to initiate resolution procedures for the banks in question, bailing in shareholders and private creditors first, and then using up whatever funds were available in national resolution and deposit insurance systems before a call could be considered.

Considerable concern was raised over whether the ESM should go so far to protect itself as to undermine the sanctity of deposit insurance in the event of such a resolution. Eurogroup Chairman Jeroen Dijsselbloem suggested that not only unsecured creditors and deposits should be subjected to radical haircuts, but accepted that deposits guaranteed by national deposit insurance should be subjected to haircuts as well. Whether Dijsselbloem himself made the suggestion or not is unknown,[1] but the fact that he actively and openly promoted it as the preferred approach to resolving Laiki and Bank of Cyprus without ESM assistance and a 'new model' for the Eurozone said a great deal about the lengths he was willing to go to push national problems back onto national governments, businesses and citizens. It also demonstrated the willingness to send a message to depositors throughout the Eurozone periphery that their deposit insurance would be worthless in the event it was needed. Indeed, it should have been known that the flow had already started. The Bank for International Settlements had released data in 2012 showing that deposits had been flowing out of Greece, Ireland and Portugal since 2010, and out of Italy and Spain since 2011 and flowing into northern European countries of Finland, Germany and Luxembourg (Bank for International Settlements 2012: 2). This state of affairs required the introduction of capital controls to stem the outflow.

Seeing that this Dijsselbloem Principle (Salmon 2013) would destabilize the entire Eurozone economy if allowed to stand, Schäuble announced the next day that secured deposits would not be touched in a resolution (Kirschbaum 2013). However, according to Austria's Finance Minister Maria Fekter, the Eurogroup finance ministers indeed discussed imposing haircuts on covered deposits, while the ECB and Austria, the Cypriot government and presumably Germany opposed it. Luxembourg Prime Minister Jean-Claude Juncker also made clear his opposition to such plans (Shields 2013).

The Cyprus Crisis was instrumental in bringing the Eurogroup to articulate in detail the relationship between national responsibility and the terms and conditions of group assistance through the ESM. The Cypriot government unsurprisingly sought financial assistance in the form of loans from the ESM in the same way that the Spanish government had done a year previously. It was willing to accept the condition of Troika supervision in principle in exchange for loans per se, but was opposed to the detailed demands on its banking sector and economic policies while negotiating the loans. But the Eurogroup's trust in Spain was higher, given its full willingness to accept ESM terms, and also because most problem banks could be absorbed by healthier ones without closure, which limited politicization. The Eurogroup insisted that ESM loans could only be made if all other measures had been exhausted, meaning haircuts by private investors and depositors, national resolution and deposit insurance funds and national public backstops, and if the assistance was combined with the closure of insolvent banks. The ESM was therefore not to be used primarily as a public backstop to national public backstops (although it formally does this), but to act as a firewall, sometimes in combination with capital controls, that prevents the collapse of a bank from having uncontrolled effects beyond the country in question.

This doubling down of reliance on national deposit insurance systems, on responsible sovereignty, results in an undersupply of financial stability when measured against the requirements of banking sector officials discussed above. The discretion of member states in granting loans to the DGSs of other countries reflects not only an undersupply of the public backstop to deposit guarantees, but an asymmetric one at the European level. Countries with higher credit ratings enjoy a stronger capacity to borrow to shore up their systems in an emergency, meaning that in order to ensure appropriate buffers, the banking systems of financially weaker countries would be forced to reduce their balance sheets more vigorously than elsewhere. It also ensures that the EU's more financially powerful countries are more fully capable of coercing national governments faced with a failing bank to close it against their will. Germany, the Netherlands and Finland recognized and showed in the 2013 Cyprus bank crisis that cost sharing in a deposit guarantee system would reduce pressure that the powerful can exert on program countries to restructure and resolve banks in trouble without resort to common European resources. What was remarkable was how far the Eurogroup was willing to go to compel the Cypriots to solve their problems with their own resources to the greatest extent possible, and with the greatest amount of national leeway possible, using the limited assistance of the ESM as a coercive tool to bring about Cypriot acceptance.

Thus, the Eurogroup's willingness to use coercion through ESM conditionality showed up fairly early, but left room for escalating demands based on the cooperative or combative nature of the Cypriot government. Its engagement with Cyprus was markedly different with its experience with the Spanish government, for example, which accepted the terms fully and without an attempt to (re)negotiate. The Eurogroup's later resort to imposition of terms on an unwilling Cypriot government was intended to preserve a measure of financial stability under continued interdependence of national economies in the Eurozone, based ultimately on national responsibility to pay for the country's own rescue in the medium to long term. This pattern came directly from Germany, after all other options had been exhausted. The decision to institutionalize to preserve interdependence and a well-functioning Eurozone did not come from the Eurogroup or its president (Campbell 2013), but from Germany alone, and unapologetically – as an October 2017 interview on his retirement as Finance Minister revealed (Chazan, Brunsden & Khan 2017).

In 2014, the Commission again attempted to get the Council to agree to a fully fledged EDIS, but changed course to pursue a harmonization of national deposit insurance systems instead, in accordance with Northern European demands to avoid the cross-border transfer of funds. The 2014 Deposit System Guarantee Directive consolidated incremental changes in line with international standards since 2010 – the mandatory establishment of deposit insurance covering 100k of deposits, the gradual shortening of payout periods from a month to seven days, and in particular reflection of German concerns – the switch to an ex ante funding system and continued exemptions for systems based on alternative, but ostensibly safer foundations (for the Germany Sparkassen in particular – see as follows).

The difficulties of moving further than this harmonization to a true EDIS were fed by differing attitudes in Germany and Italy in particular over state aid and risk-averse supervision standards, and amplified by different intensities of state-bank financial links and oversight features (Howarth and Quaglia 2016 & 2018; Cerrone 2018) In Germany, depositors are not insured directly, but indirectly through a system of institution insurance that is designed to keep the bank afloat in case of catastrophe and avoid the messy stranding of creditors and potential financial contagion that is typical for deposit insurance. It also contains a measure of mutual peer pressure and supervision designed to contain moral hazard. In the Sparkassen sector in particular, participating banks pay into a mutual insurance fund, and participate in an oversight board of all their peers in a given region. This board determines the insurance premiums, making them more expensive if it deems the bank's behaviour is too risky, and retaining the power to block a bank's further loan and investment activity if it persists. They in turn are financial liable for shortfalls in the insurance fund if they prove to be insufficient. Although public authorities were in theory also ultimately liable, the quasi political independence of the Sparkassen required ensuring that recourse to public funds was not sought. Larger banks have a similar system of mutual bank insurance, oversight that functions in addition to statutory oversight by the financial services regulator BaFin and the Bundesbank, though the institutional culture allows for riskier investment activity in accordance with the traditional market making and shaping activities of universal banks in Germany.

The existence of this system meant two things: that German Sparkassen in particular viewed any alternative system as inherently inferior. Introducing it would mean shifting to a system that opened up banks to poorer oversight, riskier behaviour and subsidization of excessive risk by other banks, by their more conservative Sparkassen and cooperative (Volksbank and Raiffeissenbank) brethren. This would not only generate moral hazard and redistribution in principle, but clearly in practice. Sparkassen saw the unbridled expansion of credit in Southern Europe during the decade preceding the Eurozone crisis as evidence that their Southern counterparts could not be trusted to run their banks properly, and that paying into the same fund would punish Sparkassen for good governance. It also saw an enormous problem in any system which would be liable for the existing inventory of non-performing loans in Southern Europe.

In this context, the German government found itself attempting unsuccessfully in 2015 to avert a renewed initiative by the Juncker Commission to introduce an EDIS. While the Commission returned to the notion of a phased-in, mutualized deposit insurance system in its November communique, Chancellor Merkel herself underlined at a Sparkasse meeting the time for EDIS had not come (Bundesregierung 2016). Schäuble undertook a successful effort to get the Council to agree to what the preconditions for negotiating EDIS would be. By June 2016, the Council had backed a list of preconditions designed to place responsibility for financial stability on banks, but within a set of supervisory standards to be embedded in EU law. They included a review of capital adequacy standards – capital banks must hold that can be bailed in (total loss-absorbing capacity – TLAC and minimum requirements for own funds and eligible liabilities – MREL) in sufficient quantity to avoid a bailout; restricting bank borrowing in accordance with Basel Committee standards (leverage ratio and net stable funding ratio); a further harmonization of insolvency law to help get rid of non-performing loans in the European banking sector; and most controversial of all, new rules to end the practice of treating national treasury bills as if they had zero risk of default (European Council 2016; Donnelly & Wessel 2018). Although Basel II capital standards linked sovereign risk weights to national credit ratings, it also allowed ratings of zero risk on the basis of internal models, which allowed banks to circumvent the regulatory implications of sovereign defaults and haircuts. Basel III standards did not change this. The practice had been further solidified in Europe through the Capital Requirement Directive (CRD-IV) of 2013 (CRD IV), which assumed a zero risk of default (Mansilla-Fernandez 2016), but was challenged again by the ESRB in 2015. Effectively, Germany had succeeded in getting the Council to promote using Basel Committee standards, existing and future (Basel Committee 2017), as a tool for downsizing risk in the European banking market. Already in 2013, the Bank for International Settlements, which hosts the Basel Committee, had noted that sovereign risk weights could no longer objectively be zero-rated (Bank for International Settlements 2013), and the ESRB (2015) had followed up by suggesting that zero-rating might not be appropriate in all cases, depending on the sovereign's credit rating. These measures put together would force banks, particularly in Southern Europe, to raise significant amounts of fresh capital or be sold to larger entities.

In this context, the German government got into a bitter dispute with the Italian government in 2016 and 2017 regarding the conditions under which it would consider an EDIS involving limited transfers between national systems. There were two components. For Germany, it was vital that Southern European banks reduce their stock of non-performing loans. It was also imperative that they reduce their holdings of national state treasury bills, which had proven to be an unreliable store of value during the Eurozone crisis. Second, sovereign risk weights had to be tackled. In Southern Europe, bank holdings of state treasuries amounted to roughly 10% of assets, more than double the average. This placed both the banks and the sovereigns in a bind, in that the holdings could not be reduced without placing state finances under stress, and leading to an uncontrolled collapse in the value of the remaining bonds held on their balance sheets. Although this should have been an impossible demand for any Southern European state, public confrontations between Italy and Germany were the ones that were visible.

The second and third German demands were that there be a clear order of which creditors would be bailed in during a resolution where deposit insurance could be deployed, and that the bail-ins actually occur in accordance with the BRRD (Donnelly 2017b). The case of junior bondholders being reimbursed by the state in lieu of deposit insurance and circumventing the requirement of a bail-in with the approval of the Commission meant that the sides in the conflict had hardened without any prospect for bridging.

The German government also managed to get the Council to agree, much like the case for the SRF, that any EDIS fund be agreed by intergovernmental agreement and therefore be outside the reach of EU law. Releasing funds would therefore require unanimity, rather than qualified majority vote as the Commission had proposed (European Council 2016). The fund itself would consist of national compartments under international law available for use in national circumstances, and cross-border transfers would be extremely limited. National funds would be responsible for half of all costs followed by national compartments, then common funds in the last instance.

By 23 November 2016, the Commission had conceded defeat and prioritized a Banking Reform Package that pushed forward part of the Council's agenda, with a focus on reducing risk with banks. This included a binding leverage ratio, a net stable funding ratio (to compel banks to find stable sources of finance rather than volatile financial markets) (European Commission 2017). Both this proposal and the assessment of the EBA recommended an increase in the volume of capital that could be bailed in (European Banking Authority 2017).

In light of poor common backstop (Brandt & Wohlfahrt 2018), attention focussed on an alternative once more. This came in the form of newly-elected French President Macron resurrecting the proposal of a finance minister, budget and European Monetary Fund for the Eurozone (Chassany 2017), and a (controversial) alternative from the Commission for the ESM to function as a European Monetary Fund within the context of EU law (Wyplosz 2017). On departing the Eurogroup as German Finance Minister in October 2017, Schäuble (2017) made it clear that the ESM could only provide sparing aid to member states (not the SRM), subject to strong conditionality for national structural reforms and fiscal conservatism, and underlining the principle of using national, not European automatic stabilizers (fiscal policy) to steer the economy. The likelihood of the German coalition of the 2017 elections deviating from that vision seems low, given the increased hostility toward mainstream politics and the strong claim of the economically conservative Free Democratic Party to the Finance Ministry.

Conclusion

This chapter outlines the great gap between the functional need for and the supply of two key elements of a prospective European Banking Union: a European deposit guarantee system and a European resolution mechanism. It outlined how distributional power politics by Germany in particular (H2) but largely within the EU led to a structure that reinforces responsible sovereignty on the financial consequences of bank insolvency (H1) with increased enforcement (H3), but in ways that were partly outside the EU at the behest of Germany (H1). The use of power to veto other options in doing so remained important (H1), as for other components of the EU's financial stability architecture.

These outcomes differ strongly from expertise and transnational actors steering toward an EDIRA with a sizeable fund capable of intervening throughout the Eurozone. By keeping the crucial financial resources outside European law, the EU reinforces responsible sovereignty and allows Germany to set effective rules on resolution. At the same time EU law is used where protecting money isn't required and others agree to an enforcement pyramid, to secure possible future access to the Fund.

Both of these projects – resolution and deposit insurance – contribute to financial stability directly by intervening at the end of a bank's life, ensuring that what is salvageable can be transferred to another institution and winding down the rest with a minimum of harm to the rest of the financial system. A number of characteristics are considered by the international policy community to be key to the design of effective institutions that do this: deposit guarantee and resolution funds that banks pay into before a crisis occurs and that resolution authorities manage with the assistance of the deposit guarantee body; wide-ranging powers of the resolution authority to restructure the assets and sell off the parts of a dying bank; clear rules for bail-ins that provide institutional investors with incentives to monitor the behaviour of the banks they invest in; an effective public backstop large enough to supplement the use of pre-paid funds and bail-ins in winding down a bank in an orderly fashion; and a good match between the powers of the competent authorities and the activity of banks for which they are responsible. The starting point of international expert bodies was that a single European market in which banks operate throughout the EU requires a European DGS, a European Resolution Authority and Resolution Fund; a single set of rules for bail-ins; and a European public backstop for large emergencies in the form of a fiscal union, or barring that, an enhanced European Stability Mechanism. None of this functionally necessary infrastructure has been developed in Europe. Instead, national responsibility for national banks has been preserved and reinforced as the main organizing principle of deposit guarantees and resolution in the EU. The consequence is a choice between lasting financial instability in Europe, or the renationalization of banking within national borders. To the extent that there are common rules, they favour a long-term ratcheting down of banking in Southern Europe and Ireland. What went wrong?

Conflicting national interests within the EU, particularly with regard to the sharing of costs between states for deposit guarantees, resolution funds and a public backstop for both of these, played a large role in Europe not agreeing on their establishment. Those countries that stood to benefit, including Southern Europe and France, favoured their introduction. Countries that would have to pay did not, and used the Cyprus Crisis and its aftermath to insist that national governments would remain responsible for their banks and the costs associated with winding down a dying bank or a zombie bank. Also noticeable is the Council's dual recognition that resolution authorities wield enormous power over banks, and that they must retain significant powers. The SRB therefore gets formal powers to decide, but in a context in which money remains national and solutions therefore tend to be national as well. The apparent mis-match between the international activity of banks and the national nature of the resolution authority is resolved in a way that benefits countries with the EU's strongest banking sectors and strongest public sector credit ratings in Western Europe: the authorities in charge of those banks will effectively make the decisions for all countries where the bank does business. Authority transfers to the European level on paper, but in practice remains with a small, select number of member states who retain the capacity to treat their own national banks with lenience (forbearance) when desired, a luxury not available to others. Both the Commission and the SRB have provided the leeway for this to happen in their interpretation of national discretion.

Chapter 2 drew three specific hypotheses about likely state behaviour in a realist institutionalist world. The first and second hypotheses, that Germany shapes European economic governance using institutions (outside the EU) determine whether cooperation takes place and in what form in response to distributional cleavages, where relative gains are important, is confirmed. The hypotheses do not shed light on what elements are 'merely' intergovernmental a priori, but institutions are nested to allow pressure to be applied from the outside where required. The more an institution is nested in other frameworks, the more likely it can be negotiated by regular intergovernmental means within that context. National positions are therefore limited. Nevertheless, intergovernmental compromises are more likely to result in institutional weakness (seen in both the EBA and SRB). The specific expectation that strong states choose individual state responsibility for regulation and financial matters, unless enforcing agreements on weaker states, also is confirmed in negotiations on the deposit guarantee and resolution directives, in addition to the handling of the collapse of the Cypriot banking sector. The institutional and policy solutions found do not establish rules beyond the nation state that tie the hands of or impose obligations on most national governments. Only countries whose banking sectors and public finances have collapsed will experience obligations – that are determined by the political negotiations of the Eurogroup rather than the transparent rules of a supranational institution. The findings in this chapter study underline that realist foundations for managing interdependence must not be discounted.

Note

1 Some analysts suspected that the Cypriot government itself had suggested the measure to protect Russian depositors from bearing the full brunt of haircuts on unsecured deposits. A significant portion of the Cypriot banking sector, and of the Cypriot economy on which it was unusually dependent, comprised deposits from Russians seeking to protect their assets from the reach of the Russian state.

References

Asmussen, Jörg. (2013) *Building banking union*. London: Speech to the Atlantic Council, 9 July.

Avgouleas, E., & Goodhart, C. (2016). An anatomy of bank bail-ins why the Eurozone needs a fiscal backstop for the banking sector. *European Economy* 2: 75.

Baglioni, A. (2016) *The European banking union*. London: Palgrave Macmillan.

Bank for International Settlements. (2012) European bank funding and deleveraging. *BIS Quarterly Review*, March.

Bank for International Settlements. (2013) *Sovereign risk: A world without risk-free assets?* BIS Papers 72.

Barker, A., & Sanderson, R. (2017) Brussels and Rome secure rescue deal for Monte dei Paschi. *Financial Times*, 1 June.

Basel Committee. (2017) The Basel Committee's work programme. 25 April.

Bernet, B., & Walter, S. (2009) *Design, structure and implementation of a modern deposit insurance scheme*. Vienna: SUERF.

Berschens, R. Kröner, A. & Hildebrand, J. (2017) Die EU kommt Deutschland entgegen. *Handelsblatt*, 4 October.

Binnie, I., & Za, V. (2017) ECB's Constancio says solution on Veneto banks must take financial stability into account. *Reuters*, 14 June.

Brandt, F., & Wohlfahrt, M. (forthcoming) A common backstop to the Single Resolution Fund. *Journal of Economic Policy Research*.

Brunsden, J. (2014) EU struggles to streamline bank failure plan for weekends. *Business Week*, 21 February.

Brunsden, J. (2017) ECB's Nouy defends handling of Banco Popular resolution. *Financial Times*, 19 June.
Brunsden, J., & Christie, R. (2013) ECB battles Germany on pace of EU plans to handle failing banks. *Futures*, 14 May.
Buell, T. (2013) ECB's Mersch: ESM could backstop resolution fund without treaty change. *Wall Street Journal*, 24 September.
Buergin, R., & Christie, R. (2013) Luxembourg's Frieden supports ESM role winding down banks. *Bloomberg*, 9 October.
Bundesregierung. (2013) *France and Germany – together for a stronger Europe of stability and growth*. Paris, 30 May.
Bundesregierung. (2016) *Rede von Bundeskanzlerin Merkel beim 25: Deutschen Sparkassentag am*. Berlin, 27 April 2016.
Business World. (2013) Calls rise for treaty changes over banks, 16 April.
Campbell, A. (2013) *Raising awareness*. Presentation to the Research Conference of the International Association of Deposit Insurers, Basel, 9–10 April.
Carnegy, H. (2014) US treasury secretary Jack Lew calls on Germany to boost growth. *Financial Times*, 19 February.
Cermak, Chris. (2013a) Asmussen: SSM, Res Mech Cld be operational by Summer 2014. *The Main Wire*, 28 May.
Cermak, Chris. (2013b) ECB's Asmussen: ESM bank backstop needs only ESM treaty change. *The Main Wire*, 25 September.
Cermak, Chris. (2013c) Schaeuble will have negotiating mandate. *The Main Wire*, 14 November.
Chassany, A-S. (2017) Macron to press case for eurozone reform despite Merkel setback. *Financial Times*, 26 September.
Chazan, G., Brunsden, J., & Khan, M. (2017) Wolfgang Schäuble feels vindicated by tough bailout policies. *Financial Times*. 8 October.
Christie, R. (2013) Constancio says Barnier plan not enough for bank failures. Bloomberg, 28 February.
Christie, R., Buergin,R. & Stagno Navarra, K. (2014) Schaeuble counters push to speed common Euro bank-failure fund. *Bloomberg*, 18 February.
Coeuré, B. (2013) *The single resolution mechanism: Why it is needed*. Speech to the International Capital Markets Association, Copenhagen, 23 May.
Coffee, J. C. (2010) *Bail-ins versus bail-outs: Using contingent capital to mitigate systemic risk*. New York: Center for Law and Economic Studies (Columbia University) Working Paper No. 380.
Coussens, W. (2012) Presentation on the Eurozone Crisis, European Central Bank, October.
Datwati, M. (2013) *Enhanced guidance for deposit insurance systems*. Presentation to the Research Conference of the International Association of Deposit Insurers, Basel, 9–10 April.
Deeg, R. (2012) *Liberal economic nationalism and europeanization: The rise of Spanish and Italian banks*. Paper for the Annual Meeting of the American Political Science Association.
Deeg, R., & Donnelly, S. (2016) Banking union and the future of alternative banks: Revival, stagnation or decline? *West European Politics* 39, 3: 585–604.
Donnelly, S. (2010) *The regimes of European integration: Constructing governance of the single market*. Oxford: Oxford University Press.
Donnelly, S. (2016) Expert advice and political choice in constructing European banking union. *Journal of banking regulation*, *17*, 1–2: 104–18.

Donnelly, S. (2017). Liberal economic nationalism, financial stability, and Commission leniency in Banking Union. *Journal of Economic Policy Reform*, doi:10.1080/17487870.2017.1400433.

Donnelly, S. (2017b) Advocacy coalitions and the lack of deposit insurance in banking union. *Journal of Economic Policy Reform*. doi: 10.1080/17487870.2017.1400437

Donnelly, S., & Wessel, R. (2018) The global financial stability architecture and EMU. In Amtenbrink, F. & Hermann, C. (eds.) *The EU Law of Economic and Monetary Union*. Oxford: Oxford University Press.

Duffy, J. (2013) France-Germany on collision course with EC. *The Main Wire*, 11 June.

The Economist. (2012) Made in Brussels: The Eurozone needs a Banking Union, but this isn't it, 17 November.

The Economist (2013) Til default do us part: A half-hearted Banking Union raises more risks than it resolves. 8 June.

Epstein, R. (2008) *In pursuit of liberalism: International institutions in postcommunist Europe*. Baltimore: Johns Hopkins University Press.

Epstein, R. (2013) Assets or liabilities? The politics of bank ownership. *Review of International Political Economy* 21, 4: 765–89.

ESRB. (2012) *Forbearance, resolution and deposit insurance*. Reports of the Advisory Scientific Committee, 1 July.

ESRB. (2015) *ESRB Report on the regulatory treatment of sovereign exposures*. Frankfurt am Main.

Eurogroup. (2014) Remarks by Eurogroup President Jeroen Dijsselbloem on the IGA on the single resolution fund, 17 February.

European Banking Authority. (2017) *Guidelines on treatment of liabilities in bail-in*. London: 5 April.

European Commission. (2017) State aid: Commission approves aid for market exit of Banca Popolare di Vicenza and Veneto Banca under Italian insolvency law, involving sale of some parts to Intesa Sanpaolo, 25 June.

European Council. (2011) *Why was the European semester created?* Special Report.

European Council. (2013) *Proposal for a Directive of the European Parliament and of the Council establishing a framework for the recovery and resolution of credit institutions and investment firms and amending Council Directives 77/91/EEC and 82/891/EC, Directives 2001/24/EC, 2002/47/EC, 2004/25/EC, 2005/56/EC, 2007/36/EC and 2011/35/EC and Regulation (EU) No 1093/2010 - General approach*. 28 June 2013.

European Council. (2016) *Council conclusions on a roadmap to complete the Banking Union*. Brussels: 17 June.

European Parliament. (2012) *EP adds pressure to end deadlock on bank deposit guarantee schemes directive*. 16 February.

European Parliament. (2014a) *Amendments adopted by the European Parliament on 6 February 2014 on the proposal for a regulation of the European Parliament and of the Council establishing uniform rules and a uniform procedure for the resolution of credit institutions and certain investment firms in the framework of the Single Resolution Mechanism and a Single Bank Resolution Fund and amending Regulation (EU) No 1093/2010 of the European Parliament and of the Council (COM(2013/0253(COD)*.

European Parliament. (2014b) *EP single bank resolution mechanism and fund: Key principles for successful negotiations*. (ECON Committee), 16 February.

European Parliament. (2017) *Single resolution mechanism*. Legislative Train Schedule.

Fekete-Györ, A. (2013) *Evolution of the deposit insurance framework: Design features and resolution regimes*. Presentation to the Research Conference of the International Association of Deposit Insurers, Basel, 9–10 April.

Financial Stability Board. (2012) *Thematic review on deposit insurance systems: Peer review report*. Basel.
Fontanella-Khan, J. (2014) European Parliament challenges plan for EUR55bn bank rescue fund. *Financial Times*, 16 January.
Goldbach, R., & Zuckerman, H. (2015) In Mayntz, R. ed., *Negotiated reform: The multi-level governance of financial regulation*. Frankfurt am Main: Campus Verlag: 139–61.
Goodhart, C., & Avgouleas, E. (2014) A critical evaluation of bail-ins as bank recapitalisation mechanisms. In Allen, F., Carletti, E., & Gray, J. eds., *Bearing the losses from bank and sovereign default in the Eurozone*. Philadelphia: FIC Press: 65–98.
Gros, D., & Schoenmaker, D. (2012) European deposit insurance: Financing the transaction. *DSF Policy Briefs*, 18.
Hadjipapas, A. (2013) Cyprus seeks to ease bailout terms in meeting with Draghi. *Financial Times*, 3 July.
Hamilton, S., & Brunsden, J. (2013) EU's Barnier says open to compromise on bank resolution law. *Bloomberg*, 17 October.
Howarth, D., & Quaglia, L. (2016) Internationalised banking, alternative banks and the Single Supervisory Mechanism. *West European Politics* 39, 3: 438–61.
Hudson, A. (2013) EU's Barnier says ESM could take on banking resolution. *Reuters*, 9 October.
International Association of Deposit Insurers. (2013) *Enhanced guidance for effective deposit insurance systems: deposit insurance coverage*. Basel, Bank for International Settlements.
International Monetary Fund. (2013) *A banking union for the Euro area: Technical background notes*. 13 February.
Jenkins, P. & Fleming, S. (2013) EU bank watchdog in governance plea. *Financial Times*, 18 November.
Jones, E. (2016) Financial markets matter more than fiscal institutions for the success of the Euro, *The International Spectator* 51: 4, 29–39.
Kapstein, E. (1994) *Governing the global economy: International finance and the state*. Cambridge, MA: Harvard University Press.
Kirschbaum, E. (2013) Schäuble says Eurozone savings deposits are safe. *Reuters*. 30 March.
Kuczynski, A. (2013) *Presentation at the research conference of the international association of deposit insurers*, Basel, April 24.
Mansilla-Fernandez, J. M. (2016) Institutions. *European Economy* 36, 1: 35–9.
Mayes, D. (2013) *Guidance on coverage and moral hazard*. Presentation at IADI Research Conference, Basel, 9–10 April.
Münchau, W. (2013) An exercise in prolonging a banking credit crunch. *Financial Times*, 23 December.
New Europe. (2016) Frankfurt raises objections on Rome's bailout. *NEOnline*, 28 December.
Pistelli, F. (1999) *International deposit insurance systems*. Rome: Fondo Interbancario di Tutela dei Depositi.
Quaglia, L., & Royo, S. (2015) Banks and the political economy of the sovereign debt crisis in Italy and Spain. *Review of International Political Economy*, *22*, 3: 485–507.
Riedhill, J. (2013) *Guidance papers on deposit insurance coverage and moral hazard*. Presentation at IADI Research Conference, Basel, 9–10 April.
Salmon, F. (2013) The Dijsselbloem principle. *Reuters*, 26 March.
Scally, D. (2012) Germans say no deal agreed on Irish debt. *Irish Times*, 18 October.
Scally, D. & Lynch, S. (2013) Germany to agree deal on bank resolution. *Irish Times*, 9 December.

Schäuble, W. (2017) *Non-paper for paving the way towards a Stability Union.*

Shields, M. (2013) Cyprus deal "mistake" can be changed: Austria's Fetker. *Reuters*, 18 March.

Spiegel, P. (2013) Cyprus President calls for bailout overhaul to save economy. *Financial Times*, 18 June.

SRB. (2017) *The single resolution board adopts resolution decision for Banco Popular*. Brussels, 7 June.

Stagno Navarra, K., Verlaine, J. & Christie, R. (2015) Juncker warns nations of danger if resolution pact not sealed. *Bloomberg*, 26 November.

Thomson, C., & Barker, A. (2014) Bank test impact of reform on debt demand. *Financial Times*, 9 January.

Tonveronachi, M. (2013) *PSL Quarterly Review* 66, 267: 371–85.

Véron, N., & Wolff, G. B. (2013) *From supervision to resolution: Next steps on the road to European banking union.* Brussels: Bruegel Policy Contribution (No. 2013/04).

Wagstyl, S., & Vasagar, J. (2014) Transcript: FT interview with Wolfgang Schäuble. *Financial Times*, 29 June.

Walsh, J. (2013) ESM will not finance legacy debt. *Irish Examiner*, 22 July.

Waterfield, B. (2013b) Move to shield UK taxpayers from Eurozone banking plan: Britain demands protection guarantee over scheme to allow closure of stricken lenders. *Telegraph*, 19 December.

Wolff, B. (2013) *Why the ESM direct bank recap is not a done deal yet*. Bruegel, Brussels, 21 June.

Wyplosz, C. (2017) *A European monetary fund?* In-Depth Analysis for European Parliament, Economic and Monetary Affairs Committee, May.

7 Realist institutionalism and international order

This chapter begins by returning to the general propositions of realist institutionalism outlined in Chapter 2, the specific hypotheses derived from them and assessing how the evidence laid out in the chapters above confirm them or not. Realist institutionalism is built on three propositions: that great powers manage interdependence by building institutions that serve their interests; that distributive gains matter greatly in their demands on others (though they will use policy ideas to guide their behaviour); and that great powers exercise economy that favours incremental change over radical solutions, and favours enforcement pyramids that use coercion and imposition sparingly, where necessary to protect and promote the system.

This in turn led to three hypotheses and associated sub-hypotheses to be tested: that Germany would reshape European economic governance to suit its interests, including the use of non-EU institutions; that distributional concerns (including its understanding of them) would dominate its demands on others; and that it would seek to establish an enforcement pyramid through incremental changes to European economic governance to achieve its ends.

The evidence supporting the hypotheses laid out in this book is considerable, and presented in Table 7.1 alongside competing theories of international relations and European integration. What stands out first of all is that the expectations of neofunctionalism – above all the means by which spillover is expected to lead to institutional development – cannot be verified. Indeed, there are new institutions that emerge out of the Eurozone Crisis, but they do not reflect the input of actors which neofunctionalism expects to be influential. Europe's institutional development attracted a great deal of international, transnational and supranational support for US-style federal institutions to correct the financial instabilities of the Eurozone, but they were not influential in any meaningful way. Even the ECB, which gained supervision responsibilities, acquired less than it and others considered necessary in order to get the job done (Coussens 2012). Instead, the EBA as a body dominated by national representatives, remained involved in coordinating national supervisors and carrying out stress tests, while the SRB, similarly dominated by national authorities, began its tenure by providing ample leeway to national authorities to manage resolutions on their own terms. Bodies and institutions within the EU that were established as part of Banking Union or a reformed

DOI: 10.4324/9780203702130-7

Table 7.1 Contending theoretical principles and results

	Realist institutionalism	*Liberal intergovernmentalism/ Liberal institutionalism*	*Neofunctionalism*	*New intergovernmentalism*
Order (Proposition 1)	Institutions backed by Great Powers to support interdependence Responsible sovereignty ***Results***: **German-led Banking Union and EMU reform** **Non-EU institutions used to change outcomes (EMS, TSCG)** **Responsible sovereignty as ordering principle of European fiscal policy, within framework of German economic policy demands.** **Sovereignty replaced by trusteeship for countries unable to borrow** **Responsible Sovereignty persists in bank supervision, resolution and deposit insurance if bank is not a European SIB**	Institutions backed by states to support interdependence Responsible sovereignty plus delegated agency ***Results:*** **EBA 2011–14**	Institutions, networks and Supranational governance Diffused power across levels Weak sovereignty ***Results:*** **Fiscal union/FDIC model of Banking Union (proposed)** **SSM initiatives by ECB**	De novo institutions Power concentrated nationally Strong sovereignty ***Results:*** **EBA & SRB governance**
Payoffs (Proposition 2)	States choose: relative gains great powers push costs on others **Results:** **Germany chooses order to sustain interdependence on own terms**	States choose: mix of absolute and relative gains **Results:** **nil**	Actors choose: absolute gains (welfare) **Results:** **nil**	Relative gains, absolute gains (welfare) **Results:** **nil**

Institutional change (Proposition 3.1)	Economy: Incremental change **Results: nesting of EMU in TSCG, ESM** **Germany adheres to EU institutions only as one possible option.** **Rejection of EU status, policy procedures, legislative demands and ECJ jurisdiction for ESM, SRF, TSCG:** **Creation of a Shadow Europe.**	Punctuated change **Results: EBA, SRB construction**	Incremental and punctuated change **Results: strengthened SSM**	Punctuated change **Results: SRB, EBA governance**
Enforcement (Proposition 3.2)	Enforcement pyramids: Imposition and coercion where incentives and persuasion fail Nested commitments **Results:** **Coercion exploited against backdrop of financial insecurity (TSCG, ESM) to reform European Semester** **Coercion for ESM recipients** **Imposition on unwilling** **ESM recipients**	Supranational supervision Incentives and persuasion Contract and convention **Results:** **Arguably ECB responsibility for supervision of SIBs, partial SRB role in resolution (unclear)**	Supranational supervision and enforcement Incentives and persuasion Supranational supervision and legal action (Commission and ECJ) **Results:** **ECB expansion of modest powers already supported by Germany (SSM)**	Open method of coordination in de novo bodies **Results:** **EBA, SRB. In overlap with RI proposition**
Power (Prop. 3.2)	Power resources used with restraint to coerce, impose decisions on others **Results:** **Extra-EU institutional design and enforcement**	Power resources determine bargaining capacity on hard rules Institutions filter capacity to achieve goals. **Results: limited EU institutional capacity**	Power resources diffused **Results: limited to ECB extension of SSM**	Governments restrain supranatural bodies **Results: EBA, SRB governance**

EMU therefore had hallmarks of continued national involvement and subsequent institutional weakness.

Second, Liberal Intergovernmentalism and New Intergovernmentalism provide insights into the politics of institutional development and system design, but they bracket new political developments that affect those outcomes. Liberal Intergovernmentalism sheds light on the interests involved and the power relations involved in negotiating new EU institutions within the context of EU law and decision-making procedures in a way that New Intergovernmentalism does not focus on, and therefore remains of particular value in shedding light on why countries want what they do. Its expectation that new institutions will be supranational can and should be modified, however, to take a wider range of institutional fixes as suggested by the New Intergovernmentalism literature, rather than supranational agents. What this amounts to, in the context of proposals to establish supranational institutions, is that intergovernmental negotiations within the EU generate weak institutions for the most part.

This can be accounted for in part because there are voting requirements that limit the capacity of powerful states like Germany to override the interests of others. Some German proposals like a Finance Minister to control national budget processes failed to get far for this reason. New Intergovernmentalism provides an explanation for the development of responsible sovereignty, but in voluntary situations that provide a great deal of national leeway. What about when there is a serious conflict about what needs to be done?

The answer, unforeseen by any of these theoretical camps, is that Germany supported responsible sovereignty – and therefore EU institutions that placed responsibility on national governments – as a component of its strategy to have member states take care of their own financial stability problems to the greatest extent possible and stop asking Germany to pay for it. Strong EU institutions not only require powers, but require resources and raise concerns about unintended future consequences of Brussels imposing solutions on national governments.

Within the context of EU laws and decision-making, however, it is difficult to see how responsible sovereignty alone in the context of directives could have come to be seen as a part of the solution to Europe's financial stability problems. It first becomes comprehensible in light of extensive demands that national administrations and banking systems take action to make their finances more resilient – demands that become debatable once (limited, conditional and Eurozone-leveraged) German financial assistance comes into discussion. Similarly, Germany's capacity to pull the strings within the Eurozone and the Troika to demand responsible sovereignty in granular detail for states in financial distress (to the extent that sovereignty was truly organized hypocrisy) makes sense in the light of Germany's financial capacity and the lengths they would go to use it to reconfiguring European economic governance.

The result was Germany's use of an overwhelming resource – money – to establish a Shadow Europe that coerces others into commitments outside the EU's institutional order (TSCG, ESM), that forces a repurposing of the EU's institutional architecture to harden those commitments (European Semester, MIP and revised EDP), that legalizes the involvement of Shadow Europe (ESM) in imposing rules on deviance, and keeps the funds (ESM, SRF and potentially an EDIS Fund) required for financial stability firmly outside of the reach of EU law and institutions. German power is thereby not justiciable by the ECJ, and although the Commission can propose changes to incorporate those institutions into EU law, it can do nothing to break into institutions founded in international, rather than EU law.

This means that the provision of international order relies on power more than existing institutions, and that great powers are willing to go to great ends to get the institutions that they want. The EU could have provided for financial stability under continued interdependence under existing institutional rules, but it would have meant a much more federal Europe with fiscal transfers from Germany – and Northern Europe more generally – to the periphery in Southern Europe and Ireland.

These findings make sense from a realist perspective on international relations, in which institutions are reflections of power, shaped by great powers periodically rather than imposing significant shackles on them. But it is a modern realism, a realist institutionalism that is distinct from the deep paradigm on which it ultimately built.

Based on the results above, the following comparison can also be made with the Europe-specific hypotheses outlined in Chapter 2. Hypothesis 1, that Germany, as a financial great power, will reshape European economic governance to manage interdependence in its own interest, stepping outside the EU if necessary, is confirmed. Rather than allow the Eurozone to collapse, to remain in gridlock, or to move in the direction of a federal fiscal union as so many supranational and transnational coalitions had demanded, Germany reshaped European economic governance to suit its own demands for responsible sovereignty.

That Germany would resort to establishing an institutional order outside the EU to do away with the need for intergovernmental and interinstitutional compromise is confirmed as well. The critical infrastructure of Banking Union and the backstop to EMU is outside the EU, at the express will of the German government. That government determinedly thwarted the massive push by European institutions, the IMF, OECD and US government and the French government for an essentially federal Europe as the guarantor of European financial stability, and imposed its own view on the rest. In most cases it needed at least one or two allies in its quest, the Netherlands and Finland in particular, but the decisions were uniquely German.

Hypothesis 2, that Germany would focus on distributional goals and try to upload its own preferences into new institutions as rule maker for others to adopt is reflected as well in the cases of the TSCG, the ESM, as well as in bank supervision and resolution. Hypothesis 3.2, that Germany would resort to coercion and imposition if necessary to secure its goals in the context of an enforcement pyramid, is confirmed in the cases of the TSCG, the ESM and the treatment of Cyprus and Greece in particular. Hypothesis 3.1, that institutional change would be incremental, nesting old institutions in new ones that provide a new purpose and new commitments for others to follow, is confirmed as well. Much of the new architecture of EMU and Banking Union is designed with this in mind. Hypothesis 3.2, that Germany would incorporate an enforcement pyramid to direct and enforce behaviour in an economic but decisive way, is also borne out by its use of the ESM and its strong shielding of that tool of leverage and sanctioning from EU meddling.

Institutional review

The package of initiatives and the sequencing had a redistributive logic that determined national positions. The preferences of national governments for what component came first, and what obligations member states would have to bear once those components were established, varied by the likelihood that they would need assistance themselves – either because their own financial system was in direct peril of collapse – or because the collapse of another country's banking system threatened to spill over into a collapse of their own. While Ireland, Spain, and the rest of Southern Europe saw a European bailout fund as Banking Union's most pressing and important feature, countries that were likely to have to pay into the fund prioritized components and features that reduced the likelihood of a payout. This not only included keeping ESM disbursements small in an emergency, but insisting that a European bank supervisor help prevent those kinds of emergencies in the first place. That could be done by ensuring that banks lend money more conservatively, that they hold on to more cash and more high-quality financial instruments to ensure that they can better weather economic and financial turbulence, and that they err on the side of caution during an economic downturn by getting rid of risky investments that could turn sour and hurt the financial position of the banks. There was no support for making a European bank supervisor responsible for the entire banking system. Instead, it was designed to be more limited, so that its initial purpose would be fulfilled. The ECB, as a European bank supervisor, was therefore a necessary precondition for Germany and other potential paymasters of Banking Union, to ensure that banks would act conservatively in the future, so that money would only be spent in the rarest of circumstances – events that no one saw coming and that were out of Europe's control.

For other matters, the logic of net payers that drove the establishment of a bank supervisor alongside the ESM was precisely that banks in Southern Europe were in trouble due to their own profligate tendencies dating back to the launch of EMU, and that they could only be helped with European money if a European supervisor simultaneously ensured that they would be less daring when lending money in the future. This logic eventually won out over international consensus and lobbying by European institutions, all of which favoured another road to financial stability that involved a common European treasury, fiscal transfers between the member states and European authority to regulate, supervise and intervene in the affairs of European banks.

In contrast, other components of Banking Union failed to acquire support by Germany in particular, as they were less central to this quid pro quo. They consequently were designed to coordinate national authorities and keep tabs on them, or they did not come into being at all. A single resolution authority, an EDIRA capable of shutting down and restructuring banks and equipped with its own fund, was considered by banking regulation experts to be essential to dealing with banks that had collapsed and needed to be shut down safely without infecting damage on the rest of the economy. But the prospect of yet another European fund for banks that were certifiably dead was more than either the German government or German banks were happy to contemplate, a position that was echoed in other countries like Finland, the Netherlands and Austria as well. Nor was anyone at the national level, among these or other countries, keen on establishing a European Resolution Authority that would have the power to take apart a bank, sell parts off to rival banks, and do this across national borders. Although a Single Resolution Board (SRB) for the Eurozone was eventually agreed on, its recommendations to the Commission remained subject to approval by the European Council and based on plans drafted by national resolution authorities. It therefore disappointed many of the proposals and recommendations that the expert community had made. Similarly, the SRF was established, but small enough that national funds come quickly into action at their own discretion and capacity, and under intergovernmental rather than EU control. Instead of European institutions and funds, each national authority and fund remained responsible for implementing resolutions. The SRB has the right to review what each of them does, and propose improvements, but plans are nationally determined. An even worse fate was in store for proposals that Europe develop an EU-wide system of deposit insurance. Again, the prospect of pan-European insurance for depositors against the loss of their savings during a bank collapse was more than the prospective paymasters of the plan could contemplate, with the result that plans to mutualize deposit insurance went nowhere.

All of this indicates that banking is high politics, in which there are high economic and political stakes for national governments and banks that decide what is considered a component of Banking Union, and under what conditions. The paymasters decide, picking and choosing what they find essential. The conditions they are confronted with are not of their choosing, and not of their liking, but their reactions represent the attempt to make the best of a bad situation, when measured against the national interest. Key here is that it is the national interest of creditor states, not that of financially precarious states that is relevant in determining capacity to act, pick and choose. The others respond. There is real and meaningful change to the EU's regulatory framework, but far less than experts deem necessary to function properly. The result is that like monetary union, the components are selected for political expediency rather than technical merit or necessity, with the result that Banking Union is unable to deal sufficiently with threats to financial stability in the EU. These threats are not only the state of the global economy, but long-term contractions of economic activity in Southern Europe. These contractions feed the doom loop of mutually reinforcing insolvency of banks and national governments in those areas, which in turn generate further economic downturn and further problems for both banks and sovereigns. Considerable national bias is built into the architecture of Banking Union that undermines the capacity of the institutions to contribute significantly more to financial stability than what the member states contribute themselves. Indeed, the chief impact of European output in the area of Banking Union is to enhance national responsibility for ensuring financial stability in the context of European guidelines and monitoring. Although the establishment of the ECB as a single supervisor is a significant exception to this trend, the national bias in the EBA and SRB limits the bank's capacity to do the job it considers necessary to fulfil its mission. In this, the ECB is put in a similar situation in Banking Union as it is in monetary union: powerful in one area, but unable to affect directly the environment in which it operates, or the behaviour of other actors – both banks and national authorities – on whom it relies to do its job properly. To the extent that it encounters national resistance to its capacity to act, as has been the case in monetary union with fiscal policy, the ECB may be forced to alleviate problems of financial instability through loose monetary policy and extraordinary liquidity injections. This book reviewed just how large that gap is, the reasons why and elaborates on the consequences.

Implications for Europe

There are two implications of the findings above for Europe and the world, and for our understanding of international relations, international institutions and great power politics more generally. I discuss first the implications for Europe, and then conclude with observations of why and how this is important for our study of international relations.

The economic and financial crisis that began in 2008 shook the world's advanced economies and challenged them to do more to ensure financial stability and resilience, both in the banking sector, and in public finance. Within Europe, the challenges were far greater. There was a mismatch between the transnational scope of banking activity on the one hand, and on the other, the primacy of national governments in banking regulation and serving as lenders of last resort to banks. The consequence was financial instability in the banking sector and a Eurozone crisis in the public sector, which became intertwined and mutually reinforcing. Only one of two outcomes could put an end to this instability: the establishment of supranational authorities and budgetary power at the European level, to provide security, regulation and oversight for a European single market, or the renationalization of authority, public finance and the activity of banks. For the first time in Europe's history, all actors, public and private, supranational and national had to choose which way to go. Not choosing would have torn Europe apart.

The path Europe chose involved one significant headline advance in supranationalism – the ECB's responsibility for part of banking supervision, but the overwhelming development reaffirms the primacy of the member states in overseeing, regulating and financing rescue plans for the European economy in time of need. As a result, Europeans continue to provide stability on a largely national basis, albeit with new instruments with the capacity to prevent total disaster. Instead of an integrated European economy with European authorities, funds and budgetary powers, Europe continues to have a network of national economies with strengthened national authorities working within the context of a thin supranational coordinating layer. The ECB acts as the flagship institution for banking supervision, and is the most impressive development toward some sort of governance beyond the state, but national supervisors remain in charge of overseeing nearly 6000 banks, for telling them whether it is acceptable to hold assets from other member states, and in cooperation with the EBA, for performing the stress tests that are so critical for ensuring that banks cleanse their balance sheets of toxic assets. The Single Resolution Board and the Commission play a role in recommending and initiating the resolution of failed banks that the ECB supervises, but national authorities are the primary resolution authorities elsewhere, even when the Commission and SRB decide. Similarly, national resolution funds and national governments remain the primary sources of capital large enough to assist with the orderly resolution of banks in the event of an emergency, particularly emergencies of a systemic nature.

The institutional underdevelopment of financial stability in Europe, due to its ordering principle of responsible sovereignty in financial matters, also potentially influences the ECB's capacity to make the most of its new powers to supervise banks, to force them to clear up their balance sheets and to raise sufficient capital to ensure their resilience to economic shocks. This is not because the ECB is not proficient or unwilling, but because pressure on banks to improve might need to be balanced against the potential unleashing of another banking and Eurozone crisis from which Europe might not recover. As one sees in the difficult relationship between the ECB and Italian banks and government, putting an end to the forbearance that prevents both crisis and recovery is easier said than done under these conditions. The fear that Europe will enter a long period of economic decline as Japan has done may very well become reality.

What is more, the most important aspects of Europe's economic policy reforms were built outside the EU, on the basis of international treaties, with the specific intent to circumvent the EU. Nor is there any reason to believe that these are temporary innovations that the EU will absorb shortly. The German desire to impose responsible sovereignty would be undermined if the institutions were brought into the EU legislative and judicial architecture. In this Shadow EU, the TSCG compels member states, with the exception of the UK, to balance their budgets and pay down their overall debts. The ESM Treaty effectively establishes a European Monetary Fund mirroring the IMF, acting and operating in much the same way, outside the EU. The Single Resolution Fund similarly remains outside the EU legal and institutional framework. Meanwhile, as the single supervisory mechanism and the single resolution mechanism try to break the link between state and bank insolvency on the bank side of the equation within the EU, the TSCG and ESM are the elements that try to break the link on the public side. States are to bring their finances into the black for the first time since the 1960s in many cases by treaty obligations and changes to their constitutions (TSCG), and to be subject to coercion and conditionality for aid if financial markets sense that they will fail to meet their targets (ESM).

None of these stability features are supranational in the sense that responsibility for economic management is transferred or pooled. On the contrary, they massively heighten national responsibility for getting national finances in order. The consequences of not doing so, as seen in Greece, Portugal and Ireland, are severe. The thrust of these treaties and mechanisms, both inside the EU and outside of it (rein)forces national authority and responsibility for ensuring financial stability in their own jurisdictions. As a consequence, one must expect an extended period of economic contraction in Southern Europe in particular as government budgets and bank balance sheets shrink in line with the obligations that governments have entered into, and the deterrent effect that Germany, the Troika and the ESM have shown against those governments (Greece and Cyprus) that have not lived up to those expectations or have outright fought them. The firmness with which political and economic tutelage has been imposed on those two countries in particular, despite their resistance, underlines to all member states the consequences of resistance – an existential threat to the survival of the country. Even more, those treaties provide far more detailed prescriptions on the acceptable limits of public policy, unlike the development of the EU to date. This means that the Shadow EU is not a radical change simply because of its non-EU nature, but because of the demands it makes on the signatories.

The defining reason why these events took place is that a single powerful country, sometimes with allies and sometimes without, demanded them of Europe in exchange for financial assistance that would avert disaster. This was not the financial assistance that most EU countries, international organizations and the US government called on Germany and the EU to support. It was the bare minimum required to prevent the total collapse of states, their capacity to repay German banks, and with it, to prevent a collapse of the Eurozone itself. Instead of a European federal government with a Secretary of the Treasury, European treasury bills and a fiscal union, Europe got a Shadow EU imposed through coercion that is far more relevant than EU rules, institutions and procedures themselves.

The German focus on ordering principles for Europe also seems to be clear. On a regular basis, the German government also made it clear that its own doctrine of national responsibility, and of responsible sovereignty, lay at the core of its vision for a renewed Europe cast on principles it would accept. At the 2014 World Economic Forum in Davos, German Finance Minister Wolfgang Schäuble stated that Germany wanted to see the EU as an organization made up of sovereign states and not a federation like the United States. He elaborated that this meant that each nation state would largely assume responsibility for its own banks, and have its own funds, with the additional EU layer. He directly rejected the suggestion that there should be stronger powers and funds (Schäuble 2014).

His parting communications on his retirement as Finance Minister in 2017 reinforce this even further. Rather than embrace French President Macron's suggestions to establish a European Minister of Finance, a sizeable European budget and to transform the ESM into an EU body acting as a European Monetary Fund, Schäuble (2017) insisted on using the ESM as a lever of conditionality to further institutionalize responsible sovereignty. Indeed, this would have further shifted

EMU powers from EU institutions to non-EU ones. Given the election results favouring nationalists and anti-government liberals, there is little reason to believe that the policy will change under his successor.

Again, the methods used to introduce those ordering principles were also clear. In negotiations over Banking Union at that time, Germany was also keen to maximize its leverage in the Council in favour of intergovernmental agreements on the modalities of bank supervision and resolution in advance of European Parliamentary elections. This leverage was required, and the approval of the EP required if the EU would accept the arrangements of the IGA outside the EU itself, but using some EU institutions to assist in the process. In that context, the Council pressured the Parliament to accept the IGA-based solution on Banking Union, noting that the Parliament would risk increasing financial instability if it did not. The Parliament had expressed great reservations in March 2014 at the IGA-based nature of the agreements, stating that they deliberately undermined the law and spirit of the treaties on the European Union by bypassing the Parliament and the normal legislative procedure.

One of the last attempts of the Parliament to push back the rise of intergovernmentalism was attached to the choice of a new Commission president after Parliamentary elections in May 2014. The Party of European Socialists in particular saw the Commission's complicity in accepting the rise of intergovernmentalism and of extra-EU institutions in Europe as the work of Manuel Barroso, who hails from the conservative European People's Party, whose replacement candidate, Jean-Claude Juncker, had negotiated many of the deals that Germany had demanded of other member states. In this, they saw the likelihood that the hollowing out of the EU and its replacement by a Shadow EU would be strengthened, not opposed.

In the drive to secure its preferred ordering principles for Europe, the German government was also prepared to go on the offensive to undermine attempts and candidates pushing for a federal or supranational alternative. In the context of negotiations in 2014 over the appointment of a new Commission President, the President of the European Parliament and member of the Socialist Party, Martin Schulz announced that he would run as a candidate to replace the incumbent President of the European Commission when his term of office expired later that year. If successful, he would have been in a position to end the Commission's reluctant support for the creation of a Shadow EU outside the legal framework of the European Union. This could have been accomplished via the Commission's sole right to propose legislation in the EU legislative context, coupled with a Commission position that EU institutions could only be used if the activities they carried out were brought inside the EU's legal architecture, where the Council and qualified majority voting rights would be restored with more balance and voluntarism to intergovernmental negotiations, where the Parliament would be able to insist on arrangements with more supranational elements, as it consistently demanded, and where the European Court of Justice would have jurisdiction to adjudicate disputes and enforce legislation. If Schulz had been successful, it would have forced the German-led coalition to choose between one of three options: accepting more supranationalism in exchange for using EU institutions to implement what remained of intergovernmental agreements, altered to become EU law; strengthening the Shadow EU even further to carry out the financial stability functions that the formal EU would not; or accepting a permanent state of financial instability, which would tear the single market apart. During this contest, on 10 March 2014, Schäuble shed light on fears in the Council that the Parliamentarian leading the opposition to the IGA model could run as a candidate for President of the European Commission, stating that Martin Schulz, who was President of the European Parliament, was *misusing his office* in order to run for the position (Euronews 2014). The controversy continued after Parliamentary elections favoured Juncker as the key candidate, only to be vehemently opposed by the UK government. At the global level, the German government lobbied for the head of the IMF, Christine Lagarde, to take the position, as a person who had shown in the Troika dealings with Greece and Cyprus that she could be trusted to uphold the principles that Germany held so dear (Taylor 2014).

Realist institutionalism and international relations

A great deal was riding on the outcome of the contest analyzed in this book, not only in concrete terms for the citizens of the EU, but for how we understand and look at not only integration and cooperation within the EU, as well as regionalism and international relations more generally. Until the Eurozone crisis, Europe had gone much further than other regions of the world in terms of not only international cooperation and regimes, but also supranational institutions with the power to constrain or displace national sovereignty. Were those advances irreversible – would international institutions constrain and shape the room for manoeuvre of even a great power like Germany, or could that great power undermine EU institutions, circumvent them and establish its own preferred vision of international order in its neighbourhood? Banking Union and EMU reform are stress tests for the power of institutions to guide member state behaviour in a particular direction, and just as importantly, to prevent them from moving in other directions. At the minimum, the rules and ethos of the European Union are built to prevent domination of one state or a minority of states over the others, and to prevent member states that disagree with validly established treaty provisions and EU law from going their own way in violation of the obligations those treaty and legal provisions impose.

The European Union is different from other regionalisms precisely because it has developed common institutions and law far more strongly than ASEAN, MERCOSUR, NAFTA, the CACM, the GCC and a few other regional organizations. These other organizations are built on the principle of national sovereignty and autonomy within the context of an international agreement (Breslin et al. 2002). None of the other regionalisms, with the exception of the Caribbean dollar area, have supranational aspects. While none of these regional organizations give definitive evidence on the question of whether institutions are the product of power (Strange 1983, 1998), or whether they significantly modify it (Krasner 1983; Krasner 1982), or whether they thoroughly transform it (Keohane & Nye

1984), Europe has always held the prospect that liberal institutionalist expectations about the hold of international regimes, and neofunctional expectations about the gradual establishment of supranationalism might be confirmed in a dramatic fashion. This would mean a lack of significant defection from existing commitments at the least (NLI) and the pursuit of deeper cooperation and supranationalism to buttress existing institutions and secure even greater gains (NF). Although neofunctionalism typically expresses these gains in terms of spillover and positive benefits, the neoliberal institutionalist conclusion that states might cooperate to insure themselves against the prospect of loss should be reflected in the Banking Union crisis by compelling evidence that states can rise above competitive, predatory and above all coercive power relations that are standard fare for the realist view of world affairs. On the contrary, if the Banking Union crisis demonstrates the latter characteristics, then it says a great deal about whether regimes and institutions can really rise above the interests of the member states indefinitely.

We should also be clear about the fungibility of power and the extent to which real hegemony can be exercised. The point of hegemony is easily overstated, even if realist tactics and strategy dominate the politics of regional integration. Germany is not attempting to establish an all-encompassing order over all policy areas, but it is imposing order in a significant range of policy issues. In the case of Europe, to the extent that hegemony is being established, it is financial hegemony, extending into broader economic hegemony as other countries are forced to shrink their economies in line with German demands (Bulmer & Paterson 2013). These are the areas in which Germany can exploit the vulnerabilities of other EU member states to establish order and to impose it if need be. Changing the EU treaties from within, in which every state has a veto that must be deterred at the very least, is beyond the scope of German capabilities. They would then have to engage in more side payments to compensate what they want, which in turn degrades their strategic goals – to constrain costs and impose national responsibility. This is not only part of EMU's legacy, but of the general pattern within the EU that the Germans pay for (the lion's share of) whatever initiatives Europe has to offer. Germany's efforts on Banking Union and on the TSCG, by reinforcing national rather than collective responsibility and resources serve to limit Germany's financial burden in a decisive way that they can live with into the future. But this is precisely where realist institutionalism is different than its other institutionalist rivals. Rather than accept such institutions, the great power builds its own to get the job done. Gulliver's giant is free of his chains – not to seek destruction or to withdraw from interdependence – but to reshape it on his own terms, whether the neighbours like it or not.

Whether that is sustainable for Europe is dubious, but remains to be seen. The scale and depth of economic reforms that the TSCG mandates and that Banking Union continues, coupled with market pressure on national governments to engage in structural reforms, budget retrenchment, internal devaluation and shifting capital from consumption to savings in the most depressed areas of the EU have never been tried before in the developed world, and rarely in full democracies. Much has been made of the comment that Europe is starting to go down the same path as Japan did in the 1990s, so that austerity and deflation are likely to persist for decades to come. That is probably true in the richer, creditor countries of Northwestern Europe. However, the Eurozone crisis, and the response of European governments under the guidance and insistence of the German government may bear greater resemblance for the southern periphery of the Eurozone, and perhaps for the newer member states of Eastern Europe to the East Asian financial crisis of 1997–1998. In that crisis, the IMF and financial markets imposed pressure on national governments to do the same things that Germany is now imposing on Southern Europe and Ireland in the context of speculative financial markets. As we now know of the East Asian Crisis, the long term result was strong fiscal conservatism and high savings rates on a national basis, buttressed by international cooperation on a regional monetary fund, rather than supranational cooperation. Fiscal conservatism and high savings rates contained inflation and unit labour costs, and fuelled export-led investment and growth, which in turn was made possible in part by investment from Japan. It is possible that at a later stage of retrenchment in Europe, that the periphery of the Eurozone will strengthen its dependence on German and other investment to fuel recovery by the 2020s. Before then though, deflation and retrenchment will have to take place. All of this will be made possible by the imposition of responsible national sovereignty at the hands of Europe's new economic hegemon.

References

Breslin, S., Hughes, C. W., Philipps, N., & Rosamond, B. (eds.) (2002) *New regionalism in the global political economy: Theories and cases*. London: Routledge.

Bulmer, S., & Paterson, W. E. (2013) Germany as the EU's reluctant hegemon? Of economic strength and political constraints. Journal of European Public Policy, 20(10), 1387–1405.

Euronews. (2014) EU officials seek pre-election Banking Union deal. 11 March.

Keohane, R. O., & Nye, J. S. (1984) *After hegemony: Cooperation and discord in the world political economy*. Princeton: Princeton University Press.

Krasner, S. D. (1982) Structural causes and regime consequences: Regimes as intervening variables. *International Organization* 36, 2: 185–205.

Krasner, S. D. (1983) Regimes and the limits of realism: Regimes as autonomous variables. In Krasner, S. D. ed., *International regimes*. Ithaca: Cornell University Press: 355–68.

Schäuble, W. (2014) *Round table interview at World Economic Forum*, Davos.

Schäuble, W. (2017) *Non-paper for paving the way towards a Stability Union*.

Strange, Susan (1983) 'Cave, Hic dragones!', in Krasner, S., ed. *International Regimes*. Ithaca: Cornell University Press: 337–54.

Strange, S. (1998) *States and Markets* (2nd ed.). London: Bloomsbury Academic.

Taylor, P. (2014) Merkel eyes IMF's Lagarde for Commission chief: sources. *Reuters*, 3 June.

Index

Note: Page numbers in italic indicate a figure and page numbers in bold indicate a table on the corresponding page.

www.ingramcontent.com/pod-product-compliance
Ingram Content Group UK Ltd.
Pitfield, Milton Keynes, MK11 3LW, UK
UKHW011012180926
475701UK00004B/690
9780367591717